TEACHING
MATHEMATICS
CONCEPTUALLY

TEACHING MATHEMATICS CONCEPTUALLY

GUIDING INSTRUCTIONAL PRINCIPLES FOR 5–10-YEAR-OLDS

BETH L. MACDONALD
JONATHAN N. THOMAS

SAGE Publications Ltd
1 Oliver's Yard
55 City Road
London EC1Y 1SP

CORWIN
A SAGE company
2455 Teller Road
Thousand Oaks, California 91320
(800)233-9936
www.corwin.com

SAGE Publications India Pvt Ltd
B 1/I 1 Mohan Cooperative Industrial Area
Mathura Road
New Delhi 110 044

SAGE Publications Asia-Pacific Pte Ltd
3 Church Street
#10-04 Samsung Hub
Singapore 049483

Editor: James Clark
Senior assistant editor: Diana Alves
Production editor: Nicola Marshall
Copyeditor: William Baginsky
Proofreader: Sharon Cawood
Indexer: Martin Hargreaves
Marketing manager: Dilhara Attygalle
Cover design: Wendy Scott
Typeset by: C&M Digitals (P) Ltd, Chennai, India

Library of Congress Control Number: 2022944707

British Library Cataloguing in Publication data

A catalogue record for this book is available from the British Library

ISBN 978-1-5297-9184-6
ISBN 978-1-5297-9183-9 (pbk)

The Mathematics Recovery Book Series

Teaching Mathematics Conceptually is the ninth book in the Mathematics Recovery series. The nine books in this series address the teaching of early number, whole number arithmetic and fractions in primary, elementary, and secondary education. These books provide practical help to enable schools and teachers to give equal status to numeracy intervention and classroom instruction. The authors are internationally recognized as leaders in this field and draw on considerable practical experience of delivering professional learning programs, training courses, and materials.

The books are:

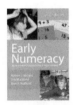

Early Numeracy: Assessment for Teaching and Intervention, 2nd edition, Robert J. Wright, Jim Martland and Ann K. Stafford, 2006.

Early Numeracy demonstrates how to assess students' mathematical knowledge, skills, and strategies in addition, subtraction, multiplication, and division.

Teaching Number: Advancing Children's Skill and Strategies, 2nd edition, Robert J. Wright, Jim Martland, Ann K. Stafford, and Garry Stanger, 2006.

Teaching Number sets out in detail nine principles which guide the teaching, together with 180 practical, exemplar teaching procedures to advance children to more sophisticated strategies for solving arithmetic problems.

Developing Number Knowledge: Assessment, Teaching and Intervention with 7–11-Year-Olds, Robert J. Wright, David Ellemor-Collins, and Pamela D. Tabor, 2012.

Developing Number Knowledge provides more advanced knowledge and resources for teachers working with older children.

Teaching Number in the Classroom with 4–8-Year-Olds, 2nd edition, Robert J. Wright, Garry Stanger, Ann K. Stafford, and Jim Martland, 2015.

Teaching Number in the Classroom shows how to extend the work of assessment and intervention with individual and small groups to working with the whole class.

Developing Fractions Knowledge, Amy J. Hackenberg, Anderson Norton, and Robert J. Wright, 2016.

Developing Fractions Knowledge provides a detailed progressive approach to assessment and instruction related to students' learning of fractions.

The Learning Framework in Number: Pedagogical Tools for Assessment and Instruction, Robert J. Wright and David Ellemor-Collins, 2018.

The Learning Framework in Number presents a learning framework across the whole K-to-5 range and provides three sets of pedagogical tools for the framework – assessment schedules, models of learning progressions, and teaching charts. These tools enable detailed assessment and profiling of children's whole number arithmetic knowledge and the development of specific instructional programs.

Teaching Early Numeracy to Children with Developmental Disabilities, Corinna F. Grindle, Richard P. Hastings, and Robert J. Wright, 2020.

This practical guide for teaching numeracy is based on core concepts from *Teaching Number* (aka 'the green book') that have been adapted for children with developmental disabilities.

Numeracy for All Learners: Teaching Mathematics to Students with Special Needs, Pamela D. Tabor, Dawn Dibley, Amy J. Hackenberg, and Anderson Norton, 2021.

Numeracy for All Learners builds on the first six books in the series and presents the knowledge, resources, and examples for teachers working with students with special needs from Pre-K through secondary school.

Teaching Mathematics Conceptually: Guiding Instructional Principles for 5–10-Year-Olds, Beth L. MacDonald and Jonathan N. Thomas, 2023.

This book is designed to clearly explain ten research-driven guiding instructional principles deeply ingrained in the Math Recovery professional learning community that fundamentally inform mathematics teaching and learning.

Table of Contents

About the Authors

Beth L. MacDonald is an Associate Professor in Early Childhood Mathematics Education in the School of Teaching and Learning at Illinois State University. After completing a Bachelor of Arts degree in Studio Art and Elementary Education (PreK-6) at SUNY Potsdam, Beth taught elementary school for 15 years and served as a K-5 Instructional Specialist for two years in southwest Virginia. In this time, Beth taught in fully inclusive elementary classrooms within Title 1 schools and within all K-5 grade levels. While teaching, Beth completed her Master of Arts in Education degree, with a focus on K-8 Mathematics Education and her Doctor of Philosophy degree, with a Curriculum and Instruction concentration and focus on Mathematics Education, both from Virginia Tech. Her research broadly focuses on PreK-5 students' development of number, particularly with subitizing activity at the center of this development. Moreover, Beth collaborates often with colleagues who examine teachers' specialized content knowledge development in mathematics/STEM, and collaborates with colleagues who examine marginalized students' number understanding development. Beth also served as a lead guest editor for a Special Issue of the *Education Sciences* journal, focusing on STEM in Early Childhood Education (www.mdpi.com/journal/education/special_issues/STEM_in_Early).

Jonathan N. Thomas is an Associate Professor of Mathematics Education and the Chairperson of the Department of STEM Education at the University of Kentucky. After completing a Bachelor of Arts degree in Elementary Education at the University of Kentucky, Jonathan was a mathematics intervention specialist in public, private, and charter schools in the Cincinnati metropolitan area. While teaching, Jonathan completed a Master of Arts in Education degree with a focus on education leadership and his Doctor of Education degree in Mathematics Education, both from the University of Cincinnati. Jonathan's research focused on responsive and equitable teaching practices in the elementary classroom as well as children's construction of mental imagery and use of gesture in foundational mathematical experiences. Jonathan has been the principal investigator on several projects, funded by the National Science Foundation, focused on these areas. Jonathan is also an associate editor of the *School Science and Mathematics* journal and a Kentucky Center for Mathematics faculty associate.

Acknowledgements

This book is a culmination of many people, including Bob Wright, Gary Stanger, Ann Stafford, Jim Martland, David Ellemor-Collins, Amy Hackenberg, Andy Norton, Dawn Dibley, and so many more scholars and educators. Extending Piaget's work and collaborating with Ernst von Glasersfeld, Les Steffe established a shift in how educators and scholars position our work. All of these scholars have been affected by Les's work. By sitting with children to learn how they reason, engage with mathematics, and talk about their learning, Les's work encouraged educators and scholars to create models that better represent the mathematics of *the child*. This shift was a critical one and informed meaningful instructional moves, curricula, and scholarship. The Math Recovery series echoes much of this work. We want to acknowledge these efforts, as this book would not have been created without them.

1

Introduction

The authors of this book have worked extensively in mathematics education for several decades, serving as educators, researchers, and teacher educators. Given these experiences, we saw a real need to make clear, direct connections between effective mathematics practices and mathematics learning theory. From this need, this book came into being. Both authors saw the Guiding Principles encapsulating these connections in meaningful ways. The Guiding Principles are features of Math Recovery teaching wherein children's strategy development and mathematics learning are at the center (Wright et al., 2006b, p. 25).

In fact, the Guiding Principles grew out of Wright's need to give voice to the instructional principles that worked best when teaching *all* students mathematics conceptually. Through their early Math Recovery work, Robert Wright and his research team began noticing and recording what instructional characteristics seemed to help children learn mathematics in meaningful and equitable ways. Interestingly, we see the Guiding Principles as direct connections to mathematics education learning theory. If anything, this speaks to us at a deeper level, as this means that the Guiding Principles delineate effective mathematics learning, as echoed in the classroom and mathematics learning theory. Many educators do not realize why particular pedagogical approaches work well or need improvement. Moreover, we realize that by bringing these Guiding Principles, which were observed in the classroom, to the foreground, we can better explain why some mathematics pedagogy is effective. From this realization, the Guiding Principles book was first conceptualized.

Purpose

The purpose of this book is not to redistribute the resources and discussions in the Math Recovery books but to help educators understand the learning theories related to these Guiding Principles and how they evidence themselves in mathematics classrooms. To meet this aim, this book organizes the Guiding Principles into three categories of effective approach to mathematics: (1) instruction, (2) planning, and (3) assessment. To do this, we provide small vignettes, tools, and connections to policies and standards. In short, this book draws on all of the Math Recovery books to allow the reader a more comprehensive lens when considering how these Guiding Principles evidence themselves explicitly in these books.

Book Structure

The Guiding Principles have introduced many of the Math Recovery books, highlighting the conceptual lens educators need to take up when using the resources in these books. This book is structured around these nine original Guiding Principles (Wright et al., 2006b, p. 26–7):

1.   Problem-based/inquiry-based teaching

The teaching approach is inquiry based – that is, problem based. Children routinely are engaged in thinking hard to solve numerical problems which, for them, are quite challenging.

2.   Initial and ongoing assessment

Teaching is informed by an initial, comprehensive assessment and ongoing assessment through teaching. The latter refers to the teacher's informed understanding of the child's current knowledge and problem-solving strategies, and continual revision of this understanding.

3.   Teaching just beyond the cutting edge (ZPD)

Teaching is focused just beyond the 'cutting edge' of the child's current knowledge.

4.   Selecting from a bank of teaching procedures

Teachers exercise their professional judgement in selecting from a bank of teaching procedures, each of which involves particular instructional settings and tasks, and varying this selection on the basis of ongoing observations.

5.   Engendering more sophisticated strategies

The teacher understands children's numerical strategies and deliberately engenders the development of more sophisticated strategies.

6.   Observing the child and fine-tuning teaching

Teaching involves intensive, ongoing observation by the teacher and continual micro-adjusting or fine-tuning of teaching on the basis of their observation.

7.   Incorporating symbolizing and notating

Teaching supports and builds on the child's intuitive, verbally based strategies and these are used as a basis for the development of written forms of mathematics which accord with the child's verbally based strategies.

8.   Sustained thinking and reflection

The teacher provides the child with sufficient time to solve a given problem. Consequently, the child is frequently engaged in episodes which involve sustained thinking, reflection on their thinking, and reflection on the results of their thinking.

9.   Child intrinsic satisfaction

Children gain intrinsic satisfaction from their problem-solving, from their realization that they are making progress, and from the verification methods they develop.

To extend this work that was first conceptualized in the mid-1990s, we have added one more Guiding Principle:

10.   Equitable mathematics practices

Ensuring that all children construct meaningful mathematical knowledge and practices requires a profound commitment to equity in our teaching practices. Accounting for and connecting to children's abilities, cultures, and lived experiences are essential for the creation of broad pathways for learning and for fostering positive identities as capable mathematical thinkers. Equity also involves addressing systems and practices that contribute to inequitable outcomes amongst children, particularly those historically marginalized in mathematical spaces.

These ten Guiding Principles frame this book and help readers make connections between instructional practices in their mathematics classrooms and mathematics learning theories. To better understand how the Guiding Principles can be utilized by readers, we have also organized them into three main themes or parts. Essentially, we envision them as explaining three aspects of an effective mathematics classroom.

Part I: Effective Mathematics Teaching

Part I consists of four chapters: Chapter 2 focuses on *inquiry-based instruction* and draws from literature grounded in constructivism, inquiry, pedagogy, mediated action, and problem-centered lessons. Chapter 3 describes *mathematics learning progressions and multiple student-created strategies* and draws from literature that explains how learning progressions can be used effectively to support multiple learning abilities. Chapter 4 discusses *relationships between mathematics teaching and learning* and grounds the discussion in literature focused on mathematics knowledge for teaching. Finally, Chapter 5 provides insight into how educators can *plan effective mathematics teaching* by drawing connections between inquiry-based approaches and three-phase planning models.

Part II: Assessments and Responsive Mathematics Teaching

Part II is organized into three chapters: Chapter 6 focuses on responsive teaching with *formative assessments* at the center of the chapter's discussion. Chapter 7 explicates how educators can *monitor mathematics learning* by examining the literature that examines teachers' noticing. Finally, Chapter 8 discusses how educators can best design *feedback and discourse in their mathematics instruction* by drawing from literature that explains intrinsic satisfaction in mathematical activity.

Part III: Inclusive and Equitable Mathematics Teaching

Part III is structured around three chapters: Chapter 9 focuses on how *grouping strategies may promote students' productive struggle in mathematics instruction*. To explain this clearly, we draw from fundamental tenets outlined in social constructivist learning theories. Chapter 10 explains how *the role of children's reflection relates to mathematics learning* by expanding on different types of abstractions set within a neo-Piagetian set of theories. Finally, Chapter 11 provides some informative and critical discussions around *equitable mathematics practices*. This chapter is an extension of the current Guiding Principles and serves to update the discussions in Math Recovery to ensure all students are provided equitable opportunities to access and construct mathematics concepts.

By dividing these principles into three main sections with learning theories that explain what effective mathematics teaching, assessments and responsive mathematics teaching, and inclusive and equitable mathematics teaching look like, we are better able to connect mathematics learning theories to mathematics teaching and learning practices. Interestingly, the teaching and learning cycle (see Figure 1.1), used in many of the Math Recovery books (e.g. Wright et al., 2006b; Wright et al., 2015), often draws on the themes of the three main sections used in this book.

In the teaching and learning cycle, as shown in Figure 1.1, these three main sections are found in more than one of the four parts of this cycle. When designing effective mathematics instruction, mathematics educators need to consider (1) where they want their students to be, and (2) how they will get there. To assess and respond to students' learning needs during and prior to/following mathematics instruction, mathematics educators need to know (1) where their students currently are in their mathematics learning, (2) where they want their students to be, and (3) how they will know their students have reached these goals. Finally, to teach students with an inclusive and equitable lens, educators need to consider all four parts of this cycle. Readers may notice that we draw on this cycle at various points in the book, referencing many aspects of how teaching and learning mathematics relate in broad and nuanced ways. Essentially, we understand that mathematics teaching and learning cannot be captured with a simple linear cycle but that they encompass a much more multifaceted set of phenomena.

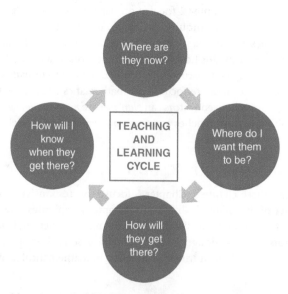

Figure 1.1   Teaching and learning cycle (Wright et al., 2006b)

Historical Roots of the Guiding Principles

Historically, these principles were first conceptualized by Robert Wright and his research team in 1996 and have remained critical in many of the Math Recovery resources and books. Before this moment, Robert Wright and his team were funded to establish the Australian Research Council (ARC), which focused on the development of a Math Recovery program. This project involved collaboration with schools in the northeast region of New South Wales. Through this work, Robert Wright successfully recruited Ann Stafford to join the research team at Southern Cross University, which allowed for more development of the Math Recovery work. Through these efforts, the New South Wales State Department of Education adopted Math Recovery as a project focusing on classroom teaching rather than specialist intervention. Due to the expanded nature of Math Recovery, Robert Wright determined a need to establish fundamental principles, which guided mathematics instruction at the classroom level. Therefore, in 1996, Robert Wright first developed the Guiding Principles for the teaching of number. These Guiding Principles were first used as the fundamental guide for Math Recovery instruction – applied to both classroom teaching and specialist intervention.

From this point forward, Math Recovery efforts have included the Guiding Principles as a lens for mathematics instruction and intervention design in multiple countries (the United States, the United Kingdom, New Zealand, and Ireland). With this lens, the resources that educators have used to better their students' mathematics learning opportunities have grown increasingly and developed into a comprehensive set of discussions and collaborations at conferences, they have informed professional book development, and extended research in mathematics education beyond most scholarly efforts in mathematics education. Given this, we found the Guiding Principles to be an area that should be expanded to allow more foci around some of the fundamental tenets of mathematics education research and practice.

Notes for the Reader on Connections to the Math Recovery Books and Mathematics Educational Standards

Throughout this book, we refer to other books in the series that connect to the Guiding Principles. We do so to allow the reader more direct connections to resources, which educators can use when designing effective mathematics instruction, assessments, and equitable and inclusive access to mathematics. The purpose of this book is not to redistribute the resources and discussions in the Math Recovery books but to help educators understand the learning theories related to the Guiding Principles and how they evidence themselves in mathematics classrooms.

In this section, we also make connections between mathematics learning theories and the mathematics standards used to inform classroom instruction and intervention design. This allows the reader to see how the Guiding Principles dovetail into current practices, standards, and research initiatives, instead of their being a separate entity, disassociated with current best practices in mathematics instruction. Given these two foci, this remaining section will be divided into a discussion on the connections between the Guiding Principles and Math Recovery books, and between the Guiding Principles and mathematics learning theories and educational standards.

Connections to Math Recovery Books

The Math Recovery books often make connections, sometimes implicitly and sometimes more visibly, between the Guiding Principles and their resources. This section provides an overview of these connections so that the reader can explore them in more detail or simply use them to link the resources with discussions in this book.

In Chapter 2, we discuss inquiry-based instruction and draw broadly on discussions which echo child-centered approaches described in the green book (Wright et al., 2006b, pp. 56–9). In this section, the green book expands on the importance of child-centered instruction by discussing key attributes of problem-center whole-class teaching. The white book (Wright and Ellemor-Collins, 2018, Chapter 5) provides explicit connections between inquiry-based instruction and number development. Finally, the brown book (Tabor et al., 2021, Chapter 11) focuses on effective practices that a constructivist teacher utilizes by comparing constructivist learning and instructional approaches to those utilized in behaviorist approaches.

In Chapter 3, we focus our discussion on mathematics learning progressions and learning trajectories. There are many examples of progressions and learning trajectories in all the books in the series. Interestingly, these tools – often considered at first blush in a linear, two-dimensional manner – are frequently used by Math Recovery specialists in a much more comprehensive manner and in relation to particular mathematical content. These discussions shift along a continuum from broad foci, considering classroom-level progressions throughout the course of a unit of study (e.g. see the white book, Wright and Ellemor-Collins, 2018; the orange book, Hackenberg et al., 2016; and the blue book, Wright et al., 2006a), to nuanced foci, considering individual student trajectories as related to an Individualized Educational Plan (e.g. see the brown book, Tabor et al., 2021; and the yellow book, Grindle et al., 2020).

In Chapter 4, we focus on relationships between mathematics teaching and learning. In the Math Recovery books, we find connections to the teaching and learning cycle (see Figure 1.1) in several of the books (e.g. see the purple book, Wright et al., 2015, p. 12; the green book, Wright et al., 2006b, p. 52; and the brown book, Tabor et al., 2021, p. 8). The green book (pp. 58–9) also discusses the role of the teacher in children's learning, and Chapter 7 in the brown book has an extensive discussion on how to better understand mathematics teaching and learning, as explained with a cognition lens.

In Chapter 5, we focus on planning effective mathematics teaching. As in Chapter 3, many of the Math Recovery books draw on planning for particular content, such as early number construction and fraction development. In fact, the sections in the brown and yellow books that focus on planning for students with Individualized Education Plans is particularly helpful.

In Chapter 6, the discussion shifts from effective teaching and planning towards effective responsive assessments that educators can use and develop in mathematics education. In particular, this chapter focuses on formative assessments in mathematics instruction. Connections again vary depending on the content the reader is interested in developing assessments for and how the reader plans to use the assessment tool (i.e. individual student focus, small group focus, whole-class focus). For instance, when assessing a classroom of students, an educator may rely on the stages of Units Coordination (assessment is located in the orange book, Chapter 3), which allows for multiple access points and multiple exit points around broad objectives. This type of assessment could be designed to inform classroom planning and teaching. Alternatively, an educator assessing a small group of students in an intervention setting may need to focus on particular actions and operations within one main concept (assessment is located in the brown book, Chapter 5). This type of assessment could be designed to monitor the progress of a group of students in a daily intervention setting and to inform changes to an intervention. Given this, Math Recovery books have developed assessments that align with different educational settings and inform different types of mathematics instruction. In particular, the initial blue and white books have included assessments. Additionally, the purple, red, and orange books have assessment tasks in each chapter.

In Chapter 7, we focus on how assessments can be used to monitor mathematics learning. Often, mathematics educators can develop their ideas about what they would like to monitor and how they would like to adapt their instruction by referring to the dimensions of mathematization. These dimensions are located in many of the Math Recovery books (e.g. the white book, pp. 16–21; the brown book, pp. 30–1; and the orange book, pp. 11–14), which inform educators as to how they can adapt their instruction to better meet students' learning needs.

In Chapter 8, we focus on an underdeveloped area in the Math Recovery books, one that draws on classroom discourse structures and the feedback associated with classroom discourse. This discussion mainly connects to the green book (p. 57) and allows readers to consider how Math Recovery can be extended to promote classroom discussion.

By Chapter 9, we shift our focus again to consider how educators can group students in ways that allow for more equitable and inclusive mathematics instruction. The Math Recovery books have a few discussions on grouping models. For instance, the purple book (pp. 18–20) describes the Rotational Group Model. Other models are described in the blue book (Chapter 1) and the green book (p. 59).

In Chapter 10, we focus on some fundamental theoretical frames (e.g. constructivist learning theories) that explain why it is critical to allow children time to reflect on their mathematics learning. Much of this is described in the brown book (pp. 32–4 and Chapter 11).

In Chapter 11, we bring to the fore a discussion on equitable mathematics practices. Even though this is a new Guiding Principle, we found equitable practices in mathematics teaching to be evident, if mostly implicit, in many of the Math Recovery books. For instance, equitable mathematics practices were described in the form of the dimensions of mathematization (e.g. the white book, Wright & Ellemor-Collins, 2018, pp. 16–21; the brown book, Tabor et al., 2021, pp. 30–1; the orange book, Hackenberg et al., 2016, pp. 11–14). They were also described in relation to assessment design (e.g. the brown book, Tabor et al., 2021, Chapter 5), planning and goal setting (e.g. the brown book, Tabor et al., 2021, Chapters 4 and 5), and scaffolded approaches (e.g. the yellow book, Grindle et al., 2021). Finally, Chapter 12 of the brown book (Tabor et al., 2021) addresses equitable practices in teaching mathematics to a wide range of children.

These chapters are designed to address multiple learning theories, the learning needs of groups of children, mathematical instructional practices, and planning and assessment practices in mathematics. Often, these conversations are not novel but here allow connections to be made between learning theories and practices in ways that have not happened before in Math Recovery. By considering these connections to the Math Recovery books, we hope the reader can consider these theory–practice relationships in the context of many of the tools and resources already developed in the Math Recovery books.

Connections to NCTM and Council for Exceptional Standards in Education

As we stated earlier, the Guiding Principles were not created from mathematics learning theories or policy and standards development. They were created from student-centered mathematics classrooms, and more importantly, from observing how classroom practices better served children's mathematics learning in these classrooms. In recent years, many policies and standards have been designed to echo these mathematics learning theories. We believe, therefore, that an overview of how the Guiding Principles clearly connect to mathematics educational policies will be helpful to readers.

Part I: Effective Mathematics Teaching

In this part, effective mathematics teaching draws on rich learning theories that include constructivist approaches, learning progressions literature, mathematics knowledge for teaching, and three-phase planning approaches. When considering these learning theories in relation to high-leveraged practices, it seems that HLP 2: Explaining and modeling content, practices, and strategies; HLP 4: Diagnosing particular common patterns of student thinking and development in a subject-matter domain; and HLP 14: Designing single lessons and sequences of lessons, can be explained by much of the established learning theories in mathematics education (Council for Exceptional Children, 2017, pp. 356 & 358). Moreover, we found that teachers may inevitably draw on effective teaching practices such as: implement tasks that promote reasoning and problem solving; establish mathematics goals to focus learning; build procedural fluency from conceptual understanding, and support productive struggle in learning mathematics (NCTM, 2014, p. 3).

Part II: Assessments and Responsive Mathematics Teaching

In the second part of the book, we discuss assessments and effective mathematics teaching by reflecting on formative assessment literature, teacher noticing, and means by which to orchestrate meaningful mathematics discourse. These key learning theories are explicated in the high-leveraged practices: HLP 1: Leading a group discussion; HLP 3: Eliciting and interpreting student thinking; HLP 6: Coordinating and adjusting instruction during a lesson; HLP 15: Checking student understanding during and at the conclusion of lessons; and HLP 17: Interpreting the results of student work, including routine assignments, quizzes, tests, projects, and standardized assessments (Council for Exceptional Children, 2017, p. 356–358). By promoting these high-leveraged practices, we suggest educators draw from responsive mathematics teaching practices, such as use and connect mathematical representations; facilitate meaningful mathematical discourse; and pose purposeful questions (NCTM, 2014, p. 3).

Part III: Inclusive and Equitable Mathematics Teaching

In the third part of the book, the focus is on how educators can provide inclusive and equitable mathematics instruction for all students. This chapter broadly draws on the literature focused on social–constructivist learning theories, children's ability to abstract their reasoning, and how power and identity play a key role in mathematics learning. To situate these discussions, we posit that high-leveraged practices such as HLP 9: Setting up and managing small-group work; and HLP 12: Learning about students' cultural, religious, family, intellectual, and personal experiences and resources for use in instruction, would best illustrate detailed standards for this important work (Council for Exceptional Children, 2017, p. 357–358). Moreover, effective teaching practices pose purposeful questions and build procedural fluency from conceptual understanding, providing details on how educators can further support all of their students' mathematics learning (NCTM, 2014, p. 3).

Conclusion

By drawing on multiple findings, learning theories, and standards, we hope to promote a rich, comprehensive discussion around how the Math Recovery Guiding Principles can frame meaningful mathematics learning in multifaceted teaching approaches. We hope this work serves multiple educational stakeholders and all students' mathematics learning needs.

References

Council for Exceptional Children (2017). News from CEC: High-leverage practices in special education. *Teaching Exceptional Children*, 49(5), 355–60.

Grindle, C.F., Hastings, R.P. and Wright, R.J. (2020). *Teaching Early Numeracy to Children with Developmental Disabilities*. London: Sage.

Hackenberg, A.J., Norton, A. and Wright, R.J. (2016). *Developing Fractions Knowledge*. London: Sage.

National Council of Teachers of Mathematics (NCTM) (2014). *Principles to Actions: Ensuring Mathematical Success for All*. Reston, VA: NCTM.

Tabor, P.D., Dibley, D., Hackenberg, A.J. and Norton, A. (2021). *Numeracy for All Learners: Teaching Mathematics to Students with Special Needs*. London: Sage.

Wright, R.J. and Ellemor-Collins, D. (2018). *The Learning Framework in Number: Pedagogical Tools for Assessment and Instruction*. London: Sage.

Wright, R.J., Martland, J. and Stafford, A.K. (2006a). *Early Numeracy: Assessment for Teaching and Intervention*, 2nd edition. London: Sage.

Wright, R.J., Martland, J., Stafford, A.K. and Stanger, G. (2006b). *Teaching Number: Advancing Children's Skill and Strategies*, 2nd edition. London: Sage.

Wright, R.J., Stanger, G., Stafford, A.K. and Martland, J. (2015). *Teaching Number in the Classroom with 4–8-Year-Olds*, 2nd edition. London: Sage.

2

Inquiry-Based Instruction

> ## Guiding Principle: Problem-based/ inquiry-based teaching
>
> "The teaching approach is inquiry based, that is, problem based. Children are routinely engaged in thinking hard to solve numerical problems which, for them, are quite challenging." (Wright et al., 2006, p. 26)

Introduction

Arguably, mathematics teaching and learning fundamentally center upon thinking and activity around some problem or challenge. The extent to which the problem space allows students to explore, reason, conjecture, connect, and create dramatically shapes the learning that will occur as well as their attitudes towards mathematics and their identity as mathematical learners. This chapter will focus on the nature and importance of inquiry-oriented learning grounded in authentic and engaging problem solving. We will examine the foundations of such learning processes and situate these ideas in the research literature, both contemporary and historic. Lastly, we will explore practical examples of inquiry-oriented mathematics teaching and learning and this principle in relation to other Guiding Principles in this book.

Inquiry

Before delving into the theoretical foundations and research literature of inquiry and mathematical problem solving, let's consider an example involving a small-group working with uncovered counters (see Figure 2.1).

TEACHER: "Now everyone is going to get a bag with counters. You should have 20 counters in your bag. Count them out loud and make sure."

[Students individually count their counters]

ALEAH: "I didn't get 20. I got 19."

TEACHER: "No, you got 20. Let me show you. [Counts Aleah's counters] One, two, three . . . 19, 20. See, you have 20."

ALEAH: "Oh yeah, I missed that one." [Touches one of the counters]

TEACHER: "OK, so I want you to put five counters on one side of your mat, and three counters on the other side. How many counters do you have on your mat altogether?"

SAMUEL: "That's easy. I got eight."

JULIE: [Touching each counter] "I think it's nine."

TEACHER: "Julie, I think you put too many out. Look at your left side. Let's count those together. One, two, three, four, five, six [Julie counts along with teacher]. See, one too many. Fix that, and you will get the right answer."

Figure 2.1 Small-group working on 8 + 3 with materials

In this example, we may notice aspects that might strike a layperson as fairly typical of how teachers interact with students in a mathematical moment. There is an introduction to the materials, a clearly posed mathematical task (i.e. 5 counters + 3 counters), and teacher support as students engage in the task. However, I suspect most readers of this book will find this exchange problematic and likely such negative perceptions connect to inquiry and problem solving, or lack thereof. Time and again, in this exchange, the teacher assumes control of the mathematical moment and of the students' problem space. Indeed, Julie's arrival at the answer, nine, creates an opportunity to examine her thinking with respect to the problem at hand. In this instance, though, the teacher relieves Julie of reasoning in the moment and, essentially, performs the mathematical thinking for her (i.e. "I think you put too many out ... Let's count together ..."). Ultimately, even in this brief exchange at the onset of a small-group instructional period, there are moments where we, as teachers, may constrain (or even eliminate) the opportunities to inquire, or more positively, create and expand such opportunities.

A Quick Note on Teaching and Critique

It is important to recognize that teaching is a highly complex endeavor, and we strongly suspect the teacher in this moment is acting in accordance with the best intentions and to the best of their capability. Teaching is hard work, and teaching well is exceedingly challenging. Nevertheless, it is important that we do not shy away from critical examination of our practice and the effects of such practice upon the mathematical learning and activity of our students. In this book, we will engage in such rigorous examination; however, we hope that it is received with a sense of our immense affinity for teachers and for the profession. The work of educators (and we count ourselves as educators) is so very important and rewarding. We hope that opening these critical spaces signals not a criticism of the teachers within but an abiding, reflective fellowship aimed at helping readers develop their practice in meaningful ways.

Meaning and Inquiry in Mathematics

Before we can grapple with the different ways that inquiry and problem solving might manifest in a mathematics classroom, we must first examine why these ideas are important in the first place. Indeed, we think it may be somewhat presumptuous to assume some consensus or broad agreement on inquiry and problem solving. Thus, we find it useful to investigate the *why* of inquiry before exploring the *how*. Fundamentally, emphasis on inquiry rests on beliefs about the nature of mathematics and the role of meaning. As Aristotle (1925) argues in the opening sentence of *Metaphysics*, "all [individuals] by nature desire to know." The quest for meaning has been rightly observed as being central to the human condition for nearly all of recorded history. More recently, on the topic of meaning, one of the pioneers of mathematics education, Brownell (1947), writes:

> We should … distinguish what I shall designate the *meaning of* a thing and the *meaning of* a thing *for* something else; for the sake of brevity, between *meaning of* and *meaning for*. I know little about the meaning *of* the atomic bomb because I lack the knowledge of chemistry and physics which are requisite to accurate understanding, but I think I know a good deal about the meaning of the atomic bomb *for* other things – for peace or for the destruction of our culture, for example … that children have meaningful experiences when they use arithmetic in connection with real life needs, relates to meanings *for* … On the other hand, just as the meaning *of* the atomic bomb is to be found in the related physical sciences, so the meanings *of* arithmetic are to be found in mathematics … They must be sought in the mathematical relationships of the subject itself, in its concepts, generalizations, and principles. In this sense a child has a meaningful arithmetic experience when the situation he deals with "makes sense" mathematically. He behaves meaningfully with respect to a quantitative situation when he knows what to do arithmetically and when he knows how to do it [*meaning for*]; and he possesses arithmetical meanings when he understands arithmetic as mathematics [*meaning of*] … Meaningful arithmetic, in contrast to meaningless arithmetic, refers to instruction which is deliberately planned to teach arithmetical meanings and to make arithmetic sensible to children through its mathematical relationships. (pp. 256–7)

In this seminal work, Brownell describes the different ways in which we may construct meaning. Here, Brownell argues for the pursuit of both meaning of and meaning for the mathematics at hand. For example, we should strive not only to help students establish a meaningful purpose for the mathematics of our classrooms (*meaning for*) but also create spaces for students to construct meaning around the mathematical ideas and processes themselves (*meaning of*). Moreover, the mechanism through which such meaning is constructed is inquiry. The willingness and freedom to inquire, to look within and seek explanation, is the activity upon which meaning is constructed.

Seeking meaning in mathematics via inquiry opens doors to discovery, within one's self and beyond, that would otherwise remain closed. Writing about the search for meaning and purpose, Su (2020) describes how mathematics may serve as a portal to truth, beauty, love, justice, and other virtues. Referred to as mathematics for human flourishing, Su grounds his vision in theory, history, and personal experience. On the topic of meaning, which is one of the virtues explored by Su, he writes:

> Learn a bunch of separate mathematical facts, and it's just a heap of stones. To build a house, you have to know how the stones fit together. That's why memorizing times tables is boring: because they're a heap of stones. But looking for patterns in those tables and understanding why they happen – that's building a house. (p. 38)

Similar to Brownell, Su describes the satisfaction, the virtue, of meaning in mathematics and how inquiry into the mathematics of the moment is the catalyst for such meaning.

What's the Problem?

Central to most any mathematical activity and deeper quest for meaning is a problem of some sort. Here, it is important to note that we use the term *problem* quite broadly to denote most any occasion for mathematical reasoning or action. Problems may be activities, tasks, or even rich verbal prompts that open opportunities for thinking mathematically. A problem may be grounded in most any mathematical domain, ranging from the foundational (e.g. determine the numerosity of two collections of counters) to the more abstract (e.g. determining the surface area of a ring torus). Mayer and Hegarty (1996) describe mathematics problems ascribing to two broad categories: routine and non-routine. They write:

> A routine problem exists when a problem solver knows how to carry out the correct solution procedure and recognizes that the solution procedure is appropriate for the problem ... Routine problems are not really problems at all because the problem solver knows what to do and how to do it. For this reason, such problems are often referred to as *exercises*. A non-routine problem exists when a problem solver has a problem but does not immediately see how to solve it. (p. 32)

The distinction being made is between facing a problem that is well understood with respect to solution processes and one that is not. Put so aptly by Mayer and Hegarty, such routine problems that are well understood and readily able to be solved aren't really problems at all. What we aim for in the spirit of inquiry and creating mathematical meaning are non-routine problems, the types of problems that, when faced, we do not immediately understand how to solve. These are the types of problems that provoke disequilibrium, or conflict, between new ideas and current conceptions (Carter, 2008) and lead to new and refined ideas. Non-routine problems are the ones that open space for exploration, creativity, and the pursuit of virtue (Su, 2020), precisely because the avenues for solution are unknown at the time of approach.

To the extent that we aim to emphasize non-routine problems as objects for inquiry-oriented learning, we wonder, then, who determines what is non-routine? For some, mathematics problems are thought of as items, external and objective, that may be transported amongst lessons and students. In a critique of this perspective, Thompson (1982) writes:

> I recently discussed with a prominent problem-solving researcher a taped interview of a missing addend problem, and commented that his behavior led me to believe it was an ill-structured problem. The other party couldn't understand how I could say that, since a missing addend problem is certainly well-structured. I remarked that from his perspective it may be, but the problem that the child was solving seemed to be ill-structured. (p. 155)

Here, Thompson affirms that how challenging (or ill-structured) a problem may be is determined by the individual solving it and not necessarily by the individual posing the problem. In their explanation of modeling students' thinking, Steffe and Thompson (2000) describe and draw a distinction between *mathematics of the student* and *students' mathematics*. The *mathematics of the student* refers to a teacher or researcher's understanding of how a student is thinking mathematically – a model, if you will. However, they argue that the *students' mathematics* is "independent of our own mathematical realities" and our understanding or model is "grounded in the mathematical realities of students as we experience them" (pp. 267–8). While this gets us into some pretty heady philosophical territory regarding shared realities, what we need to keep in mind as teachers is that our judgements regarding mathematical problems, their complexity, and level of challenge, are an estimation. We note that problems may take many different forms ranging from highly contextualized scenarios to seemingly simple (from our perspective) tasks involving collections of objects. In subsequent examples, we will present some contextualized tasks for examination; however, it is not context per se that invokes inquiry. Rather, it is the nature of the task itself and the extent to which the task is appropriately problematic such that students may engage in sustained hard thinking. Ultimately, it is the student facing such problems who determines the nature of a problem, whether or not it is routine or non-routine, and the extent to which the problem provides terrain for inquiry.

As teachers, we take on the role of *problem posers* and even though our students will be the ultimate judge regarding the nature of our problems, there are certain elements we may keep in mind as we design and pose problems aimed at facilitating inquiry amongst our students. In their description of problem-centered lessons, Wright et al. (2012) describe the importance of (1) use of strategic rather than procedural thinking, (2) tasks being perceived as problematic by the student, (3) connection to current mathematical understanding of the student, and (4) creation of opportunities to inquire and construct new mathematical understanding. Moreover, as we endeavor to identify or create problems for our students to navigate, we must not underestimate the power and importance of *problem generation* as part of the process of problem solving. Silver (1994) describes problem posing aimed at a generation of new problems:

> Problem posing can also occur at times when the goal is not the *solution* of a given problem but the *creation* of a new problem from a situation or experience … Problem posing can also occur *after* having solved a particular problem, when one might examine the conditions of the problem to generate alternative related problems. (p. 20)

While the nature of inquiry and problematic mathematics is complex and dependent in large part on the perceptions and capabilities of those engaged in such work, there are some broad design principles of which we may be mindful in our pursuit of such inquiry-oriented experiences. The National Council of Teachers of Mathematics (2014) describes elements of such instruction thusly:

1. Selecting tasks that provide multiple entry points through the use of varied tools and representations (p. 24)
2. Supporting students in exploring tasks without taking over student thinking (p. 24)
3. Encouraging students to use varied approaches and strategies to make sense of and solve tasks (p. 24)
4. Selecting tasks that allow students to decide which representations to use in making sense of problems (p. 29)
5. Advancing student understanding by asking questions that build on, but do not take over or funnel, student thinking (p. 41)
6. Helping students realize that confusion and errors are a natural part of learning, by facilitating discussions on mistakes, misconceptions, and struggles (p. 52)

The above are some key considerations for the design and implementation of inquiry-oriented mathematics learning, but note that this list is certainly not exhaustive. Rather, we might consider these elements as a jumping-off point to delve deeper into learning mathematics via inquiry that is grounded in rich problems. In the following sections, we will focus on practical scenarios and applications regarding this work.

Opening up a Task

As a practical lens through which to examine the interaction between the mathematical problem and the potential for inquiry, let's consider two tasks within the area of *structuring to 20* (Wright and Ellemor-Collins, 2018; see Figure 2.2).

TASK 1:

My granny out in the country always has a bunch of different animals in her house. One time, I asked her, "What's in your house today, granny?" She replied, three goats and four fish.

QUESTION: Not counting granny, how many legs are in granny's house? How many tails?

TASK 2:

My granny out in the country always has a bunch of different animals in her house. She has a funny way of answering questions, and never gives a straight answer. One time, I asked her, "What's in your house today, granny?" In her usual way, she replied, "Well, besides me, there are twelve legs and three tails."

QUESTION: What animals might be in granny's house?

Figure 2.2   Animal tasks

These tasks invoke a similar context and somewhat similar mathematical demand. Task 1 asks students to create three iterations of four (goat legs) and add five single units (2 goat tails and 3 fish tails). Task 2 asks students to construct units (i.e. animals) that would accommodate 15 items (12 legs and 3 tails). Of particular interest, though, is the extent to which these seemingly similar tasks open space for inquiry, exploration, and creative reasoning. In task one, students are set upon a prescribed pathway to arrive at a specific numerical outcome – 12 legs and three tails. In task two, however, there is not a prescribed pathway and solutions might diverge considerably. Consider the responses to task two (see Figure 2.3).

Jaden:	"I think she has three dogs. That would give you twelve legs and three tails."
Aliyah:	"What if she had a spider? But that wouldn't give her enough legs or any tails. I am not sure that would work."
Kimberley:	"Spider! Like a tarantula! That could work if she had a spider and three animals that had tails but no legs."
William:	"Fish have tails and no legs."
Kimberley:	"Yeah, fish! So, a tarantula, three fish, and then two more legs and no tail."
Aliyah:	"Do gorillas have tails? I don't think so, but they have two legs. So, a tarantula, three fish, and a gorilla is twelve legs and three tails, right?"
Jaden:	"Do birds have tails? They have tail feathers, so that means they have tails. You could do something with birds since they have two legs and a tail. You could do three birds, that's six legs and three tails. And then you could add a bug, like a big cockroach, then you have twelve legs and three tails."
William:	"What about a snake? Could we do one with a snake? That's just like a long tail and no legs."
Aliyah:	"Snakes don't have a tail. That's its body. Ask the teacher, he will tell you."

Figure 2.3   Conversation around animal task 2

For this task, we see students engaging with the task and creating novel conjectures aimed at exploring the boundaries of what the task parameters will permit (e.g. any kind of animal). The open nature of this task allows for students to approach it with a spirit of inquiry and meaning-making that likely would not occur in the more constrained first task. We might think of this distinction as the difference between the routine (task 1) and the non-routine (task 2). Further, the spirit of play embodied in the conversation is indicative of virtues described by Su (2020) which emerge when students are given the opportunity to freely inquire and explore mathematically.

400 – 198: A Tale of Two Implementations

In the example from the preceding section, we explored how two somewhat similar tasks might enhance or constrain students' inquiry into the mathematical moment. However, the implementation and guidance around a specific task also influence the potential for inquiry. Let's examine the task 400 – 198. Returning to the ideas presented by Thompson (1982) around perceptions of task structure, some might look at this problem and think of the standard algorithm – particularly if the task is presented in a vertical configuration. However, 400 – 198 is arguably very ill-suited to the standard algorithm (think of all the borrowing and carrying) and there are other, more efficient strategies students might bring to bear on this task. Consider the scenarios in Figure 2.4.

400 – 198	$\begin{array}{r}400\\-198\end{array}$
Teacher: "Think about this one." [*presents 400 – 198 written horizontally*] "What could you do with this one?" **Kabrey:** "That's a hard one." **Teacher:** "Well, where could you get started?" **Kabrey:** "I guess I could line it up and subtract." **Teacher:** "Sure, that's one way. Is that the way you want to go?" **Kabrey:** "Not really. That's a ton of borrowing. It's almost like four-hundred minus two-hundred, though." **Teacher:** "Tell me more about that. What do you see there?" **Kabrey:** "Well, if I think about it like four-hundred minus two-hundred, then the answer is two-hundred. Except it's not. There's two missing because of the one-hundred ninety-eight." **Teacher:** "OK, so what about those two that are missing?" **Kabrey:** "I'm not sure about that. Since it's subtraction, I am thinking I have to take those away, so the answer would be the 198." **Teacher:** "That's interesting. So, you are thinking that 198 plus 198 is 400. Wonder if there is any way we could know for sure?"	**Teacher:** "Think about this one." [*presents 400 – 198 written vertically*] "What could you do with this one?" **Kabrey:** "That's a hard one." **Teacher:** "What side should you start on? The ones?" **Kabrey:** "Yeah, the ones." **Teacher:** "Ok, so what do we do with the ones?" **Kabrey:** "I can't take eight from zero, so I have to make the zero a ten. Then the zero next door becomes a nine." **Teacher:** "That's it. You're getting it." **Kabrey:** "Ten minus eight is two." [*writes 2*] "Nine minus nine is zero." [*writes zero*] "Four minus one is three [*writes 3*]. So, 302, right?" **Teacher:** "But what about that four? Does that need to change?" **Kabrey:** "I guess so." [*crosses out the 4*] **Teacher:** "What should it turn into? Here's a hint, you had to borrow from it." **Kabrey:** "Does it go down one?" **Teacher:** "Yes! So, what is your answer?" **Kabrey:** "202?"

Figure 2.4   400 – 198: Two examples

In the examples, we see a teacher working with a student, Kabrey, around a common task of 400 – 198; however, the exchanges are quite different. Beginning with the task itself, the vertical presentation on the right acts as something of a suggestion, or primer, with respect to the standard algorithm. Just arranging the task in that configuration steers the conversation towards that algorithm. The horizontal presentation on the left, however, removes that suggestion and signals a more open field for Kabrey to approach the task. As we design and plan the mathematical tasks for instruction, we do well to consider how task presentations may lead students toward particular avenues for solving. There may be moments when such leading is desirable; however, if our goal is to create space for inquiry and meaning-making, we do well to present problems which minimize such implicit leading and suggestion.

Diving deeper into the moment, we see some real differences in task implementation on the part of the teacher. In the exchange on the left, we see much less explicit leading and funneling toward a particular strategy (i.e. "Tell me what you see there"; "Wonder, how could we know for sure?"). In these talk moves around the task, the teacher creates space for student inquiry. Particularly noteworthy is Kabrey's initial idea of using the standard algorithm. The teacher refrains from evaluating this choice, but merely asks, "Is that the way you would like to go?" The purpose with that question, ostensibly, is to encourage Kabrey to think carefully about the affordances and constraints of the algorithm for that particular task. Ultimately, Kabrey elects to think about the task in a different manner, and the teacher deftly creates space for that reasoning.

Contrast the exchange on the left to that on the right. At the onset, the teacher funnels the child toward the standard algorithm (i.e. "What side should you start on?") and then proceeds to direct questioning towards progress through the algorithm. The nature of the questions is also noteworthy in that the questions are considerably more closed in nature, often requiring little besides yes/no responses from the student ("But what about the four? Does that need to change?"). In this exchange, we see how the potential for inquiry may be intentionally (or perhaps unwittingly) removed or minimized at the level of the individual task.

Lastly, in exchange on the left, we note that Kabrey does not arrive at the correct solution (202); rather, she offers a solution of 198. Again, the teacher withholds evaluation of that answer and positions a key question as a *wondering* ("Wonder if there is any way we could know for sure?"). While some may see this lack of evaluation and certitude as problematic, the result in this moment is that it provides opportunity for further mathematical thought on the task. Specifically, the teacher invites Kabrey to look into the problem through a different lens to examine her own thinking. Perhaps this might involve thinking about the sum of 198 + 198. Perhaps Kabrey creates a representation (e.g. an empty number line) to further examine the task and her own thinking. The point here is that a seemingly well-structured and straightforward arithmetic task becomes an opportunity for exploration, meaning-making, and ownership through skillful presentation and probing. This careful reading of the moment with the intent to open (rather than constrain) space for inquiry and meaning can make tremendous impact even when considering an individual task.

The Role of Realistic Context

In the preceding example, we examined how an individual task could be positioned to either enhance or constrain inquiry-oriented problem solving. The task in question (400 – 198) did not incorporate a particular context. Rather, it is what some might call a *bare-number* task. There are, however, many different ways that teachers may frame or contextualize mathematics problems to give them some additional meaning beyond bare numbers. Sometimes referred to as real-world problems or doing mathematics in context, establishing some realistic situation or frame for thinking mathematically can be quite useful for creating rich problem-solving space and room for inquiry. In their description of Realistic Mathematics Education (RME) theory, Van den Heuvel-Panhuizen and Drijvers (2014) write:

> Although "realistic" situations in the meaning of "real-world" situations are important in RME, "realistic" has a broader connotation here. It means students are offered problem situations which they can imagine. This interpretation of "realistic" traces back to the Dutch expression "zich REALISEren," meaning "to imagine." It is this emphasis on making something real in your mind that gave RME its name. Therefore, in RME, problems presented to students can come from the real world but also from the fantasy world of fairy tales, or the formal world of mathematics, as long as the problems are experientially real in the student's mind. (p. 521)

From this perspective, meaningful, or *realistic*, mathematical tasks don't necessarily have to be arranged within a literal world, but rather realistic such that the context may be explored in one's imagination, including games and puzzles of a fantastical nature. Of course, this doesn't preclude grounding tasks in lived reality, but it also doesn't limit us to such perspectives either.

Diving deeper into these ideas surrounding RME, there are particular principles that might inform our thinking with respect to leveraging context and realism for inquiry. Echoing our earlier examination of mathematical meaning, the *reality principle* refers to the notion that:

> mathematics education should start from problem situations that are meaningful to students, which offers them opportunities to attach meaning to the mathematical constructs they develop while solving problems … teaching starts with problems in rich contexts that require mathematical organization. (Van den Heuvel-Panhuizen and Drijvers, 2014, p. 523)

Simply put, good problem contexts should facilitate reasoning and meaning-making with respect to the mathematical ideas in play. Relatedly, the *activity principle* asserts that students be considered "active participants in the learning process [and that] mathematics is best learned by doing mathematics" (Van den Heuvel-Panhuizen and Drijvers, 2014, pp. 522–3). In the context of inquiry and problem solving, rather than leading and funneling students towards particular ways of thinking, this principle invites us to create space for students to think and act mathematically and to trust that they can do so within a properly posed task. In summary, RME puts forth a vision of context that is broad enough to encompass not only the physical world but also our imaginations, is predicated on the creation of mathematical meaning, and trusts that students best learn by acting and doing – engaging in rich problem solving via inquiry and exploration.

Now that we have some conceptual framing with respect to doing mathematics in context, let's examine what this might look like in a practical situation. Let's examine two somewhat similar contextualized tasks and how each might provide space for inquiry and problem solving (see Figure 2.5).

CLIMBING STAIRS

Sometimes when we go up and down stairs, we go one step at a time. Sometimes, we might skip one or more steps depending on how fast we are moving. At times, we might even jump from a certain point all the way to the bottom of the stairs.

Imagine we are in a big stairway and each step has a number (1, 2, 3, 4, 5, 6, and so on). Also, imagine that we can either climb (one-step-at-a-time) or jump (either 2, 3, or 4 steps at a time).

We climbed 12 steps and took two jumps. We are now at step 18; on what step might we have started and why?

What are the fewest jumps it would take to climb 100 stairs (starting at step 1)? What are the most jumps?

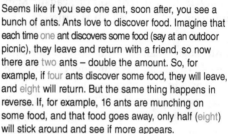

ANTS EVERYWHERE

Seems like if you see one ant, soon after, you see a bunch of ants. Ants love to discover food. Imagine that each time one ant discovers some food (say at an outdoor picnic), they leave and return with a friend, so now there are two ants – double the amount. So, for example, if four ants discover some food, they will leave, and eight will return. But the same thing happens in reverse. If, for example, 16 ants are munching on some food, and that food goes away, only half (eight) will stick around and see if more appears.

If 24 ants are munching on some food and that food goes away, how many ants are sticking around? How could you figure this out?

What math story could you write about this scenario where ants arrive and leave and, at the end of the story, there are 16 ants waiting for some food?

Figure 2.5 Tasks in context

Both tasks invoke some contextualized frame for mathematical activity and reasoning – either doing and undoing knots or the prospect of ants doubling at an outdoor picnic; however, the contexts are employed somewhat differently. Doing and Undoing Knots invokes the notion of tying and untying as something of a metaphor for mathematical action, while Ants Everywhere is a much more literal, albeit somewhat fantastical (e.g. ants gathering friends), narrative structure enrobing the mathematical tasks. Both are adaptable and could accommodate mathematical exploration along many different paths. For example, what if *doing* was adding 13 to some number and *undoing* was subtracting 13? What if, instead of each ant gathering one friend, they gathered three friends? The point is that context can operate productively at different levels, ranging from a loosely attached metaphor to a highly specific problem scenario.

Another common feature of these tasks is the manner in which each task creates space for students to generate new problem parameters and scenarios within the given context. In Doing and Undoing Knots, it's imagining different ways of *doing* and *undoing* aside from doubling and creating problem spaces to explore those different ways. In Ants Everywhere, students are asked to create a storyline involving iterations of doubling and halving of their own design. This aspect of task design and use of context drives to the heart of inquiry and is aligned with the virtuous mathematical pursuit of creativity (Su, 2020). The opening of terrain for students to explore and extend the boundaries of the context *via students' own generation of new tasks and problem parameters* is a key avenue for students to actively inquire into a particular mathematical idea or concept.

Realism and Fermi Problems

As a special type of realistic mathematical experience, *Fermi problems are* extremely open-ended tasks that provide students with expansive terrain for inquiry and exploration. Such tasks typically involve opportunities for estimation and modeling, but the fundamental design element of a Fermi problem is that the task is formulated:

> in such a way that the problem solvers not immediately associate the problem with a known strategy or procedure on how to solve it, but rather urge the problem solvers to invoke prior experiences, conceptions, constructs, strategies and other cognitive skills in approaching problems. (Ärlebäck, 2011, p. 1011–12)

Indeed, a key part of solving a Fermi problem is developing the problem itself. Consider one example of such a task put forth by Ärlebäck (2009):

> On the street level in the Empire State Building, there is an information desk. The two most frequently asked questions to the staff are:
>
> • How long does the tourist elevator take to the top floor observatory?
> • If one instead decides to walk the stairs, how long does that take?
>
> Your task is to write short answers to these questions, including the assumptions on which you base your reasoning, to give to the staff at the information desk (p. 342).

This task certainly meets the RME criteria for realism given the specificity and practicality of the context. Moreover, this task also aligns with the RME activity principle in that it positions students as active participants in their own learning and reflects a notion that mathematics is best learned via authentic practice. However, the Fermi problem is especially noteworthy in that it asks even more of students than, say, task varieties exemplified by Figure 2.5 (i.e. Doing and Undoing Knots; Ants Everywhere). Fermi problems begin with some initial formulation of the problem itself, along with explicit examination and testing of assumptions that drive such formulations. There is typically some important fact-finding that must occur as part of this process. In the example from Ärlebäck, students may choose to investigate typical elevator speeds, average stair-climbing rates, the positioning (i.e. floor number) of the observation deck, typical elevator wait times for this experience, and on and on. Even before the student moves on to the task mathematically, there is so much terrain to explore and space for inquiry into the nature of the task itself. Certainly, most (or perhaps even many) tasks that we pose as teachers can be as expansive as Fermi problems. Such problems represent, perhaps, the zenith with respect to inquiry opportunities.

Connecting and Reflecting

Inquiry and problem solving are inextricably connected to other practices put forth in this book. Arguably, inquiry fundamentally informs each of the chapters that follow. However, we find it useful to identify and highlight a few connections we feel are particularly noteworthy such that your continued reading experience may be richer and more deeply coherent. Likely, you will note additional connections of your own as you make your way through the chapters that follow.

Discussed in detail in Chapter 3, learning progressions and the extent to which teaching builds upon and supports children's mathematical conceptions and reasoning provide a meaningful lens for the operationalizing of inquiry-oriented learning. This is reflected in and informs the RME *level* principle which describes how realistic and meaningful experiences should accommodate students' construction of increasingly sophisticated strategies and ways of thinking as they grow mathematically. Relatedly, the most productive problems are those positioned at the edge of a student's capability, and Chapter 9 provides a key examination of such task-positioning and the role of productive struggle in mathematics learning.

Particularly germane to our exploration of inquiry and problem solving are the ideas related to instructional planning presented in Chapter 5, where we consider the teaching and learning cycle and how that cycle may inform planning – specifically, the planning of lesson launches, explorations, and discussions. As you read that chapter and engage with the examples therein, we encourage you to return to this chapter and consider the extent to which inquiry and rich problem solving provide a foundational worldview for the planning of instruction and activity around such instruction, including our own actions as teachers.

Lastly, key ideas in this chapter related to inquiry, the role of meaning, pursuit of virtue, the nature of mathematical problems connect us to the themes of equity examined in Chapter 11. For example, as we endeavor to create (or refine within our curriculum materials) rich and realistic contexts in which to explore mathematical ideas, we do well to consider how such contexts reflect or match with the lived experiences, or identities, of our students. We might consider how such tasks create avenues for access for different constituencies in our classrooms and what resources may be needed to enhance such access. We might consider how power is distributed amongst students and ourselves as we negotiate rich problem spaces. Lastly, we might consider how we frame and define achievement in such problem spaces – how are right and wrong, success and failure defined, and who falls along which path? Indeed, there is an elemental connection between mathematics for inquiry and creating equitable spaces for students' practice of mathematics and these ideas can live in concert with one another.

Questions for Reflection

To conclude this examination of inquiry via problem solving, we find it useful to consider a few key questions that might guide us in this area. Note, these questions are designed, we hope, to challenge you a bit and, like a productive mathematical task, may not lend themselves to easy answers. Our goal with these ideas is to prompt you to ponder as you put them into practice.

- To what extent do the problems you pose students allow for inquiry and exploration? Are there opportunities for divergent thinking, creativity, and multiple pathways towards solutions, or do they guide and funnel students towards one particular strategy or way of reasoning?
- How and to what extent are these ideas of inquiry, meaning, and problem solving reflected in your mathematics curriculum? If they are not well reflected, how might you work toward this vision for mathematics learning in your classroom? If they are well reflected, how might you further refine such experiences?
- How do you see yourself and your role as students inquire and problem-solve to construct mathematical meaning? What sorts of things do you say and do in those moments? Do they

create and sustain inquiry? If not, what might you do differently? How do the questions you may ask in these moments reflect the spirit of inquiry in this chapter?

- When you design, refine, adapt, or modify mathematics problems in context, how do you consider the relative affordances of a context? How do you think about realism? Is there room for creativity and imagination within a given context?
- How and to what extent do the mathematical problems and experiences connect with the lived experiences of your students? Do they create or constrain access for student groups, and if they constrain access, what resources or supports might you provide to offset this?
- What do you do when students grapple with problems and experience difficulty? How do you balance mathematical struggle and progress in those moments?

References

Aristotle (1925). *Aristotle in 23 Volumes* (translated by H. Tredennick). Cambridge, MA: Harvard University Press.

Ärlebäck, J.B. (2009). On the use of realistic Fermi problems for introducing mathematical modeling in school. *The Mathematics Enthusiast*, 6(3), 331–364.

Ärlebäck, J.B. (2011). Exploring the solving process of group solving realistic Fermi problems from the perspective of the anthropological theory of didactics. In M. Pytlak, T. Rowland and W. Swoboda (Eds), *Proceedings of the Seventh Conference of European Research in Mathematics Education* (pp. 1010–20). University of Rzeszów, Poland.

Brownell, W.A. (1947). The place of meaning in the teaching of arithmetic. *Elementary School Journal*, 47(5), 256–65.

Carter, S. (2008). Disequilibrium and questioning in the primary classroom: Establishing routines that help students learn. *Teaching Children Mathematics*, 15(3), 134–7.

Mayer, R.E. and Hegarty, M. (1996). The process of understanding problems. In R.J. Sternberg and T. Ben-Zeev (Eds), *The Nature of Mathematical Thinking* (pp. 29–53). New York: Routledge.

National Council of Teachers of Mathematics (NCTM) (2014). *Principles to Action: Ensuring Mathematical Success for All*. Reston, VA: NCTM.

Silver, E.A. (1994). On mathematical problem posing. *For the Learning of Mathematics*, 14(1), 19–28. Published by: FLM Publishing Association.

Steffe, L.P. and Thompson, P.W. (2000). Teaching experiment methodology: Underlying principles and essential elements. In R. Lesh and A.E. Kelly (Eds), *Research Design in Mathematics and Science Education* (pp. 267–307). Hillsdale, NJ: Erlbaum.

Su, F. (2020). *Mathematics for Human Flourishing*. New Haven, CT: Yale University Press.

Thompson, P.W. (1982). Were lions to speak, we wouldn't understand. *Journal of Mathematical Behavior*, 3(2), 147–65.

Van den Heuvel-Panhuizen, M. and Drijvers, P. (2014). Realistic mathematics education. In S. Lerman (Ed.), *Encyclopedia of Mathematics Education* (pp. 521–5). Dordrecht, Netherlands: Springer.

Wright, R.J., Ellemor-Collins, D. and Tabor, P.D. (2012). *Developing Number Knowledge: Assessment Teaching and Intervention for 7–11-Year-Olds* [Red Book]. London: Sage.

Wright, R.J. and Ellemor-Collins, D. (2018). *The Learning Framework in Number: Pedagogical Tools for Assessment and Instruction*. London: Sage.

Wright, R.J., Stanger, G., Stafford, A.K. and Martland, J. (2015). *Teaching Number in the Classroom with 4–8-Year-Olds*, 2nd edition. London: Sage.

3

Mathematics Learning Progressions and Multiple Student-Created Strategies

Guiding Principle: Incorporating symbolizing and notating

"Teaching supports and builds on the child's intuitive, verbally based strategies and these are used as a basis for the development of written forms of arithmetic which accord with the child's verbally based strategies." (Wright et al., 2006, p. 27)

Introduction

When supporting and building on children's reasoning and strategies, teachers often incorporate a framework, a trajectory, or a progression so they are better prepared to leverage students' strategies in their teaching. Some frameworks, trajectories, or progressions are research driven and stem from children's reasoning (Sarama and Clements, 2009) and some stem from curricula materials, wherein publishing companies use state standards. Often, educators even create their own frameworks, trajectories, or progressions (Empson, 2011). In fact, all three of these terms draw from different research studies, are used in very different ways, and can help educators plan and teach in very different ways (Ellis, 2014; Ellis et al., 2014; Weber et al., 2015).

For example, the National Research Council (2007) defines a *learning progression* as "descriptions of successively more sophisticated ways of thinking about a topic that can follow one another as children learn about and investigate a topic over a broad span of time" (p. 214). Given the successive nature of broad learning goals in a learning progression, many argue this term takes on a macro lens. Wright and Ellemor-Collins (2018) describe their Learning Framework in Number as a system which has "several major features" connected "into a coherent approach [for] instruction in children's number knowledge" (p. 5). The systematic frame of the Learning Framework in Number suggests that children's learning is not linear, and designs instructional materials in a connected manner. Finally, Sarama and Clements (2009) define a *learning trajectory* as:

> … descriptions of children's thinking as they learn to achieve specific goals in a mathematical domain, and a related, conjectured route through a set of instructional tasks designed to engender those mental processes or actions hypothesized to move children through a developmental progression of levels of thinking. (p. 9)

Learning trajectories tend to focus on the actions or mental processes that instructional materials are designed to engender in children. This suggests educators should use a micro lens when building upon children's learning, as evidenced by their actions and mental processes.

To better distinguish between how these tools are defined and used, Weber and colleagues (Weber et al., 2015) explain that progressions document children's movement between and through standards or benchmarks, whereas learning trajectories document children's emergent strategy development and the sophistication of these strategies. This chapter takes up all three tools to illustrate why each type of tool might be helpful for different reasons.

We first focus on the terms used in research by introducing two math educators planning and teaching children third grade mathematics. It is not our hope that particular language is used, but that when we talk about using progressions, frameworks, or trajectories, we are clear as to how we are using these tools. Next, we discuss the development and use of learning progressions, frameworks, and trajectories in the research and in the classroom. Finally, we describe classroom situations where all learning tools are most beneficial.

Educators Using Learning Progressions, Frameworks, and Trajectories

Two mathematics educators (Mr. Young and Ms. Sulton) sit together one afternoon and plan a series of lessons for the next week. In this situation, these two educators have very different past educational experiences. Mr. Young is in his first year of teaching third grade mathematics. Ms. Sulton is in her 23rd year of teaching third grade mathematics. The educators use curriculum materials and the *Learning Framework in Number* (Wright & Ellemor-Collins, 2018) materials. Both educators teach children with multiple abilities and do not group their students for mathematics instruction. To begin planning, Mr. Young opens the teacher guide provided by the curriculum publisher. In this guide, an opening activity is given with the traditional problem that connects a past lesson to the current lesson. Ms. Sulton looks at the lesson and explains that children often don't see this opening problem as related to the past lesson. Mr. Young and Ms. Sulton then consider early multiplication and division strategies that children might use in the current lesson and what strategies children used in past lessons. By connecting her children's strategies from the past lessons, Ms. Sulton is able to group her students into different types of strategy development that they are evidencing. Ms. Sulton explains to Mr. Young how they can draw from the dimensions of mathematization (see Figure 3.1) to build from their students' strategy development.

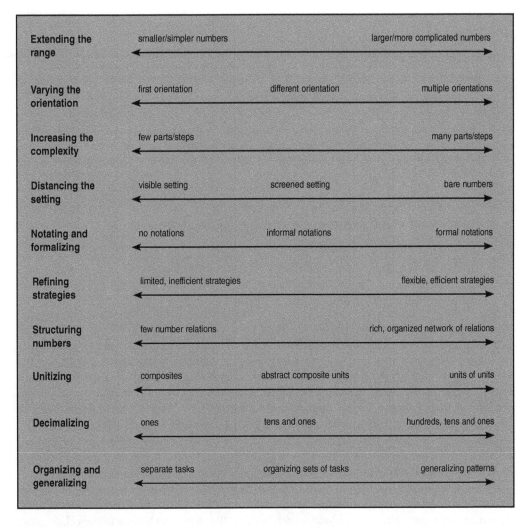

Figure 3.1 Dimensions of mathematization

Source: Wright and Ellemor-Collins, 2018, p. 18

Mr. Young opens up the state standards, drawn from the *Common Core State Standards for Mathematics* (NGA Center and CCSSO, 2010), and wonders what standards his children are moving through in these lessons. Here, he documents standards that he expects the children to meet and what this means for his own educational goals. In particular, he notes that his third grade students will "[i]nterpret products of whole numbers" and "[i]nterpret whole-number quotients of whole numbers" (2010, 3.OA.A.1 & 3.OA.A.2; see Figure 3.2). He considers carefully how these standards might explain the strategies the children in his class are developing and how he can leverage this development. Mr. Young determines that he needs to differentiate his instruction in the classroom but is uncomfortable not using the curriculum materials and does not yet understand how the *Learning Framework in Number* book relates to the curriculum.

CCSS.MATH.CONTENT.3.OA.A.1

Interpret products of whole numbers, e.g. interpret 5 × 7 as the total number of objects in 5 groups of 7 objects each. For example, describe a context in which a total number of objects can be expressed as 5 × 7.

CCSS.MATH.CONTENT.3.OA.A.2

Interpret whole-number quotients of whole numbers, e.g. interpret 56 ÷ 8 as the number of objects in each share when 56 objects are partitioned equally into 8 shares, or as a number of shares when 56 objects are partitioned into equal shares of 8 objects each. For example, describe a context in which a number of shares or a number of groups can be expressed as 56 ÷ 8.

Figure 3.2   Represent and solve problems involving multiplication and division

Note: Standards 3.OA.A.1 and 3.OA.A.2 from the *Common Core of State Standards for Mathematics*

Source: © Copyright 2010. National Governors Association Center for Best Practices and Council of Chief State School Officers. All rights reserved.

In this situation, Ms. Sulton is also considering her children's emerging strategies and how they are developing from perceptual counting towards more abstract multiplication strategies. Ms. Sulton is implicitly drawing from a trajectory that she has developed from her past teaching experiences and from the framework provided in the *Learning Framework in Number*. Because of her experience teaching third grade for so many years, she is comfortable diverging from the curriculum and understands implicitly how the *Learning Framework in Number* materials connect to the curriculum. By drawing on both (her children's learning trajectory and the learning framework), she plans at the micro level and places her students' strategy development in the foreground of her instruction. Comparatively, Mr. Young is considering his children's strategies at a macro level. Here, he connects them broadly to his state standards and to the curriculum objectives, goals, and activities. His planning seems to draw from a progression provided to him through the state standards and curriculum. Mr. Young has not yet taught mathematics to children in third grade and has not yet developed an understanding of how children's counting relates to their multiplicative reasoning.

Given these different ways that trajectories, frameworks, and progressions are used, Mr. Young and Ms. Sulton are discussing two important goals for the children in their classrooms. First, when using trajectories and frameworks, educators can build on the strategies children in their classrooms evidence. This allows educators the opportunity to develop children's mathematics in meaningful ways. It also allows educators opportunities to differentiate instruction for varying types of learning in flexible ways. Second, when using progressions, educators can draw from state standards and curricula to understand the broad system of development that children move within. This allows educators to develop overarching goals that keep their children moving forward towards benchmarks in their mathematical development. By using all these tools, educators can connect the strategies their children develop to nuanced instruction and broad benchmarks. Both of these lenses are important when teaching mathematics. Interestingly, researchers also use these tools in very different ways. In the next section, we draw from learning theories to explain how these tools are used in research and have extended the mathematics education field.

Learning Progressions, Trajectories, and Frameworks

Learning progressions, trajectories, and frameworks are tools used in the last few decades by educators and educational researchers. Historically, "stages" and "levels" documenting children's mathematics development began with Jean Piaget's work (e.g. [1941] 1965) in early childhood development. This work suggested that children developed stages of learning through their ability to make sense of their perceptual experiences (von Glasersfeld, 1995). Through this development, Piaget also explained how mathematics was an outcome of one's psychological development in terms of their ability to interpret their perceptual world and make sense of it. Building upon this work and others, Gagne (1968) examined learning hierarchies and levels of children's addition and subtraction. From this important work and others in the research field, reform-oriented instruction was developed (Lobato and Walters, 2017). Given these new instructional materials, educators were able to place children's learning at the center of the classroom. However, limitations still existed. In short, educators were not yet able to use a micro lens to document their children's mathematics development over time (Lobato and Walters, 2017).

Since the turn of the 21st century, mathematics educational researchers have taken up several theoretical frames to examine children's learning. By doing so, they have found that different tools are helpful for different research and educational goals. In Table 3.1, Lobato and Walters' (2017) examination of seven different types of learning progressions and trajectories in mathematics and science education research is organized for our consideration. In the table, we describe how each of the seven tools is characterized, its purpose, and its benefits and limitations. For example, schemes and operations are one type of learning trajectory characterized by a focus on children's learning processes with a micro and macro lens. This tool is beneficial because educators can use it to document their children's mathematics learning in a multifaceted way. Its limitation is that schemes and operations are often developed in small-group settings or environments where educators and one student are solving problems together. This may prevent an educator from using the tool in a whole-class setting.

Table 3.1 Comparing trajectories, progressions, and frameworks in research

Types of Tools	Characteristics of Tools	Educational Purpose
Cognitive levels	Distinct types of student cognition are ordered in a hierarchical level approach	This tool can be used at a macro level, considering broad levels of cognitive sophistication. It can explain how children's strategies become more sophisticated over long periods of time and can also inform diagnostic assessment tools. The tool is limited by the implicit development of learning from one level to the next

(Continued)

Table 3.1   (Continued)

Types of Tools	Characteristics of Tools	Educational Purpose
Levels of discourse	Development of sophisticated levels of communication are placed on a continuum	This tool can be used at micro and macro levels. For instance, it can be used by educators to consider day-to-day shifts in children's communication and engagement in a mathematics discussion and how these shifts illustrate broader forms of mathematical reasoning over time. The tool can also help educators connect their children's home language to their school language. The tool is limited by the need for children to develop and use particular vocabulary, which happens more often in science classrooms than mathematics classrooms
Schemes and operations	Learning process development, which evidences different degrees of sophisticated strategies	This tool can be used at both micro and macro levels. Often, these processes illustrate holistic development but allow educators more fine-grained understandings of their students' strategy development. This tool is not lock-step, meaning educators may find their children progress in different directions, providing them opportunities to revisit more rudimentary processes to be used for sophisticated learning later. These tools are limited because they are often developed with small groups of children or in one-on-one learning environments
Hypothetical learning trajectory	Learning processes and instructional processes are combined in a series of tasks. These trajectories are grounded in children's learning and educators' decision making	This tool can be used at both micro and macro levels. Often, the processes engender students' strategy development, but also consider how educators make sense of these and develop instructional goals for the children in their classroom. This tool is considered a living document, as it should be revised continually by educators to allow for children's strategy development to be in the foreground of mathematics instruction. This tool begins with educators' conjectures of their children's strategies. This tool is often limited because it can stand apart from state standards and not seem meaningful to educators
Collective mathematical practices	Community learning is ordered through children's mathematical practices	This tool is used at the macro level. It can be used by educators considering how the children in their classroom take learning processes "as-shared." This tool provides a sequence of practices that show educators the "normative" processes children engage in. It often includes helpful representations, social norms, and mathematical community expectations
Curricular coherence	Ordering broad learning targets for children over the course of several years	This tool is used at the macro level and draws from broad research findings. Often, state standards (CCSSM, 2010) and the NCTM Process Standards (NCTM, 2000) are described as a type of curricular coherent tool. This tool can be inconsistent because it draws on several research findings
Observable strategies	Strands documenting levels of children's strategy development	This tool is used at the macro level and describes children's proficiency levels. This tool draws from children's observable strategies. Because children's observable actions are foregrounded and their cognitive development backgrounded, educators sometimes disregard the children's cognitive development. Limitations also include the fact that one strategy might result in multiple proficiencies

Source: Based on Lobato and Walters, 2017

Note: CCSSM – Common Core State Standards for Mathematics; NCTM – National Council of Teachers of Mathematics

Another tool discussed in Table 3.1 is the collective mathematical practices tool, which is often used at the macro level and documents mathematical community practices. The tool is helpful for educators designing instruction at the classroom level, wherein normative processes are foregrounded and individual strategies are backgrounded. The tool is limited in that nuanced mathematical learning is not the focus, preventing an educator's next steps from serving a child's individual mathematical learning needs. In sum, these tools are described by Lobato and Walters (2017) as types of trajectories, progressions, or both trajectories and progressions. Depending on the goals of a mathematics educator, some tools may be more appropriate than others.

In the final sections of this chapter, we connect these varying learning trajectories, progressions, and frameworks to the mathematics classroom. First, we discuss how the components of these tools relate to the mathematics classroom. Next, we discuss how they can be used by educators when they are planning and teaching mathematics. We end with questions for reflection and connections to ways that educators can use these tools to promote equitable mathematics learning.

Components of Learning Progressions, Trajectories and Framework in Classrooms

Revisiting the Case of Mr. Young and Ms. Sulton

When using these tools, educators often use part of one tool and part of another. In our earlier example, Mr. Young and Ms. Sulton used components of four tools: (1) the schemes and operations, (2) the hypothetical learning trajectory, (3) curricular coherence, and (4) observable strategies. Ms. Sulton draws from the *Learning Framework in Number*, which explains possible mental processes (schemes), operations, and dimensions of mathematization (to inform instructional decision making). These are components of the scheme and operations tool and the hypothetical trajectory tool. Mr. Young often drew from the state standards and the curriculum materials (curricular coherence) to plan his mathematics lessons.

When the two educators met to discuss their mathematics lesson plans, they were able to connect their ideas with the observable strategy tool. This allowed Ms. Sulton a way to connect to Mr. Young's curricula focus so that she could discuss what she noticed in her children's solutions, language, drawings, and strategies as evidence of the children's possible mental processes. Mr. Young focused on benchmarks and tasks more than his students' mental processes. This is very common with an educator who has never taught a subject before. Given this, the observable strategies tool gave Mr. Young a means to make connections between the micro lens Ms. Sulton used in her planning and the macro lens that he used in his planning.

By using all types of components from these tools, educators are given an opportunity to focus on their children's strategies, build upon them, and consider them within a larger system of development. To better understand these tools, we will discuss two more classroom examples: the cases of Ms. Phillips and Mr. Rosenfeld.

The Case of Ms. Phillips

Ms. Phillips has taught kindergarten for four years. She does not co-plan with a colleague and uses the curriculum loosely. As the children in her class explore mathematics concepts, she often walks around to take notes of children's observable actions. She often sits with children and asks them questions, prompting them to explain why and how they came to a particular solution. When planning, Ms. Phillips often uses her past teaching experience in kindergarten, her notes, and the mathematical practices (NGA Center and CCSSO, 2010) or the National Council of Teachers of

Mathematics process standards (NCTM, 2016). The details of these practices and process standards are outlined in Figure 3.3. Her instructional decision-making draws from components of three tools described in Table 3.1: (1) observable strategies, (2) collective mathematical practices, and (3) schemes and operations. For instance, when Ms. Phillips walks around the room and takes notes, she is capturing her children's observable practices. In isolation, this tool can be limited for educators because it places children's mental processes and cognitive development in the background. However, because Ms. Phillips also draws on her past teaching experiences in kindergarten, she is able to connect these observable strategies to how children develop meaningful mathematical practices. This connection is also considered more broadly with the NCTM's *Process* standards (2016) and the *Common Core State Standards for Mathematics* practice standards (NGA Center and CCSSO, 2010).

PS1: Problem Solving

- Build new mathematical knowledge through problem solving
- Solve problems that arise in mathematics and in other contexts
- Apply and adapt a variety of appropriate strategies to solve problems
- Monitor and reflect on the process of mathematical problem solving

PS2: Reasoning and Proof

- Recognize reasoning and proof as fundamental aspects of mathematics
- Make and investigate mathematical conjectures
- Develop and evaluate mathematical arguments and proofs
- Select and use various types of reasoning and methods of proof

PS3: Communication

- Organize and consolidate their mathematical thinking through communication
- Communicate their mathematical thinking coherently and clearly to peers, teachers, and others
- Analyze and evaluate the mathematical thinking and strategies of others
- Use the language of mathematics to express mathematical ideas precisely.

PS4: Connections

- Recognize and use connections among mathematical ideas
- Understand how mathematical ideas interconnect and build on one another to produce a coherent whole
- Recognize and apply mathematics in contexts outside of mathematics

PS5: Representation

- Create and use representations to organize, record, and communicate mathematical ideas
- Select, apply, and translate among mathematical representations to solve problems
- Use representations to model and interpret physical, social, and mathematical phenomena

MP1 Make sense of problems and persevere in solving them.

MP2 Reason abstractly and quantitatively.

MP3 Construct viable arguments and critique the reasoning of others.

MP4 Model with mathematics.

MP5 Use appropriate tools strategically.

MP6 Attend to precision.

MP7 Look for and make use of structure.

MP8 Look for and express regularity in repeated reasoning.

Figure 3.3   Comparing NCTM Process standards with CCSSM Practice standards

Note. PS – "problem solving", MP – "mathematical practices"

Having walked around the classroom to note her children's observable strategies, Ms. Phillips uses them for both the collective classroom practices tool and the scheme and operations tool. The first tool provides Ms. Phillips with a macro lens to determine the development her class is making throughout their kindergarten year when they are developing meaningful practices and processes. In particular, Ms. Phillips notes that her students first began kindergarten by making sense of problems and persevering when solving them but struggled to reason abstractly and quantitatively (see Figure 3.3, MP2). Given this, she designed tasks that encouraged the children in her class to solve problems with manipulatives, talk about them, and draw on paper their solutions. This provided the children with opportunities to represent their thinking in multiple ways, while also stepping away from the perceptual material they used in their initial solutions.

Ms. Phillips also used these observable strategies to note the potential mental processes (schemes) and operations they were using to solve problems. For instance, she began to note one day after reading the book *Ten Black Dots* (Crews, 1995) that some children were capable of using varying grouping strategies to construct "ten" and some students relied on only one or two grouping strategies to construct "ten." Ms. Phillips interpreted this as students' ability to use finger patterns, spatial patterns, and small units of ten. In future lessons, Ms. Phillips planned on tasks that encouraged students to partition larger units and doubles to ten in a figurative manner. This would mean that Ms. Phillips would engage students in counting tasks wherein some perceptual items are covered (see Wright and Ellemor-Collins, 2018, pp. 75–80).

By carefully considering the strategies her children use when problem solving, Ms. Phillips is also focused on the Problem Solving process standard (see Figure 3.3, PS1). In this standard, Ms. Phillips realizes that the children in her class need to "[a]pply and adapt a variety of appropriate strategies to solve problems" (NCTM, 2016). By making these connections, between collective mathematical practices and possible mental processes, Ms. Phillips is given the opportunity to design meaningful tasks while also differentiating these tasks to provide access to multiple students and build upon their strategies in the classroom.

The Case of Mr. Rosenfeld

Mr. Rosenfeld is a fifth-grade teacher with 17 years of teaching experience. Mr. Rosenfeld has taught fourth grade for 13 of these years and has looped up with his students from fourth grade to fifth grade the past four years. Mr. Rosenfeld plans with his colleagues but prioritizes his past teaching experience with his students when determining their mathematics development. Given this unique perspective, Mr. Rosenfeld draws on what many describe as a vertical trajectory, by considering the cognitive levels the children in his class evidence on the diagnostic assessments that he develops. Mr. Rosenfeld also engages the children in his class in classroom discourse and considers their language development as indicative of their mathematical understanding. By using both of these instructional strategies, Mr. Rosenfeld draws on the components of two tools (see Table 3.1): (1) Cognitive Levels and (2) Levels of Discourse.

For instance, when working with his students, Mr. Rosenfeld notes that children in his class are evidencing addition and subtraction facts up to 100, early multiplication and division actions, or varying degrees of ability to use multiplication basic facts. By noting these variances in children's mathematical activity, Mr. Rosenfeld is able to design two different types of lessons. First, Mr. Rosenfeld designs group activities that support some of the broad goals he might have for his children. Second, Mr. Rosenfeld designs some whole-class tasks that have multiple access points and opportunities for a high ceiling effect (see Caldwell et al., 2014, p. 8 for more on effective task designs). By being aware of both, Mr. Rosenfeld can engage in a "Launch, Explore, Discuss" lesson (see Chapter 5). Essentially, this means that the children in his class can explore the task(s), discuss their solutions in small groups, and finally engage in a whole-class discussion, connecting their mathematical ideas.

When engaging in a whole-class discussion, Mr. Rosenfeld also attends to the children's discussion as falling into varying degrees of autonomy. There are several frameworks that Mr. Rosenfeld could draw on, but he chooses one developed by Hufferd-Ackles and colleagues (2004, pp. 88–90), as this looks at four areas of discourse (questioning, explaining mathematical thinking, source of mathematical ideas, and responsibility for learning), and four levels (levels 0–3) of student autonomy in a discussion (see Chapter 8 for more information on mathematics discourse).

This framework showed Mr. Rosenfeld that the children varied in levels of student autonomy but mainly drew from the "explaining mathematical thinking" category at level 3 (indicating more student autonomy) and from the "responsibility for learning" category at level 2 (indicating a student-to-teacher and student-to-student discussion). Moreover, the types of "questioning" and "mathematical ideas" seemed to stem from level 1. This told Mr. Rosenfeld that he should promote student-to-student questioning by asking students to add to other students' mathematical ideas and use these mathematical ideas to guide his mathematics lesson. In subsequent lessons, he also began noting which children in his class were engaging with the discussion, in what way, and at which level.

By using broad cognitive levels, Mr. Rosenfeld is better equipped to determine children's cognitive levels and use them to design small-group and whole-class instruction. By combining this with the discourse trajectory developed by Hufferd-Ackles and colleagues (2004), Mr. Rosenfeld focuses on how to engage all of the children in his class by placing their ideas, questions, thinking, and learning at the center of his instruction, and so gives them the opportunity to connect the ideas they are constructing in small groups in a whole-class setting.

Using Concrete, Pictorial, and Abstract Progressions

When using these educational tools in the classroom, it is a teacher's goal to build upon the children's intuitive, verbally based strategies and use them as a basis for instruction. Often, general educators use these tools in the ways described, but sometimes educators who work with children with multiple abilities and learning needs feel conflicted as to how to use the tools in this way. In fact, Grindle et al. (2020) explain that there is often a debate between educators about how to approach teaching children with different mathematics needs. These are characterized as either "constructivist" or "systematic" approaches (p. 33). Constructivist teachers often utilize more inquiry-based instruction whereby children draw on their own experiences and their sense-making is made center. On the other hand, educators who intend to teach those with different learning needs might use more teacher-directed instruction. These two approaches seem to be at odds with each other, but Grindle et al. (2020) posit that there are opportunities for the two approaches to overlap.

For instance, when teaching children with multiple learning needs, teachers may begin by developing instruction around children's exploration and sense making with concrete materials (Grindle et al., 2020) before progressing towards pictorial representations and then abstract symbols. Often when educators design instruction around such a linear trajectory, children's sense making is not first designed to be at the center of the mathematics instruction. However, by engaging in concrete materials in this way, children's ability to make sense of problems becomes the focus of the lesson. Thus, by designing lessons in a systematic manner with a trajectory, educators are given the opportunity to bridge some systematic means for instruction with some constructivist approaches.

This type of progressive instructional move is often described in the dimensions of mathematics as "distancing the setting." By distancing the setting, educators take up their children's mathematics development and determine what type of material (e.g. concrete, pictorial) that they want their children to develop, which can stand in for the materials they are currently relying upon. Essentially, by using the dimensions of mathematics, educators find themselves relying more heavily on their children's sense making. In the following example, we will follow Ms. Snarr's use of concrete, pictorial, and abstract materials with a small group of students.

The Case of Ms. Snarr, a Mathematics Specialist

Ms. Snarr is a mathematics specialist working with children identified as requiring mathematics support in third grade. Ms. Snarr has noticed that her students often use counting-on strategies when adding and subtracting with concrete materials but struggle without them. This suggests a mismatch in their development of procedures and conceptual understandings with counting. Given this, Ms. Snarr decides to use manipulatives to begin where her children are successful in their mathematical activity. She provides her students with some double-digit addition and subtraction problems and with base-ten blocks. Here, she is able to help the children develop precise language when describing their strategies. She also documents details of their current strategies with concrete materials.

To transition the children towards more abstract activity, Ms. Snarr must help them take a step away from the concrete material. This can be done by using pictorial representations/material or by covering the concrete material (an example of distancing the setting from perceptual material). By distancing the setting even further, children can also create actions and visual motor patterns on the screen or mat to avoid relying on pictorial material (an example of distancing the setting from pictorial material). In these transitions, we describe pictorial material as types of finger patterns, dot patterns, and area models. Often, Ms. Snarr also draws on virtual manipulatives, allowing children more engagement with the figurative material. To help connect actions with concrete material (e.g. base-ten blocks) to actions with figurative material (i.e. virtual manipulatives of base-ten blocks), Ms. Snarr asks children to predict the solution by acting on the figurative material and then testing out their predictions by revisiting the concrete material. For example, Ms. Snarr asks the children in a group to solve the problem 35 – 17. She first asks them to use a number line (see Figure 3.4). She turns off the "show answer option" and has the children put the first number as "17" and the ending number as "35."

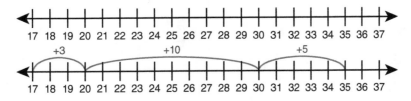

Figure 3.4   Number line engagement to illustrate figurative/pictorial material use

Using the number line, all the children individually determine the solution and then explain to their partners in their groups why they think their solution is accurate (see Figure 3.4). Then, the children test out their solutions with base-ten blocks. One group of children start by placing four base-ten blocks and five cubes on their mats before changing one base-ten block into ten cubes and then removing one ten block and seven cubes (see Figure 3.5).

Tens	Ones	Tens	Ones

Figure 3.5 Base-ten block engagement to illustrate concrete material use

A second group of children use the base-ten blocks differently. They begin with the subtrahend to count up towards the minuend (see Figure 3.6). They then go on to create 17 with one base-ten block and seven cubes. The children then add three cubes to make ten cubes and then add five more cubes to make a total of 15 cubes. At this point, the children count on, "8, 9, 10, 11, 12, 13, 14, 15, 16, 17, 18, 19, 20, 21, 22, 23, 24, 25". Next, they add one more base-ten block to make a total of 35. By counting the blocks below, they are able to determine the difference between the minuend and the subtrahend. This strategy is not one grounded in traditional procedures but is more closely aligned to the children's actions with the number lines.

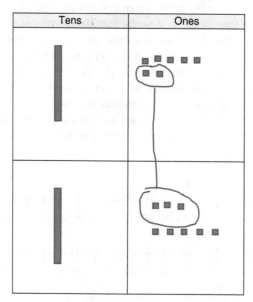

Figure 3.6 Base-ten block engagement to illustrate a solution with concrete material use

By using different materials, the children are developing different actions and acting on different parts of the problem. For instance, in the base-ten blocks, the first group of children are encouraged to act on the subtrahend (second number) in the problem. Here, they also need to regroup one of the tens, providing connections to more traditional procedures. The second group of children and all the children using the number line construct the difference by creating groups that add up from the subtrahend to the minuend (first number). In these solutions, children are developing actions that serve non-traditional procedures that are more conceptual in nature because the difference is being constructed and is the focus of the children's engagement with the materials. By discussing and reflecting on their actions, all the children are more prepared to construct symbolic procedures.

To make connections between the children's actions with concrete materials, pictorial materials, and symbols, Ms. Snarr takes the children's reflections one step further by having them document their strategies. She asks the children to solve a second problem, 28 – 9. The children first solve the task without writing and then use the number line to document their strategies on the number line. Next, she asks them, "What was your thinking there?" (question taken from Wright et al., 2012, p. 115) to elicit their thinking in numbers and words (see Figure 3.7). Some of the children explain that they first added one to the nine and subtracted the ten from the thirty-eight (28 – 10 = 18). Next, they add the one back to their total difference to find a total of 19. When they write this out, they try to make sense of their solution with the traditional procedure. They first break down the 28 into one ten and eighteen. By doing this, they are able to subtract the nine from the number line more readily (18 – 9). They can match the 10 – 0 to the ten jump on the number line and the 18 – 9 to the eight and one jump on the number line. By connecting this to the traditional procedure, the children can also connect their conceptual actions with their regrouping of two tens into one ten and one set of ten ones.

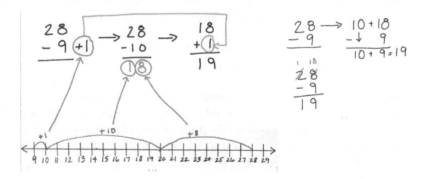

Figure 3.7   Strategy connections between symbols and figurative/pictorial materials

By making connections between concrete materials, pictorial materials, and abstract symbols, children are able to construct conceptual groundings for procedural understandings in a systematic manner. Educators working with children who have not yet constructed "ten" as an abstract object to act upon, might need to use different concrete materials (e.g. popsicle sticks, unifix cubes) that they can group into groups of ten. This grouping activity might then be a focus for educators, prompting them to use very different pictorial and abstract representations *or* to use the same pictorial and abstract representations but with different goals in mind. By beginning with children's activity in a concrete manner, educators have the opportunity to make micro-adjustments to their instruction grounded in their children's strategies in order to develop their children's verbal and abstract representations of their thinking.

Connections to Other Math Recovery Books

Throughout this chapter, we have related many of the discussions to other books in the Math Recovery series. In particular, we want to draw on more detailed sets of strategies, teaching practices, and resources that this book is not intended to discuss.

The following books provide details of students' number strategies and tasks that teachers can use to distance the setting, extend the range of numbers, and increase the complexity of a task:

- The purple book, *Teaching Number in the Classroom with 4–8-Year-Olds* (Wright et al., 2015): Focus on the last pages of Chapters 3–10 (pp. 51–2, 70, 91, 110, 134, 159–60, 176–7, 205) and on p. 11 there is an Early Number Learning Framework.
- The green book, *Teaching Number: Advancing Children's Skills and Strategies* (Wright et al., 2006): Focus on Table 1.1, pp. 9–21, and pp. 69–70.
- The red book, *Developing Number Knowledge: Assessment, Teaching and Intervention with 7–11-Year-Olds* (Wright et al., 2012): Focus on pp. 11–19.
- The blue book, *Early Numeracy: Assessment for Teaching and Intervention* (Wright et al., 2006): Focus on Chapters 2 and 4.
- The orange book, *Developing Fractions Knowledge* (Hackenberg et al., 2016): Focus on Chapter 2 and pp. 8–11.
- The white book, *The Learning Framework in Number: Pedagogical Tools for Assessment and Instruction* (Wright and Ellemor-Collins, 2018): Focus on Chapters 1 and 4.
- The brown book, *Numeracy for All Learners: Teaching Mathematics to Students with Special Needs* (Tabor et al., 2021): Focus on Chapter 5 in which the Learning Framework in Numbers is used to inform IEP development, and on Figure 1.1.

These books provide detailed frameworks, trajectories, and progressions and how to use them when teaching, planning, and assessing children. We did not cover details around planning as they will be discussed more fully in Chapter 5. How an educator plans with these tools is the essence of how these tools are used in a math classroom. For instance, when planning for an inquiry-based classroom, many structures can be used and, based on these structures, educators have the potential to use tools in very different ways.

In addition to the areas where these Math Recovery resources can help teachers engender sophisticated strategies from students, the white book also has many details on how a framework can be used for planning, teaching, and assessment purposes. For instance, in Chapter 1, Wright and Ellemor-Collins (2018) organize the framework into nine domains with three distinct types of pedagogical tools (assessments, models of children's thinking, and progressions). By incorporating these different tools, educators can use task-based interviews to determine how their students might solve problems. Their solutions can be compared to typical models of student learning in number and then placed along a progression where benchmarks of children's learning in number can give educators a direction. The scope of the white book is quite powerful and gives educators both micro and macro lenses while making their students' strategies central to their planning and instruction. By bringing students' reasoning front and center in their planning and using the frameworks, trajectories, and progressions, the educator "builds on the child's intuitive, verbally based strategies and these are used as a basis for the development of written forms of arithmetic" (Wright et al., 2015, p. 8).

Questions for Reflection

As you begin to take up this principle in your own mathematics classroom, these are some questions to consider:

- Which type of trajectory, progression, or framework do you use and why? How might new tools help you focus on different aspects of children's mathematics learning?
- How do you envision children's mathematics learning development? How does this align or not align with the tools you use?
- We know that changes in children's language and written forms of arithmetic evidence their ability to develop flexible, abstract ways of thinking. In what ways do children in your classroom progress from a reliance on concrete/perceptual material towards more abstract strategies?

Equity Concerns

As you consider the wide diversity in students' abilities to reason mathematically, you may find some trajectories, progressions, and frameworks afford you perspectives on the equity of your children's mathematics learning.

- When using benchmarks in mathematics learning, are you drawing on those that best represent your children's mathematical experiences?
- When interpreting children's strategy development, we often frame this development with standards that draw from majority populations and from our own experiences. We often do not begin with the culture of the children in our classroom. Take time out of your busy schedule and sit with children to better understand their home cultures and their home experiences related to the mathematics. By putting this at the center of your use of trajectories, progressions, and frameworks, your planning and teaching may allow for more inclusivity for the diversity of children in your class.

References

Caldwell, J.H., Kobett, B. and Karp, K. (2014). *Putting Essential Understanding of Addition and Subtraction into Practice: Pre-K-2*. Reston, VA: National Council of Teachers of Mathematics.

Crews, D. (1995). *Ten Black Dots*. Hong Kong: South China Printing Company.

Ellis, A.B. (2014). What if we built learning trajectories for epistemic subjects? An elaboration on Hackenberg's musings on three epistemic algebraic students. *Epistemic Algebraic Students: Emerging Models of Students' Algebraic Knowing, 4*, 199–207.

Ellis, A.B., Weber, E. and Lockwood, E. (2014). The case for learning trajectories research. In P. Liljedahl, C. Nicol, S. Oesterle and D. Allan (Eds), *Proceedings of the 38th Conference of the International Group for the Psychology of Mathematics Education and the 36th Conference of the North*

American Chapter of the Psychology of Mathematics Education (Vol. 3, pp. 1–8). Vancouver, Canada: PME.

Empson, S.B. (2011). On the idea of learning trajectories: Promises and pitfalls. *The Mathematics Enthusiast, 8*(3), 571–96.

Gagne, R. M. (1968). Presidential address of division 15 learning hierarchies. *Educational Psychologist, 6*(1), 1–9.

Grindle, C.F., Hastings, R.P. and Wright, R.J. (2020). *Teaching Early Numeracy to Children with Developmental Disabilities*. London: Sage.

Hackenberg, A. J., Norton, A. and Wright, R. J. (2016). *Developing Fractions Knowledge*. London: Sage.

Hufferd-Ackles, K., Fuson, K.C. and Sherin, M.G. (2004). Describing levels and components of a math-talk learning community. *Journal for Research in Mathematics Education, 35*(2), 81–116.

Lobato, J. and Walters, C.D. (2017). A taxonomy of approaches to learning trajectories and progressions. In J. Cai (Ed.), *Compendium for Research in Mathematics Education* (pp. 74–101). Reston, VA: National Council of Teachers of Mathematics.

National Council of Teachers of Mathematics (NCTM) (2016). *Process*. Standards and Policy. Retrieved November 12, 2021 from www.nctm.org/Standards-and-Positions/Principles-and-Standards/Process

National Council for Teachers of Mathematics (NCTM) (2000). *Principles and Standards for School Mathematics*. Reston, VA: NCTM.

National Governors Association Center for Best Practices and Council of Chief State School Officers (NGA Center and CCSSO) (2010). *Common Core State Standards for Mathematics*. Washington, DC: Authors.

National Research Council (2007). *Taking Science to School: Learning and Teaching Science in Grades K-8*. Washington, DC: National Academies Press.

Piaget, J. ([1941] 1965). *The Child's Conception of Number* (Translated by E. Duckworth). New York: The Norton Library.

Sarama, J. and Clements, D.H. (2009). *Early Childhood Mathematics Education Research: Learning Trajectories for Young Children*. New York: Routledge.

Tabor, P. D., Dibley, D., Hackenberg, A. J. and Norton, A. (2021). *Numeracy for All Learners: Teaching mathematics to students with special needs*. London: Sage.

von Glasersfeld, E. (1995). *Radical Constructivism: A Way of Knowing and Learning*. London: RoutledgeFalmer.

Weber, E., Walkington, C. and McGalliard, W. (2015). Expanding notions of "Learning Trajectories" in mathematics education. *Mathematical Thinking and Learning, 17*(4), 253–72.

Wright, R.J. and Ellemor-Collins, D. (2018). *The Learning Framework in Number: Pedagogical Tools for Assessment and Instruction*. London: Sage.

Wright, R.J., Ellemor-Collins, D. and Tabor, P.D. (2012). *Developing Number Knowledge: Assessment, Teaching, & Intervention with 7-11-Year-Olds*. London: Sage.

Wright, R.J., Martland, J., Stafford, A.K. and Stanger, G. (2006). *Teaching Number: Advancing Children's Skill and Strategies*, 2nd edition. London: Sage.

Wright, R.J., Stanger, G., Stafford, A.K. and Martland, J. (2015). *Teaching Number in the Classroom with 4–8-Year-Olds*, 2nd edition. London: Sage.

4

Relationships between Mathematics Teaching and Learning

> ### Guiding Principle: Engender more sophisticated strategies
>
> "The teacher understands children's numerical strategies and deliberately engenders the development of more sophisticated strategies." (Wright et al., 2006b, p. 27)

Introduction

Early-grade-level teachers often enact teaching practices that are designed outside the context of their children's learning and development. By considering children's responses and actions during a mathematics lesson, teachers can better understand their children's strategy development and how to deliberately engender the development of more sophisticated strategies. This chapter focuses on this relationship between mathematics teaching and students' mathematics learning. To examine the relationship in detail, in this chapter:

- First, we expand on the *history* of how mathematics teachers' knowledge has been studied and on related pedagogical theories in mathematics education.
- Next, we examine the mathematics learning theories that explain *children's development of mathematical strategies*. By exploring both mathematics teachers' knowledge and children's

mathematics learning, we are better able to consider the relationship between mathematics teaching and children's mathematics learning.

- Finally, we examine classroom vignettes that enable us to consider teachers' instructional moves and students' strategies in concert.

The Teaching and Learning Cycle

The teaching and learning cycle (Wright et al., 2006b, p. 52; Wright et al., 2015, p. 12) informs many of the Guiding Principles and brings forward four broad pedagogical questions (see Figure 4.1):

- Where are the children now?
- Where do I want them to be?
- How will I get them there?
- How will I know when they get here?

By focusing on these questions, teachers can make explicit connections between their teaching and their students' learning. For the purpose of this chapter, we will focus on the question, "Where do I want them to be?" Some aspects of this question bridge gaps between teaching, planning, and student learning (measured with assessments).

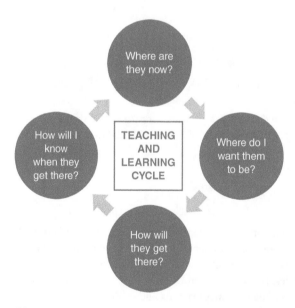

Figure 4.1   Teaching and learning cycle

Source: Wright et al., 2006b

When teachers focus on "Where do I want them to be?" they are required to have "sound mathematical knowledge, and … knowledge of how children's learning of mathematics progresses" (Wright et al., 2006b, p. 53). In this chapter, we unpack what it means to have a combination of these two types of knowledge by explaining the theories that address mathematics knowledge of teaching or MKT. Next, to better understand how to guide children's mathematical development, we briefly focus on learning theory that explains children's mathematics learning. Finally, with these theories in place, we describe teaching practices and student practices. By unpacking the teaching and learning cycle in this way, we are better able to explain why and how effective teaching practices can be leveraged to support conceptual student learning.

Mathematics Knowledge for Teaching: Tensions between Content and Pedagogy

As elementary teachers learn how to teach mathematics, they form different types of knowledge. Shulman (1981, 1987) first described this knowledge as "pedagogical content knowledge", which he characterized as a combination of "particular kinds of content knowledge and pedagogical strategies" (Shulman, 1987, p. 5). In the 1980s, educational leaders and policy makers were attempting to reform teaching so that teachers were considered as professionals. Associated standards and measures were developed to determine the degree of teachers' instructional effectiveness, which encouraged educational researchers, teacher teachers (i.e. professional development leaders), and educational stakeholders to reconsider the knowledge needed for effective teaching. By shifting teaching from a personal, artful style of communication with students towards an effective use of content knowledge and pedagogical knowledge, teachers' knowledge base was now being considered to be comprehensive and multifaceted.

Building on Schulman's work, Deborah Ball and colleagues (2008) extended pedagogical content knowledge (and the related subdomains) to mathematics teaching (see Figure 4.2). In particular, their mathematics teacher education findings identified six separate domains that elaborated on Schulman's framework and described the unique contributions that pedagogical knowledge and subject matter knowledge made to teachers' *mathematical knowledge for teaching* development.

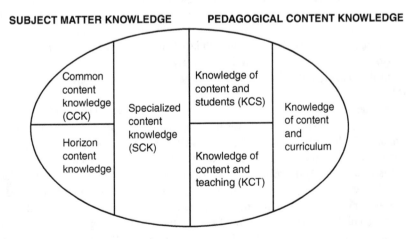

Figure 4.2 Domains of mathematical knowledge for teaching

Source: Ball et al., 2008

The subject matter knowledge subdomains included (1) *common content knowledge* (a common understanding of mathematics, allowing errors to be noted), (2) *horizon content knowledge* (an awareness of how mathematics content across/within grade levels is related), and (3) *specialized content knowledge* (an understanding of the mathematics that children construct, allowing for a nuanced degree of student conceptions). These three subdomains mapped out the unique contributions that teachers' subject matter knowledge made to their mathematics teaching.

The pedagogical content knowledge subdomains included three more types of knowledge: (4) *knowledge of content and students* (knowledge of students' common errors), (5) *knowledge of content and teaching* (knowledge of mathematics and teaching), and (6) *knowledge of content and curriculum* (related curricular knowledge similar to horizon content knowledge). Taken as a whole, these six subdomains emphasize the importance of both pedagogy and content in teachers' mathematical knowledge development. Ball et al. (2008) explain that each subdomain plays an important role in the efficacy and development of teachers' mathematics instruction. However, teacher educators often experience tension when designing professional development; these tensions often rest on whether their professional development should focus on teachers' mathematics content knowledge development or focus on teachers' pedagogical knowledge development. With limited timeframes and opportunities for meaningful learning opportunities, teacher educators often handle these tensions by designing professional development that incorporates both for professional development participants. In order to leverage both types of teachers' knowledge development, teacher educators often place students' mathematics learning at the center of the professional development.

Students' Mathematics Learning: A Guiding Force for Teaching Moves

By examining how teachers learn and reason when teaching mathematics, we also have to consider how students learn and reason when being taught mathematics. Piaget ([1941] 1965) first began examining young children's mathematics learning by observing young children in problem-solving contexts. Extending behavioral science, Piaget (e.g. 1937, 1945) used stimulus–response learning theories (where animals learned reflexively by developing life-saving responses to particular stimuli) to explain that humans had a three-part response (as cited by von Glasersfeld, 1995, p. 64).

Scheme theory resulted from this work by Piaget (e.g. [1937] 1971, [1945] 1951). As shown in Figure 4.3, students (1) perceive a mathematical situation, (2) develop an action or activity to solve the situation, and (3) develop an expected result (as cited by von Glasersfeld, 1995, p. 65). Often, children experience learning when an expected result and a perceived result are not the same. Piaget (as cited by Glasersfeld, 1995) described this experience as disequilibrium or cognitive dissonance. For example, when children begin counting items (e.g. cups on a table), they often skim or skip the cups that they are counting, resulting in different numbers than their peers. Through their reflection on their counting, children may say, "I counted seven cups!" and "I counted six cups!" With different results, children may experience disequilibrium because they realize that they should each have finished their acts of counting with the same counted number.

Figure 4.3   Scheme theory

Source: **Based on von Glasersfeld, 1995**

When children experience disequilibrium, they have to *accommodate* their schemes. Accommodation means that children will need to change one of the three parts of their thinking. When children's expected result and perceived result align, children experience equilibrium, and their schemes are *assimilated*. Assimilation allows children to abstract their reasoning further (as cited by von Glasersfeld, 1995). For example, when considering the counting example, children who arrived at different counted number words may realize their actions did not exactly account for each cup located on the table. Each child may recount the cups to determine how they can change their actions to experience equilibrium. Once children in this scenario experience equilibrium, they assimilate their scheme by internalizing their actions. Internalization of actions happens over several perceived experiences and may first be evidenced by their ability to use actions, words, or finger patterns to stand in for the physical counting of the cups.

By stepping away from using manipulatives and other concrete objects, children are more likely to anticipate their solutions and be aware of their strategies (Piaget, [1977] 2001). This awareness enables children to share their thinking, to make connections between their strategies and those of others, and to become fluent problem solvers. By recognizing that children learn mathematics in a progressive manner (Bruner, 2004; Clark, 2018; Illeris, 2018), teachers are better equipped to develop mathematics knowledge for teaching.

Effective Mathematics Teaching and Student Mathematics Practices

When considering what teachers' knowledge of mathematics includes and how children learn mathematics, we can explain why particular teaching and student practices are related and effective. By becoming aware of connections between teaching and learning, teachers can be mindful when developing their mathematics knowledge for teaching. Thus, this section will first explain effective student strategies, described in *The Learning Framework in Number* (Wright and Ellemor-Collins, 2018) and student practices, as outlined in the *Common Core State Standards for Mathematics* (NGA Center and CCSSO, 2010), before explaining how particular teaching practices from *The Learning Framework in Number* and *Principles to Action* (NCTM, 2014) may leverage these student practices.

Effective Student Strategies and Practices in Mathematics

Each Math Recovery book outlines students' strategies in such a way that allows educators opportunities to understand how previous actions and results from students' actions can be used to leverage future actions and more sophisticated strategy development. For example, in *Developing Number Knowledge* (Wright et al., 2012), the authors provide details about children's counting development by labeling seven mental strategies that children use when counting to solve addition/subtraction problems. For example, children may begin by "jumping" (pp. 103–4) by beginning from one number before jumping tens and then ones. Wright et al. explain that by learning how to jump, children are then equipped to "over-jump" (compensating for an overshoot of a jump), "jump to the decuple" (jumping to a decuple before jumping by tens and ones), and "split-jump" (splitting tens and ones before jumping by ones). By developing schemes that include "jumping" as an effective action for adding and subtracting, students are better equipped to refine these strategies and develop conceptual understandings of procedures. These strategies are detailed and align only with particular domains or content (i.e. conceptual place value). Thus, it is also important for teachers to understand effective student practices, regardless of the domain they are working within.

In the United States, student practices have been outlined as critical for students' success in mathematics. These practices are grounded in two foundational research-driven documents. First are the National Council of Teachers of Mathematics' process standards (NCTM, 2000), which outline processes to yield effective learning opportunities, in particular: (1) problem solving, (2) reasoning and proof, (3) communication, (4) representation, and (5) connections. Second, these practice standards draw on the National Research Council's report Adding It Up! (2001). This report details student practices that yield mathematical proficiency, in particular: (1) adaptive reasoning, (2) strategic competence, (3) conceptual understanding, (4) procedural fluency, and (5) productive disposition. The *Common Core State Standards* (NGA Center and CCSSO, 2010) included eight effective student practices in mathematics learning (see www.corestandards.org/Math/Practice):

- Make sense of problems and persevere in solving them.
- Reason abstractly and quantitatively.
- Construct viable arguments and critique the reasoning of others.
- Model with mathematics.
- Use appropriate tools strategically.
- Attend to precision.
- Look for and make use of structure.
- Look for and express regularity in repeated reasoning.

These practices are broad and do not align with a particular learning goal or grade level. Essentially, students might use these processes to solve a problem or evidence mathematical activity, regardless of the mathematical content or grade level. The mathematical proficiency practices can inform teachers of the characteristics of effective actions and broad learning goals.

By utilizing detailed, student-constructed strategies and the broad characteristics of students' learning processes, teachers can develop effective teaching practices that are grounded in working models of students' mathematical knowledge. Moreover, these working models can be understood as having the potential to engender more sophisticated student learning in mathematics, which can inform teachers of their students' learning development. The next section therefore examines how teachers can leverage their teaching practices to engage students in effective mathematical practices.

Leveraging Mathematics Teaching Practices to Develop Students' Mathematics Strategies

In *The Learning Framework in Number* (Wright and Ellemor-Collins, 2018), three broad elements are considered essential when developing a working model of students' mathematical knowledge: assessments, learning progressions, and teaching charts. In this chapter, we will focus on the dimensions of mathematization in the teaching charts. Wright and Ellemor-Collins (2018) outline ten dimensions of mathematization. When leveraging teaching practices to develop students' mathematics strategies, three of these dimensions are used most often:

- Extending the range
- Increasing the complexity
- Distancing the setting. (2018, p. 107)

After discussing these three dimensions, we will compare them to the NCTM's effective teaching practices (NCTM, 2014). These eight practices are broad and explain the relations between particular teaching moves, such as the dimensions and students' particular strategy development, and broad student practices.

Extending the Range

Often, tasks are designed with a range of arbitrary numbers. When teachers are intentional about which range of numbers students are given at different points in their mathematics learning, they are able to utilize a working model of students' reasoning to develop more sophisticated strategy development. In particular, Wright and Ellemor-Collins (2018) break down these number ranges into broad ranges, wherein students add in the "range of 1 to 5 through to adding numbers in the thousands" and finer grained ranges, wherein students structure numbers from 1 to 20 in four ranges (2018, p. 19). Thus, these ranges vary in size for different domains and strategy use.

Increasing the Complexity

Often, students develop more sophisticated strategies because tasks require them to manage more complex parts in the task (Wright & Ellemor-Collins, 2018). Therefore, by determining how each student reasons through a task, teachers can make informed decisions about the ease with which students solve problems. For example, Wright and Ellemor-Collins explain that a task can be made more complex by requiring children to manage more addends, regrouping, or a remainder. These progressions are, of course, not the only ones available to teachers. Teachers often increase the complexity of a task by changing the constraints. For example, in the Bubble Gum Task, adapted from the *Principles to Action* toolkit (NCTM, 2014; see Figure 4.4), once students solved the first part of the task – determining the size of gum each friend chewed – students are next asked to show, re-justify, and re-explain their solutions with this new information. By adding this second part to the task, its complexity increases by building on the schemes children have developed in their first solution.

Part 1: Four friends each bought a roll of bubble gum tape (1 foot in length). Francis chewed 2/3 of his gum. Carter chewed 4/9 of her gum. Sydney chewed 4/6 of her gum. Jamal chewed 3/4 of his gum. Use the first number line to show which friend(s) chewed the most gum, the smallest piece, and/or the same amount of gum.

Part 2: After deciding who chewed different amounts of gum, Jamal and Francis realized they had started with twice as much gum (2 feet in length) as Carter and Sydney's gum length (1 foot in length). Given this, use the second number line to now show which friend(s) chewed the most gum, the smallest piece, and/or the same amount of gum.

Figure 4.4   The bubble gum task

Source: Adapted from the Principles to Action Toolkit (NCTM, 2014)

Distancing the Setting

The third dimension of mathematization described by Wright and Ellemor-Collins (2018), distancing the setting, refers to teachers distancing an instructional setting, encouraging students to step away from a reliance on concrete materials. This dimension echoes the need for students to anticipate their solutions and be aware of their strategies. Wright and Ellemor-Collins explain that progressions within this dimension might include the following:

1. Manipulating the materials
2. Seeing the materials but not manipulating them
3. Leaving the materials behind a screen
4. Solving tasks posed in a verbal or written form without materials, which we refer to as bare number tasks. (2018, p. 19)

By designing tasks that distance students from settings that include concrete materials, teachers encourage students to develop a procedural fluency that is grounded in engagement with conceptual understandings.

Effective Teaching Practices

Resulting from a call to unify teaching and learning practices in mathematics education, the NCTM (2014) provided teachers with eight effective teaching practices. Broadly, these teaching practices were developed for multiple educational stakeholders, in the hope of addressing a wide range of school communities (NCTM, 2014). In particular, the goal of the teaching practices was to fill a "gap" in mathematics education by clearly explaining the effective teaching of mathematics whilst aiming to encourage the aforementioned student practices (NGA Center and CCSSO, 2010) in their students. On the basis of this goal, the authors of *Principles to Action* (NCTM, 2014) categorized the literature around student learning into six different types of effective mathematics experiences:

1. Engage in challenging tasks that involve active meaning making.
2. Connect new ideas with prior knowledge/informal reasoning.
3. Acquire conceptual knowledge as well as procedural knowledge.
4. Construct knowledge through discourse, activity, and interactions with meaningful problems.
5. Receive descriptive and timely feedback.
6. Develop awareness of themselves as learners, thinkers, and problem solvers. (NCTM, 2014, p. 9)

By examining student learning in this way, the authors of *Principles to Action* posited that teachers are better able to create effective teaching practices. The authors therefore used these six categories of student learning to create the following framework of eight effective teaching practices:

1. Establish mathematics goals to focus learning.
2. Implement tasks that promote reasoning and problem solving.
3. Use and connect mathematical representations.
4. Facilitate meaningful mathematical discourse.
5. Pose purposeful questions.
6. Build procedural fluency from conceptual understanding.
7. Support productive struggle in learning mathematics.
8. Elicit and use evidence of student thinking.

By considering the relationship between students' and teachers' effective practices, we can think closely about how students' strategy development should inform teachers' moves, both in the moment and before a teacher steps in front of the children. In the following section, we consider how teachers use students' effective mathematics practices and strategies to inform their teaching.

Examining the Relationships between Mathematics Teaching and Learning in Action

This section will explain the relationships between mathematics teaching and learning by examining classroom situations where (1) teachers planned to allow students to engage in effective practices or (2) responded to students' practices to promote effective practices.

Visiting Classroom Situations to Examine Teachers' and Students' Practices

In the first grade classroom situation taking place in the fall of the academic term, Jessica, the teacher, is using ten frames to help her students explore different number representations and early addition/subtraction concepts (see Table 4.1).

It seems Jessica is using ten frames (mathematical representations) to engage her students in their building procedural fluency from conceptual understanding. In particular, Garrett (one of the first grade students) uses these representations as a mathematics tool when reasoning quantitatively. His reasoning brings a unique additive solution to the problem, opening up the opportunity for several students in the classroom to use their conceptual understanding and to build procedural fluency.

In the second part of the lesson, the students do not connect their representations to their reasoning as much, suggesting they may have developed mental actions to support their reasoning with 10 and 1, but not with 10 and 6. Moreover, in this section Jessica begins posing purposeful questions to the students: "Where are we getting all these? I want to hear how we are figuring these numbers out. Can someone raise their hand to tell me their math thinking?" These questions prompt students to discuss and share their reasoning and suggest to the students that there may be more than one strategy for solving these problems. This move is particularly powerful because students are now reflecting on both their own actions and the actions of their peers, allowing them to compare strategies.

Table 4.1

Classroom Scenario	Effective Practices
Jessica: We are going to be working with 10 frames today when we go back to the carpet, so it is very important for you to listen. We know this is 10 because it is a 10 frame, and then Garrett knew that three on the top and three on the bottom equals six, so he added 10 plus six equals 16.	***Teaching Practices:*** Uses and connects mathematical representations
Class: Several students are saying out loud that six and 10 is 16.	Builds procedural fluency from conceptual understanding
Jessica: Wow, you know you are adding, Garrett – adding is kind of your thing.	Poses purposeful questions
Garrett: Math is my favorite thing in school.	
[In the next part of the lesson, Jessica transitions the class to the carpet spots at the front of the room. Jessica puts up a pocket chart. She has the Bridges curriculum manual in her hand and references it often during the lesson. Jessica is putting 10 frames representing teen numbers in the pocket chart. The 10 frames have bug pictures in patterns of five on them.]	***Student Practices:*** Uses appropriate tools strategically
Jessica: (Reading from the manual) I want you to look up here at these cards that show more than 10 bugs, and we are going to figure out ways to find out how many we have.	Reasons abstractly and quantitatively
Class: Students vocalize quantities. Several different responses.	
Jessica: How many bugs do I have?	
Class: Students begin speaking out loud, responding with different teen numbers.	
Jessica: (Points to a card. Shares all the responses heard from students.)	
Jessica: Where are we getting all these? I want to hear how we are figuring these numbers out. Can someone raise their hand to tell me their math thinking?	
Jessica: Maybe I shouldn't have all of these cards up here. (She takes down all the cards except one in order for students to focus on one frame to respond to.)	
Jessica: We are going to listen to Evan.	
Evan: 10 plus one is 11.	
Jessica: 11. That is great math thinking, Evan. Does anyone have another way to come up with 11?	

Source: Excerpt from Miller, 2019, pp. 148–9. Using conceptual understanding to build procedural fluency.

In the next excerpt, the lesson starts with the class preparing to do an activity called Number Rings (see Table 4.2). Instructions are that each student puts +1 in the center of the ring. Then when they get the thumbs up from Jessica, they can put any number they would like in the ring. Students are getting supplies to do the ring activity and going to their seats to begin working. The rings have an open center, where students record a number they are adding to each of the numbers written on the ring. The numbers 0–9 are written on the ring. Students record the sum around the outside of the ring.

Table 4.2

Classroom Scenario		Effective Practices
Jessica:	(Supports a student with this activity by providing her Unifix cubes to build the number written on the ring and then add one cube to that number to be able to determine the total. Once Jessica checks a student's board, she allows the student to choose a number for the center.)	***Teaching Practices:*** Builds procedural fluency from conceptual understanding
One student:	(Writes +100.)	Supports productive struggle in learning mathematics
Jessica:	(Goes around the room. She provides Unifix cubes to additional students who need to have the cubes in order to determine the sum of two numbers. For students requiring Unifix cubes to solve, Jessica is telling them to now place two Unifix cubes in the center to do +2 to each number written on the ring after completing +1.)	Implements tasks that promote reasoning and problem solving ***Student Practices:***
One student:	(Places +10 inside the ring.)	Makes sense of problems and perseveres in solving them
One student:	(Places +5 inside the ring.)	Looks for and expresses regularity in repeated reasoning
One student:	(Chooses +100 to place inside the ring. This is a bit out of reach for this student, but he is motivated to figure out the correct sums.)	Reasons abstractly and quantitatively

Source: Excerpt from Miller, 2019, p. 176. Promoting reasoning and problem solving.

In this excerpt, there is no dialogue, but it is evident that Jessica is working to understand the children's mathematical strategies and engender the development of more sophisticated strategies. She is doing this by implementing tasks that promote reasoning and problem solving. These tasks are also designed to promote students' productive struggle, and to build procedural fluency from conceptual understandings. In response, students seem to be making sense of problems and persevering in solving them, while also looking for repeated reasoning and reasoning abstractly. Thus, by drawing from students' reasoning, teachers, like Jessica, are more equipped to design tasks that promote sophisticated strategies.

Revisiting the Classroom Situations to Examine Students' Strategy Development

In these classroom situations, we broadly examined teachers' practices (NCTM, 2014) to determine how students develop effective mathematics practices (NGA Center and CCSSO, 2010). However, to develop specialized content knowledge and knowledge of content and teaching (Ball et al., 2008), let's revisit these same classroom situations to examine them more closely. This will allow us to develop an insight into Jessica's instructional choices and task design.

Remember that this classroom situation takes place in a first grade classroom in the fall academic term. Jessica, the teacher, is working with ten frames to help students develop conceptual understandings around ten and some more. The following three dimensions we are examining are from the white book:

1. Extending the range
2. Increasing the complexity
3. Distancing the setting. (Wright and Ellemor-Collins, 2018, p. 107)

We explained these dimensions earlier in the chapter. The students' strategies we are considering are more nuanced and represent strategies from many of the Math Recovery books. By considering this interaction at such a granular level, we are better able to exemplify the students' learning as sophisticated, or not sophisticated, in development (see Table 4.3).

In this classroom situation, Jessica, the teacher, transitions the students from one setting to another, distancing the setting. In particular, she takes the visual ten frames and places them in a pocket chart so the students can see the arrangements of dots but not in close proximity. She is implicitly discouraging them from touching the dots. This promotes the students' development of finger patterns, physical actions, verbal utterances, and/or imagined actions. In particular, by distancing the students from the materials, but not removing the materials, Jessica promotes students' partitioning (i.e. segmenting) of visible patterns (i.e. four and two, five and one more) and then gets them to combine (i.e. two and two, and six to make ten) or compare patterns (i.e. four and two compared to five and one) using several 10 frame grids. Thus, by distancing the setting, Jessica is able to encourage students in her class to visualize the actions associated with grid patterns when answering questions such as "How many dots?"

In the second classroom situation, Jessica has taught the students the Number Rings activity. The instruction is that each student is to put +1 in the center of the ring. Then when they get the thumbs up from Jessica, they can put any number they would like in the ring. Students are getting supplies to do the ring activity and going to their seats to begin working. The rings have an open center, where students record a number they are adding to each of the numbers written on the ring. The numbers 0–9 are written on the ring. Students record the sum around the outside of the ring (see Table 4.4).

In this classroom situation, the teacher uses two dimensions. By allowing students to choose a number for the center of the ring, they are given a task where the range is extended, and the complexity is increased. For instance, the range is extended because now the students are operating on the numerals 0–9 with a higher addend. In particular, the addend is one of their choosing. This gives the students an opportunity to determine how they would like to extend the range of this task. Students are now also asked to use the operations that they found to be successful in the first part of the task and to refine these for numbers in a higher range. Thus, this additional part of the task extends their strategies and potentially promotes disequilibrium.

Given these two short excerpts, it seems evident that by asking students purposeful questions that allow them to discuss their reasoning, they are better equipped to develop more sophisticated strategies. Additionally, when designing tasks, it is beneficial to consider how the three dimensions can promote productive struggles, build procedural fluency from conceptual understandings, and develop quantitative and abstract reasoning.

Table 4.3

Classroom Scenario		Dimensions
Jessica:	We are going to be working with 10 frames today when we go back to the carpet, so it is very important for you to listen. We know this is 10 because it is a 10 frame, and then Garrett knew that three on the top and three on the bottom equals six, so he added 10 plus six equals 16.	***Dimensions:*** Distancing the setting
Class:	Several students are saying out loud that six and 10 is 16.	
Jessica:	Wow, you know you are adding, Garrett – adding is kind of your thing.	***Student Strategies:***
Garrett:	Math is my favorite thing in school.	Partitioning visible patterns to 6 (p. 111)
[In the next part of the lesson, Jessica transitions the class to the carpet spots at the front of the room. Jessica puts up a pocket chart. She has the Bridges curriculum manual in her hand and references it often during the lesson. Jessica is putting 10 frames representing teen numbers in the pocket chart. The 10 frames have bug pictures in patterns of five on them.]		Combining patterns using 6-grids and 10-grids (p. 113)
Jessica:	(Reading from the manual) I want you to look up here at these cards that show more than 10 bugs, and we are going to figure out ways to find out how many we have.	
Class:	Students vocalize quantities. Several different responses.	
Jessica:	How many bugs do I have?	
Class:	Students begin speaking out loud, responding with different teen numbers.	
Jessica:	(Points to a card. Shares all the responses heard from students.)	
Jessica:	Where are we getting all these? I want to hear how we are figuring these numbers out. Can someone raise their hand to tell me their math thinking?	
Jessica:	Maybe I shouldn't have all of these cards up here.	
(She takes down all the cards except one in order for students to focus on one frame to respond to.)		
Jessica:	We are going to listen to Evan.	
Evan:	10 plus one is eleven.	
Jessica:	11. That is great math thinking, Evan. Does anyone have another way to come up with 11?	

Source: Excerpt from Miller, 2019, pp. 279–80. The strategies are from Wright et al., 2006b. The dimensions are from Wright and Ellemor-Collins, 2018

Table 4.4

Classroom Scenario		Dimensions
Jessica:	(Supports a student with this activity by providing her with Unifix cubes to build the number written on the ring and then add one cube to that number to be able to determine the total. Once Jessica checks a student's board, she allows the student to choose a number for the center.)	***Dimensions:*** Extending the range
One student:	(Writes +100.)	Increasing the complexity
Jessica:	(Goes around the room. She provides Unifix cubes to additional students who need to have the cubes in order to determine the sum of two numbers. For students requiring Unifix cubes to solve, Jessica is telling them to now place two Unifix cubes in the center to do +2 to each number written on the ring after completing +1.)	***Potential Student Strategies:*** Counting up from
One student:	(Places +10 inside the ring.)	Counting by tens and ones
One student:	(Places +5 inside the ring.)	
One student:	(Chooses +100 to place inside the ring. This is a bit out of reach for this student, but he is motivated to figure out the correct sums.)	Counting by tens and hundreds

Source: Excerpt from Miller, 2019. The strategies are from Wright et al., 2006b. The dimensions are from Wright and Ellemor-Collins, 2018

Connections to Other Math Recovery Books

Throughout this chapter, we have related many of the discussions to other books in the Math Recovery series. In particular, we want to take a moment to show and describe these connections below. This is done to allow teachers to draw on more detailed sets of strategies, teaching practices, and resources that this book is not intended to discuss.

The following books provide details of students' number strategies and tasks that teachers can use to distance the setting, extend the range of numbers, and increase the complexity of a task:

- The purple book, *Teaching Number in the Classroom with 4-8-Year-Olds* (Wright et al., 2015): Focus on Chapters 3–10.
- The green book, *Teaching Number: Advancing Children's Skills and Strategies* (Wright et al., 2006b): Focus on Chapters 5–10.
- The red book, *Developing Number Knowledge: Assessment, Teaching and Intervention with 7–11-Year-Olds* (Wright et al., 2012): Focus on Chapters 3–8; 11.
- The blue book, *Early Numeracy: Assessment for Teaching and Intervention* (Wright et al., 2006a): Focus on Chapters 8 and 9.
- The orange book, *Developing Fractions Knowledge* (Hackenberg et al., 2016): Focus on Chapters 4–13.
- The white book, *The Learning Framework in Number: Pedagogical Tools for Assessment and Instruction* (Wright and Ellemor-Collins, 2018): Focus on Chapters 1 and 6.

- The yellow book, *Teaching Early Numeracy to Children with Developmental Disabilities* (Grindle et al., 2020): Focus on Chapters 2–3, in particular where Math Recovery is being adapted for students with disabilities.
- The brown book, *Numeracy for All Learners: Teaching Mathematics to Students with Special Needs* (Tabor et al., 2021): Focus on Chapter 5 in which the Learning Framework in Numbers is used to inform IEP development.

These books provide detailed tasks, assessments, and discussions around how tasks and assessments relate to meaningful instruction. Assessments are not covered in Chapter 4 of this book, as it will be discussed more fully in Chapter 6. Assessments are the guiding force when making connections between teaching and learning. Moreover, they are critical in determining the particular student strategies your students may be constructing, while also helping teachers reflect on their own instructional practices. In addition, the green book discusses what a whole-class lesson might include. For instance, there are explanations around how to design "short sessions" and "problem-solving sessions" in mathematics (p. 60). The authors point out that the teacher's role is merely to "guide the discussion" and that "[a]ll children's strategies are valued." A helpful tip is that "[i]ncorrect responses are regarded as valuable opportunities to learn about children's thinking" (p. 60). By bringing students' reasoning front and center in a classroom, the teacher allows students' reasoning to guide the lesson. This is critical when understanding that "children's [mathematical] strategies … deliberately [engender] the development of more sophisticated strategies" (Wright et al., 2015, p. 7). In short, by making students' reasoning front and center in the classroom, the teacher is more equipped to develop more sophisticated strategies.

Questions for Reflection

As you begin to take up this principle in your own mathematics classroom, these are some questions to consider:

- What does it mean for a student to develop a "sophisticated strategy?" What goals and objectives do you have in your own mathematics teaching? How do they inform you of your students' goals?
- Where is your own pedagogical development? Do you want to grow in learning more about mathematics, your students' mathematics, or your mathematics instruction?
- How do you envision a mathematics classroom? What is the same or different in this classroom compared to what was described in this chapter? How do these differences relate to your students' strategy development?

Equity Concerns

As you consider the wide diversity in students' abilities to reason mathematically, you may find some practices are equitable and some are not:

- How might you pose purposeful questions to allow emergent bilingual students access to a discussion?
- What differences in strategies might you expect when children are identified with a learning difference?
- How might you rearrange the physical components (e.g. concrete manipulatives, paper and markers) to allow students opportunities to revisit physical actions?

References

Ball, D.L., Thames, M.H. and Phelps, G. (2008). Content knowledge for teaching: What makes it special? *Journal of Teacher Education, 59*(5), 389–407.

Bruner, J. (2004). A short history of psychological theories of learning. *Daedalus, 133*(1), 13–20.

Clark, K.R. (2018). Learning theories: Constructivism. *Radiologic Technology, 90*(2), 180–2.

Grindle, C.F., Hastings, R.P. and Wright, R.J. (2020). *Teaching Early Numeracy to Children with Developmental Disabilities.* London: Sage.

Hackenberg, A.J., Norton, A. and Wright, R.J. (2016). *Developing Fractions Knowledge.* London: Sage.

Illeris, K. (2018). An overview of the history of learning theory. *European Journal of Education, 53*(1), 86–101.

Miller, C.H. (2019). The Impact of Add+ VantageMR Professional Development: A study on teacher implementation following professional development. Doctoral dissertation, University of Minnesota.

National Council of Teachers of Mathematics (NCTM) (2000). *Principles and Standards for School Mathematics.* Reston, VA: National Council of Teachers of Mathematics.

National Council of Teachers of Mathematics (NCTM) (2014). *Principles to Action: Ensuring Mathematical Success for All.* Reston, VA: NCTM. https://pubs.nctm.org/view/book/9780873539 043/9780873539043.xml

National Governors Association Center for Best Practices and Council of Chief State School Officers (NGA Center and CCSSO) (2010). *Common Core State Standards for Mathematics.* Washington, DC: Authors.

National Research Council and Mathematics Learning Study Committee (2001). *Adding It Up: Helping Children Learn Mathematics.* Washington, DC: National Academies Press.

Piaget, J. ([1945] 1951). *Play, Dreams and Imitation in Childhood* (C. Gattegno & F.M. Hodgson, Trans.). London: Routledge.

Piaget, J. ([1937]1971). *The Construction of Reality in the Child.* (M. Cook, Trans.). New York: Ballatine Books.

Piaget, J. ([1941] 1965). *The Child's Conception of Number* (B. Inhelder, Trans.). New York: W.W. Norton.

Piaget, J. ([1977] 2001). *Studies in Reflecting Abstraction* (R.L. Campbell, Trans.). New York: Taylor and Francis.

Shulman, L. (1981). Disciplines of inquiry in education: An overview. *Educational Researcher, 10*(6), 5–23.

Shulman, L. (1987). Knowledge and teaching: Foundations of the new reform. *Harvard Educational Review, 57*(1), 1–23.

Tabor, P.D., Dibley, D., Hackenberg, A.J. and Norton, A. (2021). *Numeracy for All Learners: Teaching Mathematics to Students with Special Needs.* London: Sage.

von Glasersfeld, E. (1995). *Radical Constructivism: A Way of Knowing and Learning.* London: RoutledgeFalmer.

Wright, R.J. and Ellemor-Collins, D. (2018). *The Learning Framework in Number: Pedagogical Tools for Assessment and Instruction.* London: Sage.

Wright, R.J., Ellemor-Collins, D. and Tabor, P.D. (2012). *Developing Number Knowledge: Assessment, Teaching and Intervention with 7–11-Year-Olds.* London: Sage.

Wright, R.J., Martland, J. and Stafford, A.K. (2006a). *Early Numeracy: Assessment for Teaching and Intervention,* 2nd edition. London: Sage.

Wright, R.J., Martland, J., Stafford, A.K. and Stanger, G. (2006b). *Teaching Number: Advancing Children's Skill and Strategies,* 2nd edition. London: Sage.

Wright, R.J., Stanger, G., Stafford, A.K. and Martland, J. (2015). *Teaching Number in the Classroom with 4–8-Year-Olds,* 2nd edition. London: Sage.

5

Planning Effective Mathematics Teaching

> ### Guiding Principle: Selecting from a bank of teaching procedures
>
> "Teachers exercise their professional judgment in selecting from a bank of teaching procedures each of which involves particular instructional settings and tasks, and varying this selection on the basis of ongoing observations." (Wright et al., 2006, p. 27)

Introduction

Planning plays a key role in the instructional experience and this chapter will focus on how planning and students' mathematical activity interact with one another. We will situate planning in the research literature, examining productive approaches to planning that emphasize inquiry-oriented learning and that are responsive to students. Lastly, we will explore practical examples of instructional planning in the classroom and connect such planning to other ideals of mathematics teaching and learning.

Assumption of Autonomy

Prior to diving into contemporary ideas of instructional planning, let's examine some historical perspectives of such planning. In the middle of the last century, instructional planning was considered a fairly linear process where teachers identified objectives, selected or designed activities in support of those objectives, organized those activities, and created some mechanism for the evaluation of learning (Tyler, 1950). Moving forward in time, Popham and Baker (1970) described planning as the consideration of four components: (1) instructional goals, (2) materials and resources, (3) evaluation, and (4) students' interests. This last signifies a recognition of the importance of including the students themselves in the planning process. Embedded in these historical investigations of planning is the assumption that teachers have some degree of autonomy to design and shape an intended learning experience. The first few words of this Guiding Principle read, "Teachers exercise their professional judgement" and this exercise of judgement is absolutely essential for the consideration and enactment of meaningful, relevant, and productive instructional planning. While established learning goals (e.g. standards), curricula, and other instructional resources most certainly guide and inform the planning process (Castro-Superfine, 2009), teachers serve as mediators of these components to shape and organize them into experiences that are meaningful and relevant for students in a particular classroom. Moving more deeply into this chapter, we write with the assumption that you have agency to formulate and act upon your professional judgement in the classroom. If that is not the case, then we encourage you to present this chapter to decision makers to underscore the importance of providing such professional autonomy. In either event, professional autonomy and judgement are key elements of the foundation upon which productive planning rests.

Planning, Teaching, and Learning

A good place to ground our discussion of planning and how it relates to teaching and learning is to revisit the teaching and learning cycle presented in this book (and others within this series; see Figure 5.1).

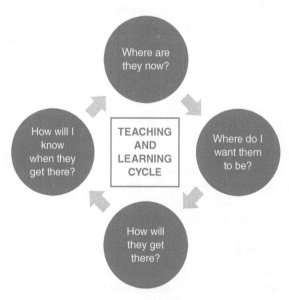

Figure 5.1 Teaching and learning cycle (Wright et al., 2006b)

As you might expect, planning primarily involves the cycle element of "How will they get there?" In other words, what manner of instructional experience will propel my students toward an intended mathematical learning goal? Here, we find it useful to consider such experiences, referred to as a "teaching cycle", in terms of three broad components: (1) Launch, (2) Explore, (3) Discuss (see Figure 5.2).

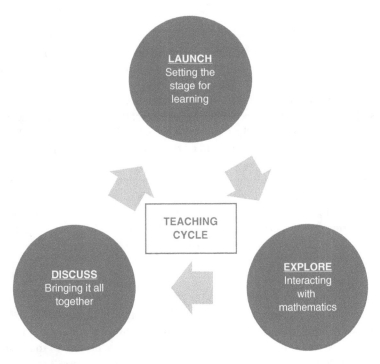

Figure 5.2 Teaching cycle

As an adaptation of a framework (Launch, Explore, Summarize) put forth by the authors of *Getting to Know Connected Mathematics* (Lappan et al., 2002), Launch, Explore, Discuss provides a productive yet accessible structure to engage in the work of instructional planning. Specifically, we can think of such plans as existing in three "acts."

Act 1 – Launch

This is the part of the lesson where we devise experiences that set the stage for mathematical learning that is to come. Perhaps we introduce a context or some novel task that captivates students' imagination, connects to their lived experiences, or engages them in some way. We may use movement or visuals in these moments, but the primary goal of a good launch is to draw students into the learning experience. The launch is also an opportunity to gauge students' initial understanding of the mathematical activities to come, perhaps by posing an open-ended question and allowing students to think/pair/share. Lastly, it allows teachers to set the stage for the more in-depth explorations that follow. Indeed, teachers do well to consider each of the planning components (Launch, Explore, Discuss) in concert with one another and to ensure strong connections between and across components. The launch to a lesson is an often overlooked, yet crucial planning element, and maximizing the opportunities provided by the launch will pay dividends throughout the lesson.

Act 2 – Explore

This is the body of the lesson where students dive more deeply into the mathematical experience itself. Explorations provide the opportunity for students to examine an idea more closely and analyze (and perhaps generalize) a particular concept, process, or skill. Explorations may occur at the individual level, but more often they involve collaboration amongst students with embedded opportunities to problem solve and persevere, to reason mathematically, and to construct viable mathematical arguments and critique the thinking of peers (NGA Center and CCSSO, 2010). From a planning perspective, tasks and activities should be rich and complex enough such that students are able to engage in varied ways and examine concepts and ideas via differing perspectives and using different strategies. Depending upon the nature of the exploration, it may not be necessary for all participants to complete every aspect of the task. Rather, teachers operate as facilitators during this part of the lesson, asking key questions, listening closely to the explanations of students, and observing their activity. Using this information, teachers make decisions, in the moment, to dive deeper into particular aspects of the exploration, move to other ideas, and consider when to move to the next act.

Act 3 – Discuss

Sometimes referred to as summarizing, this is focused on the orchestration of discussion amongst students of key ideas in the lesson. Perhaps this discussion involves considering previous activity or is organized around a new, related task. Sometimes, the Discuss portion of the lesson will begin with a key, open-ended question for students to consider in smaller groups. These discussions may be structured and sequenced such that they maximize productive discourse (Smith and Stein, 2011; see Chapter 8). Regardless of format, though, the key aspect is the connection of lesson activity to mathematical goals – reflecting upon one's own activity and the activity of others with respect to such goals to solidify viable ideas and conclusions while also identifying new learning and strategies. As students interact with one another and the teacher via discussion, this is also an opportunity for informal yet authentic assessment regarding what was learned and what mathematical experiences should follow.

Additional Planning Considerations

While the Launch, Explore, Discuss structures describe a productive approach to designing and organizing learning experiences which provide the instructional heart of a lesson, other aspects of the teaching and learning cycle should also be considered in the planning process. Specifically, these are learning goals, objectives, and standards (i.e. "Where do I want them to be?"), and assessment (i.e. "How will I know when they get there?") should influence the design of the teaching cycle (see Figure 5.3).

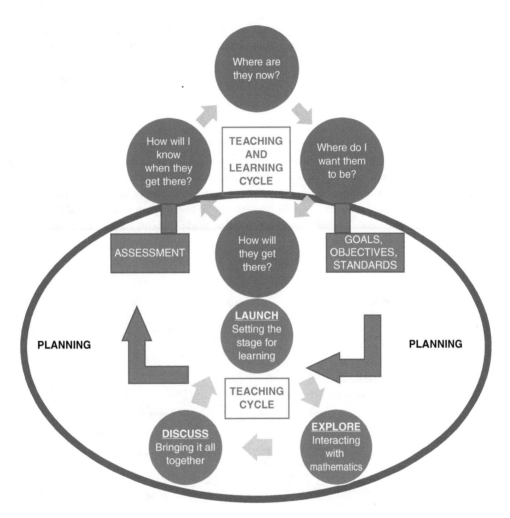

Figure 5.3 Teaching, learning, and planning

From this perspective, comprehensive planning must begin by identifying a particular learning goal (perhaps a key standard or objective), and some idea of how students' achievement of (or progress toward) that goal will be ascertained. We will examine these components in other chapters, but our purpose here is to illustrate the importance of grounding the planning process both in learning goals and related assessment. Indeed, by planning in this manner, teachers may create designs that are (1) engaging and coherent, (2) solidly connected to key goals, and (3) match well with an assessment to measure achievement or progress. Certainly, curricula and other instructional resources provide teachers with platforms from which to engage in these planning activities; however, in our experience, such materials vary in quality. More importantly, teachers' exercise of professional judgement and autonomy provide the occasion to shape and adapt these resources in order to meet the specific mathematical needs of a given classroom. Even the best of materials may benefit from a careful examination of specific tasks, models, and sequence of activities to ensure that the mathematical experience is coherent – that it *launches* in an engaging way, that it provides students with rich opportunities to *explore* ideas, concepts, and strategies, and that it concludes with some *discussion* around these ideas and what was learned.

Planning in Context

Thus far, we have presented a framework for instructional planning and a broad model for how one might structure a coherent teaching cycle via three components – launch, explore, discuss. In the coming sections, we will consider additional layers of planning complexity, but before doing so, let's examine a specific plan designed for a specific context. The following plan was designed for a small-group mathematics intervention lesson involving four first grade students (see Figure 5.4).

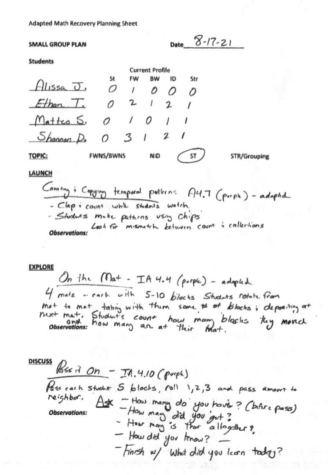

Figure 5.4 Small-group intervention plan

For this small-group lesson plan, the teacher has adapted a design from the U.S. Math Recovery Council teacher handbook and has, ostensibly, grouped students of relatively similar profiles with respect to the Learning Framework in Number (Wright and Ellemor-Collins, 2018). In this lesson, the teacher is focusing on students' early counting, and has determined that all of the students are working from the *emergent* counting stage. In this stage, students "cannot count visible counters [and the] student either does not know the number words or cannot coordinate the number words with counters" (Wright and Ellemor-Collins, 2018, p. 75). In short, the students are still developing the capacity to determine the numerosity of a physical collection. The teacher has assembled a series of three activities from *Teaching Number in the Classroom with 4–8-Year-Olds* (Wright et al., 2015).

The *launch* activity tasks students with listening to the teacher clapping some number and constructing that number using physical materials. The *explore* activity involves students moving to different spaces and determining the numerosity of changing collections of blocks. Lastly, as a context to *discuss* key mathematical ideas, the students are to roll a prepared die (1, 2, 3) and pass along some portion of their collection of blocks to a neighbor (who then determines the number of her/his new collection). Important to this component are the identified probing questions (i.e. "How many is that altogether? How did you know?") including the summarizing question of "What did you learn today?" (See Wright et al., 2015 for a more detailed description of activities.)

Connecting the Pieces

From this collection of activities, we observe a launch which draws students into the theme of constructing and counting collections in a novel way (i.e. teacher handclaps), followed by an exploration involving movement and peer interaction around the continued construction and counting of physical materials. The lesson concludes with an activity and explicit questions aimed at students' task-oriented thinking and overall learning with respect to the experience. First off, there is an internal coherence to this lesson (focus on constructing and counting physical collections across the lesson components). Certainly, lessons (and particularly intervention lessons) may be organized around varying concepts and ideas. For example, a teacher may launch with a numeral identification activity, and then move to an exploration focused on counting and arithmetic reasoning. However, it is worthwhile to consider the connective tissue amongst lesson components, and the extent to which we may link the launch, explore, and discuss portions of a lesson in some way is advantageous in that it results in a more coherent experience for the students involved. Perhaps there is a common tool or setting or the task range is similar. Whatever the connective tissue, instructional designs with components that relate in some way are often beneficial.

Zooming in on the Launch Component

Considering the launch task of this lesson, counting and copying temporal patterns (Wright et al., 2015, task A.4.7), the emphasis on somewhat novel movement and sound (i.e. clapping) may draw students into the lesson. Indeed, successful launch activities should seek to engage students from the onset and such movements/sounds are one possible design avenue. Another way to evaluate the strength of a launch activity is the extent to which it provides some initial view of students' mathematical thinking with respect to a particular concept or idea. In this instance, the teacher notes the potential for mismatches between counts (of claps) and constructed collections. Arguably, this is the most challenging task. As students are currently operating at the emergent counting stage (Wright and Ellemor-Collins, 2018), keeping track of and reconstructing (via counters) a clapped sequence is arguably more removed from perceptual materials than the task groups that follow, both of which involve counting collections of physical blocks. From this perspective, the launch may prove to be too far "beyond the [students'] current levels of knowledge" (Wright et al., 2015, p. 7; see Chapter 3). From this perspective, the launch task group of this lesson may not provide much additional insight into the students' mathematical thinking because the distance between the task demands and the students is simply too large. In any event, when planning a lesson launch, considerations of engagement and task demand (with respect to students' capabilities) are both productive lenses for design.

Zooming in on the Explore Component

Continuing our focus on task demand with respect to students, this task group focuses on student movement to different mats around the room, taking some number of blocks with them such that they create a new collection of blocks upon arrival which are then to be counted (Wright et al., 2015, task IA 4.4). Arguably, this task group is better matched with the students in that it is positioned just beyond their cutting edge of arithmetic reasoning. Specifically, this task involves establishing the numerosity of a physical collection which is the next stage of arithmetic development on the Learning Framework in Number (Wright and Ellemor-Collins, 2018). As such, this task group should promote healthy disequilibrium amongst students, but likely not reach the threshold of frustration due to an inordinate distance between the task and the students. Further, the use of movement is a novel feature to this task that also allows for the natural creation of varied collections for students to count. We can reasonably assume that this part of the lesson will provide terrain for students to problem solve and persevere, to reason mathematically. However, as mentioned, rich explorations (particularly those involving multiple students) should provide opportunities for students to reason with their peers and with the teacher, to construct viable mathematical arguments and critique the reasoning of others (NGA Center and CCSSO, 2010). While the teacher may intend to engage students in such discussions, this design element is not made explicit in the plan. One possible refinement would be to create and list probing questions that might provoke discussion amongst the students. For example, the teacher might pause the activity at a key moment and ask students to describe, in their own words, how they are determining the numerosity of the collections. From there, students may be paired and asked to identify how each others' strategies are the same and how they are different (if at all). These are but two possible prompts that might promote productive discussion and reflection, and likely there are many others. Nevertheless, rich explorations tend to have some manner of interactive component amongst participants that adds depth to the consideration of a particular idea, concept, or strategy.

Zooming in on the Discuss Component

In this component, we do see an emphasis on interaction and discussion via the listing of specific prompts. Similar to the explore component, the task group is focused on creating and counting physical collections of blocks (Wright et al., 2015, task IA 4.10), but in this lesson component the key aspect seems to be on probing questions around the tasks. Not only do these questions provide the teacher with some understanding of the students' current arithmetic reasoning at the conclusion of this lesson, they also provide a concluding occasion for students to verbalize and reflect upon their own thinking as well as how their thinking may have changed (if at all) during the lesson (i.e. "What did you learn today?"). One possibility for further refinement of this component might be to create spaces for students to interact with one another with respect to their lesson experiences (e.g.

to partner up and try to describe each other's strategies; to the group, Are the strategies the same, are they different? Why?). Another possibility might be to create additional reflective space for thinking about the arithmetic concepts at hand (e.g. Which task that you solved was the easiest? Which task that you solved was the hardest? Why?). The goal for a productive discussion should be for students to thoughtfully examine the events of the lesson and to provide the teacher with some manner of insight into what was learned and what might come next instructionally. At times, doing this in the context of a specific task or task group may be advantageous, but productive discussions do not always have to occur in the context of a specific mathematical task – sometimes they may just be a well-structured conversation around the preceding lesson activities.

Parting Thoughts and the Value of Task Detail

In the example small-group intervention plan above, we see some aspects of planning that are productive and coherent, and others that would benefit from refinement. One concluding observation on this plan is that, in each component (Launch, Explore, Discuss), the teacher maps out an instructional activity but does not actually list specific tasks. Listing actual mathematical tasks, or at least a few examples, on the lesson plan accomplishes several design goals. As opposed to generating tasks in the moment, creating and listing tasks as part of the design process allows for mindfulness regarding task sequence, structure, and fit with students. It allows teachers the time to anticipate students' activity and identify moments of disequilibrium (which may then lead to a key probe, prompt, or collaboration amongst students). While the teacher may not list every task in a particular lesson, creating examples of the actual tasks to be posed in a particular component allows for a richer planning experience as well as for more intentional lesson implementation.

Designing for Classroom Instruction

The example above provided a window into some basic planning elements in the context of a small-group intervention lesson. However, classroom instruction, typically involving far more students, creates both new planning opportunities and challenges. As such, additional lenses and structures may be useful to consider planning activities in such a complex context. Drawing inspiration from historical explorations of inquiry-oriented science instruction (Karplus and Thier, 1967), the *5E framework* provides a structure to design instruction coherently and thoughtfully while maintaining a connection to assessment processes (Bybee et al., 2006). In the following sections, we will explore how this framework might be purposed for productive instructional planning.

The "Five E" Instructional Model

As one might suspect, this instructional model consists of five components, each beginning with the letter "E." The components are: Engage, Explore, Explain, Elaborate, and Evaluate. *Engage* is similar to the notion of Launch described earlier in this chapter. This is the initial part of the lesson aimed at promoting curiosity and drawing students into the learning experience as well as gauging prior knowledge of a particular mathematical idea. *Explore* is, again, quite similar to the explore component described in earlier sections where rich activities and tasks provide terrain for varied student experiences and interactions around a mathematical concept. *Explain* is unique to this model and provides an opportunity to focus students' activity and talk on a particular aspect of the learning experience.

Sometimes misunderstood as allocating instructional space for teacher explanation or lecture, explain in this context actually refers to focused and guided student explanations or discourse around a key feature of the lesson. *Elaborate* refers to opportunities within the lesson to extend and connect students' mathematical thinking to other ideas and concepts as well as to challenge and/or scrutinize such ideas. Lastly, *Evaluate* refers to some mechanism or strategy, either formal or informal, to determine students' progress toward an identified learning goal. Further, this component also provides an opportunity for students to evaluate their own progress and reflect upon their learning with respect to a particular lesson experience.

An Example from Practice

Math Lesson Plan

Name: XXXXXXXX _____ Date: XXXXX _____ Lesson Length: 45 mins _____
School: XXXXXXXX _____ Grade Level: 5th _____ # of Students: 18
Subject: Math _____ Topic: Modeling Multiplication of Decimals

Objective
Students will be able to model equations involving decimals multiplied by decimals.

Math Standard
KY.5.NBT.1 8
Operations with decimals to hundredths: a. Add, subtract, multiply, and divide decimals to hundredths using:
• concrete models or drawings • strategies based on place value • properties of operations • the relationship between addition and subtraction; b. Relate the strategy to a written method and explain the reasoning used.

Engage

-remind students of what was learned about decimals and models in the previous week
-prompt students to prepare their materials (open workbook page)
-engage in brief re-teaching of multiplying decimals and of modeling decimal place values

Explore and Explain

-present the objectives, tools, and success strategies for this lesson, asking the essential questions
-ask, How can you model decimal multiplication?
-demonstrate the strategy using the workbook problems and the accompanying video from curriculum materials
-ensure students understand the concept of using hundredths grids to model decimal multiplication by checking their workbook problems

Elaborate

-show students the directions of the workbook tasks and walk through an example problem
-check for questions and allow them to work independently to solve. Some may need additional modeling
-provide scaffolding and support for those who need more time to arrive at an understanding of the general concept; suggest further challenges for those who exceed expectations using bonus problems or additional workbook practice

Evaluate

-check the submitted workbook assignment for accuracy of models and equations:
***Below Criteria** is unable to complete all six problems or does not have appropriate answers*
***Meets Criteria** is able to complete all six problems with appropriate answers*
***Above Criteria** is able to complete all six problems accurately and to complete a bonus problem*

Figure 5.5   Whole-class lesson plan using the 5E model

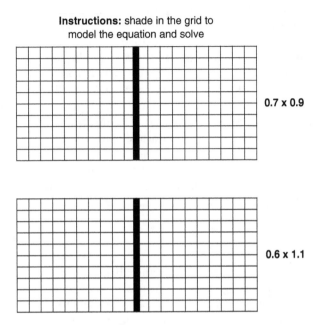

Instructions: shade in the grid to model the equation and solve

0.7 x 0.9

0.6 x 1.1

Figure 5.6   Example workbook tasks from whole-class lesson plan

In the lesson plan (see Figure 5.6), the teacher designed an instructional experience modeling decimal multiplication. Looking critically at each of the 5E components of the plan, we observe some baseline coherence around this mathematical topic, but also find space for meaningful refinement.

Engage

As planned, this part of the lesson centers on reminding and reteaching students key ideas and preparing materials for the learning to come. While not necessarily unproductive activities, this design does not embody the ideals of a well-designed Engage portion of the lesson. One possibility might be to engage students in an open-ended small-group task focused on decimal multiplication in context. For example, students might be presented with a fast food restaurant nutritional guide, asked to select their favorite item, and to determine the actual caloric distribution across carbohydrates, protein, and fat. Perhaps an even more productive beginning might be to task groups of students with identifying instances of decimal multiplication (or decimal use more broadly) in their experiences: Where do students encounter such mathematical ideas in their lives and what sense might they make of these encounters? In any event, a good Engage provides students with an opportunity to initially connect with an idea in a meaningful way and also allows the teacher to see into students' connections to make some determination of prior knowledge or familiarity with that concept.

Explore and Explain

Note, in this plan, the teacher elects to combine these components into a single set of activities primarily, but not entirely, organized around demonstrations and student activities within the context of curriculum materials (see Figure 5.6 for curriculum task examples). While these activities provide nominal terrain for students to explore decimal multiplication using a specified model, the potential for varied strategies and discourse is minimal. As such, a more productive approach might be to task student groups using three different models/strategies (i.e. area, grid, algorithm) to solve a small number of tasks (perhaps in context) and to describe the advantages and disadvantages of each approach. This design has the benefit of providing both consideration of varied problem-solving pathways and creating space for student discourse at the small-group level. While certainly not the only productive design for the Explore component of the lesson with these goals, the activity described above represents the spirit of this aspect of lesson design. Similarly, with respect to the Explain component, there is some reference to solve and share tasks from the curriculum materials, but primarily this part of the lesson appears somewhat teacher-centric with respect to mathematical talk. Mentioned earlier, the focus with this aspect of planning is not upon teachers' explaining ideas, strategies, or concepts, but rather students doing so with one another in a structured and supportive way.

Elaborate

While there is some mention of unspecified "further challenges" for those who may complete lesson tasks early, much of this design appears oriented around independent work and providing support for such work. Rather, the aim of this component should be to extend the mathematical ideas of the lesson experience and/or connect ideas and strategies to other concepts and topics. As such, one viable connection that might be made is to explore linkages between the models for decimal multiplication and the concept of area as it applies to geometric domains. For example, students might be asked to think, pair, share regarding the prompt, "How do the grid and area models for decimal multiplication connect to finding the area of a rectangle?" Further, the teacher might ask students what other mathematical concepts and ideas they see as being connected to their work in this lesson. This prompt may lead to further linking opportunities that were, perhaps, unanticipated by the teacher.

Evaluate

While this component of the presented plan does specify some check for accuracy with respect to submitted work (on tasks within the curriculum), there seems to be a missed opportunity for students to demonstrate their reasoning as well as engage in some manner of self-assessment of their own learning. Perhaps one productive pathway might be to add prompts such as:

- "Do you think using a model to solve a decimal multiplication task is helpful or not? Why?"
- "What model, grid, or area, do you think is most helpful for decimal multiplication and why?"
- "What is the most important idea that you picked up from today's lesson on decimal multiplication?"
- "If you had to explain decimal multiplication using a model to a friend, where would you start? What would you say or do first?"

Such example prompts allow the teacher to better understand students' learning with additional depth as well as provide students with the opportunity to explore and reflect upon their own thinking and connections.

Revising the Plan

From the discussion above, we gather that the initial lesson design (Figure 5.5) provides a foray into planning via the 5E structure; however, there are a number of opportunities, described in the preceding sections, for significant refinement. As such, a revised version of this plan might incorporate many of those suggested elements (see Figure 5.7). Indeed, throughout each of the components, the revised plan appears to better reflect the aims and the spirit of instructional planning that attends to the ideas of initial engagement, rich exploration, and student-driven explanations, elaboration, and connections across mathematical concepts, and reflective assessment and evaluation by both teacher and students. One final item to consider on this front is the inclusion of specific tasks (or example tasks) themselves within the plan. Note, the examples make reference to tasks in curriculum materials, but often teachers find it useful to list specific mathematical tasks (or examples of representative tasks) on the lesson plan itself. Depending upon how one may use the plan in the act of teaching, having access to such tasks may provide some in-the-moment mathematical grounding and minimize haphazard or hastily created problems and tasks.

Math Lesson Plan

Name: XXXXXXXX _____ Date: XXXXX _____ Lesson Length: 45 mins _____
School: XXXXXXXX _____ Grade Level: 5th _____ # of Students: 18
Subject: Math _____ Topic: Modeling Multiplication of Decimals

Objective
Students will be able to model equations involving decimals multiplied by decimals.

Math Standard
KY.5.NBT.1 8
Operations with decimals to hundredths: a. Add, subtract, multiply, and divide decimals to hundredths using:
• concrete models or drawings • strategies based on place value • properties of operations • the relationship between addition and subtraction; b. Relate the strategy to a written method and explain the reasoning used.

Engage

At table groups, ask students to identify where they see decimals in the world around them and share out – probe for instances where students might encounter decimal multiplication (or other arithmetic operations). Share some images of decimals from real-world contexts.

Explore and Explain

EXPLORE: Prompt: Ask students to describe/demonstrate area model, grid model, algorithm for decimal multiplication; Each table group select 4 of the share/solve tasks from Envision text and solve each task using three different strategies – area, grid, algorithm
EXPLAIN: Ask table groups to describe why they choose the tasks they did, which method(s) seemed to work best for a given task, and why

Elaborate

Think/Pair/Share – How do the models we have used connect to finding the area of a rectangle?
Think/Pair/Share – What connections do you see between the models (area/grid) and the algorithm?
Think/Pair/Share – What other math ideas or concepts do you see as being connected to our work today on decimal multiplication and why?

Evaluate

Individually, choose 4 of the 6 problems from the Envisions text and then respond to the following prompts: (1) "If you had to explain decimal multiplication using a model to a friend, where would you start? What would you say or do first?" (2) What is the most important idea that you picked up from today's lesson on decimal multiplication?

Figure 5.7   Whole-class lesson plan using the 5E model – revised

Connecting and Reflecting

Connecting to Other Practices

Returning to ideas from earlier sections regarding the teaching and learning cycle (see Figure 5.3), we want to reaffirm the idea that instructional planning does not occur in a vacuum. Rather, such planning is fundamentally situated within and shaped by other elements of teaching and learning. Perhaps most connected to the practice of planning are the formulation of instructional goals and the evaluation or assessment of learning outcomes. On the topic of goals, often these will be driven (to some extent) by specified learning objectives (e.g. state standards); however, there is typically some design autonomy regarding what is foregrounded or emphasized (e.g. "I Can" statements) with respect to an objective; further, attention to goals also provides occasion to consider what manner of mathematical practices might be emphasized in a learning experience. For example, in the lesson above (Figure 5.7), the teacher did not explicitly identify any key mathematical practice, but from the activities, we might assume that students' reasoning abstractly and quantitatively as well as students' construction of viable mathematical arguments (to name but a few practices embodied in this plan) were goals that this teacher had in mind (NGA Center and CCSSO, 2010). On the topic of assessment, mentioned earlier, this aspect of teaching and learning should be directly related to the identified goals and learning outcomes and, ideally, provide opportunities to move beyond mere correctness of response and delve deeply into students' reasoning and conceptual understanding of a mathematical idea, strategy, or practice. Further, assessment is most fully realized when it also provides opportunities for students to reflect upon and assess their own thinking with respect to a lesson experience.

Moving to processes and concepts a bit further afield but quite important to instructional planning, there are a number of topics discussed in this book that should inform instructional planning. Inquiry-oriented instruction (examined in Chapter 2) as an orientation for lesson design is essential when mapping the experiences of a particular teaching cycle (e.g. Launch, Explore, Summarize; 5Es) and the extent to which those experiences provide students with opportunities to immerse themselves in the meaningful inspection of concepts and ideas. Similarly, monitoring students' activities and thinking via professional noticing (described in Chapter 7) is an important practice to ensure that the instructional plan, as implemented, is not overly rigid, but rather is responsive to students in the moment. For most learning experiences, mathematical discourse and feedback from students (explored in Chapter 8) is an important component of the instructional design. Structuring coherent discussions such that they provide insight into students' reasoning and build towards a particular mathematical idea are often key to maximizing a particular lesson. Lastly, considerations of equity (examined in Chapter 11) should be deeply influential to the planning process. The extent to which lesson experience provides equitable access for students, the manner in which power is distributed in a particular part of the lesson, how lenses of "right" and "wrong" may inadvertently shape our interpretations of students' thinking, and the manner in which the lived experiences or identities of our students are reflected in our teaching are but a few examples of how equity concerns impact instructional planning. Arguably, every chapter in this book connects to and shapes how we consider lesson design, and these are just a few linkages to consider and explore as you refine your own planning processes.

Questions for Reflection

To conclude this exploration of instructional planning, we offer a series of questions that one might consider throughout the design process. We freely admit that these questions are complex and come with no easy answers. Rather, these are presented as ideas to ponder in one's attempt to create a robust learning experience.

Lesson Goals

- What is the primary aim of the lesson experience? What do you want students to know and be able to do at the end of the lesson?
- What sorts of mathematical practices do you want students to engage in as they pursue your lesson goals?
- What is your sense of students' mathematical understanding of the lesson topic? Is this the first time they have seen this topic? What prior knowledge might they have and on what evidence are you basing this assumption?

Launch/Engage

- To what extent do the initial moments of the lesson draw students into the learning experience?
- To what extent are these initial moments connected to the learning that follows?
- To what extent do these initial moments provide opportunities for insight into students' mathematical thinking?

Explore/Explain

- What specific mathematical tasks will students face in the lesson? What opportunities do students have to explore within the bounds of these tasks? Are there varied ways students might solve or think about these tasks?
- What opportunities do you provide within your lessons for students to use representations or models in their mathematical activity?
- What opportunities do you provide for students to engage in mathematical discourse, to reason with one another and the teacher about their ideas and the ideas of their peers? How might such discussion be organized and structured, and what prompts might you pose to foster rich discussion?

Elaborate

- Where does the mathematical concept or central idea of the lesson exist relative to other mathematical concepts or ideas? What mathematical topic or idea most naturally follows the focus of the lesson at hand, and how might you help students see this natural extension without merely explaining or telling?
- What other mathematical concepts or ideas may be connected to the lesson at hand? What connections do you see? What connections might your students see?

Evaluate/Assess

- To what extent does the assessment or evaluation relate to the learning goals of the lesson?
- Does the assessment of students' learning provide you with some insight into students' reasoning beyond mere correctness of response?

- Does the assessment provide students with an opportunity to use varied strategies or approaches to reason and solve mathematically with respect to the learning goals?
- Do students have an opportunity to reflect upon and gauge their own progress with respect to the learning experience?

Equity Concerns

- Does every student have access to the mathematical experiences of the lesson? What resources and supports are needed at the individual level? To what extent does the learning experience create opportunities for all students to participate?
- How and to what extent do notions of "right" and "wrong" factor into the lesson experiences? Are certain strategies and approaches being signalled as more desirable than others? If so, is this intentional with respect to your learning goals? Is there created space for novel or invented approaches?
- To what extent are the identities and lived experiences of students reflected in lesson activities? How might you describe the overall relevance of the lesson to the participating students?
- How is power being shared and distributed in the different components of the lesson? Who gets to talk and when? Are there moments when decision-making might be shared between you and your students? Are there moments when you might let students decide upon some aspect of the learning experience?

References

Bybee, R.W., Taylor, J.A., Gardner, A., Scotter, P.V., Powell, J.C., Westbrook, A. and Landes, N. (2006). *The BSCS 5E Instructional Model: Origins, Effectiveness, and Applications*. Colorado Springs, CO: BSCS. www.fremonths.org/ourpages/auto/2008/5/11/1210522036057/bscs5efullreport2006.pdf

Castro-Superfine, A.M. (2009). Planning for mathematics instruction: A model of experienced teachers' planning processes in the context of reform mathematics curriculum. *The Mathematics Educator*, 18(2), 11–22.

Karplus, R. and Thier, H.D. (1967). *A New Look at Elementary School Science*. Chicago, IL: Rand McNally.

Lappan, G., Fey, J.T., Fitzgerald, W.M., Friel, S.N. and Phillips, E.D. (2002). *Getting to Know Connected Mathematics: An Implementation Guide*. Glenview, IL: Prentice Hall.

National Governors Association Center for Best Practices and Council of Chief State School Officers (NGA Center and CCSSO) (2010). *Common Core State Standards for Mathematics*. Washington, DC: Authors.

Popham, W. and Baker, E. (1970). *Systematic Instruction*. Englewood Cliffs, NJ: Prentice-Hall.

Smith, M.S. and Stein, M.K. (2011). *5 Practices for Orchestrating Productive Mathematics Discussions*. Reston, VA: National Council of Teachers of Mathematics.

Tyler, R. (1950). *Basic Principles of Curriculum and Instruction*. Chicago, IL: University of Chicago Press.

Wright, R.J. and Ellemor-Collins, D. (2018). *The Learning Framework in Number: Pedagogical Tools for Assessment and Instruction*. London: Sage.

Wright, R.J., Martland, J., Stafford, A.K. and Stanger, G. (2006). *Teaching Number: Advancing Children's Skill and Strategies*, 2nd edition. London: Sage.

Wright, R.J., Stanger, G., Stafford, A.K. and Martland, J. (2015). *Teaching Number in the Classroom with 4–8-Year-Olds*, 2nd edition. London: Sage.

6

Formative Assessments

Guiding Principle: Initial and ongoing assessment

"Teaching is informed by an initial, comprehensive assessment and ongoing assessment through teaching. The latter refers to the teacher's informed understanding of children's current knowledge and problem-solving strategies, and continual revision of this understanding." (Wright et al., 2006, p. 26)

Introduction

To assess a child, many educators believe that learning ends so assessments can begin. Often, this traditional way of viewing assessments suggests that the teacher is evaluating the children in their classroom with tests and quizzes. The primary goal of these types of assessments is to inform educators of *what* mathematics children know and their degree of accuracy. Often, these are the tools used to assign a summative grade to a child on a report card. However, these types of assessments are not the only way to understand what mathematics knowledge children have constructed. A second type of assessment can be embedded into daily instruction, where educators can make "in-the-moment" instructional decisions that better support effective mathematics teaching for children's learning needs. These assessments often appear as interviews, exit slips, classroom discussions, observations of children solving rich mathematics tasks, and so on. The primary goal of these assessments is to inform educators of *how* children developed mathematical knowledge. These types of assessments inform educators of more accurate inferences of the mathematical understandings that the children in their classroom have constructed.

Defining Assessments and Feedback in Constructivist Learning Theories

In research, these integrated assessments are described as *formative assessments*, which are often characterized simply as assessments *for* learning (Van de Walle et al., 2019). Comparatively, the more traditional, *summative assessments*, are characterized as assessments *of* learning. Wiliam (2010) unpacks formative assessments further by describing three components educators must engage in when creating formative assessments: (1) determine what the children currently *understand*, (2) determine the *learning goals* for the children, and (3) determine how the children *reach these goals*. Given these three components, educators can use formative assessments to understand their children's mathematics understandings and the varied paths they create when reaching their mathematical goals.

Formative assessments do not need to be educator driven. They can also be used by children to provide feedback to their own mathematics learning (Black and Wiliam, 1998). In fact, Ernest (1999, as cited by Yeh et al., 2017) explains that feedback is essential when children are trying to determine how accurate their actions are when constructing conceptual understandings. Given this, many educators believe that feedback is at the heart of formative assessment design and enactment. Historically, feedback was first considered by early 20th century educators to only include how children were rewarded and punished when learning in school (Wiliam, 2018). These limited views were found to have small effects on children's mathematics learning. Once learning included constructivist perspectives, which centrally positioned children in their own mathematics learning, feedback became more closely tied to their own mathematics learning and understandings (Lee et al., 2020).

By extending feedback to promote children's meaning-making in mathematics, formative assessments can provide feedback to teachers, students, and student peers. In fact, Lee and colleagues (Lee et al., 2020) analyzed 25 research projects and found that formative assessment feedback initiated by the learner had a much larger impact on a child's mathematics learning than educator-initiated feedback. This finding was interesting because it explains the importance that children's active learning has with formative assessments in a mathematics classroom. To unpack this further, Yeh et al. (2017) explain that to use formative assessments, educators must shift their focus from children developing accuracy goals with memorized procedures towards children constructing conceptual understandings. This does not mean that educators should not focus on procedural understandings but that they should focus on how children construct procedural fluency. In short, children's meaning making can be formatively assessed with their development of meaningful procedures and conceptual understandings in mathematics.

Procedural Fluency and Conceptual Understanding Goals

To assess procedural fluency, educators must consider the strategy development children are constructing over time (Yeh et al., 2017). This suggests that the accuracy of children's solutions plays a smaller role, while flexibility in how children can reason through a problem has a larger role. We provide two examples that illustrate how children's procedural fluency can be assessed in meaningful ways. First, we discuss problem-based activities, and then we discuss comparison activities.

Problem-Based Activities as Assessments

This might be embedded in children's problem solving where they are asked to solve tasks that evoke meaningful contexts, applications, and representations. By shifting the task away from problems that require only one type of procedure towards tasks that have multiple entry points and multiple exit points, children draw from their own actions and strategies. For example, Ms. Stone engages her third-grade children in the following task (see Figure 6.1).

Haakan's rectangular swimming pool is 30 feet by 25 feet, and Kiesha's is 35 feet by 20 feet. Whose swimming pool is larger in area? How do you know? If one swimming pool is larger, how much larger is this pool?

Figure 6.1 Swimming pool task

To engage in the task, the children are given base-ten blocks and paper to record what they do with their blocks. As the children engage in this problem-based activity, Ms. Stone walks around the room to record the children's activity, language, drawings, and procedures (more about how to organize anecdotal notes from an observation below). In this example, Ms. Stone walks over to a student drawing two arrays (see Figure 6.2). The arrays are meant to represent what a third-grade child has done to solve this problem with their base-ten blocks. Here, Ms. Stone can see the child has made connections between their base-ten blocks, drawings, and procedures. By making these connections, the child is also able to critically reflect on the separate parts they multiplied and see how the distributive property impacts the changes in the swimming pool areas.

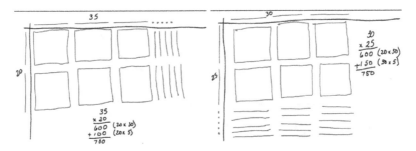

Figure 6.2   Solutions with arrays and partial products

Note: **Representions of solutions and procedures used to solve the swimming pool task**

Ms. Stone observes another student writing the problem in a simpler form by first considering 35 twice, as equal to 70 and 25 thrice, as equal to 75 before adding zeros on the end (see Figure 6.3). Ms. Stone can infer from the child solving the problem in this way that the child is drawing from procedures and conceptual relations between numbers. However, this child may not be drawing from the distributive property. This is a very different exit point for this child.

For instance, the first child enters the task with blocks and drawings of arrays related to multiplication and exits the task with opportunities to construct the foundational knowledge necessary for the distributive property. Moreover, this first child is able to construct actions that allow Ms. Stone to build towards a partial products procedure. The second child enters the tasks with an ability to double and triple some double-digit numbers. This child also understands that by adding a zero in the ones place of one factor, a zero needs to be added to the solution. Ms. Stone can connect this to area models that represent partial products and to procedures used in the traditional algorithm.

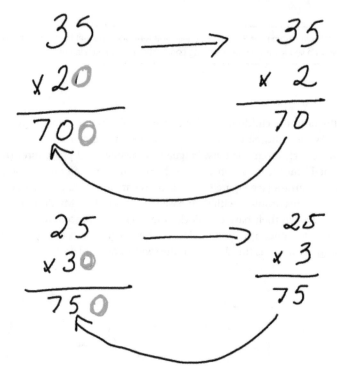

Figure 6.3 Solutions with doubling/tripling and using place value

Note: Doubling and tripling to solve the swimming pool task

As a result of the teacher posing this problem, children are asked to critically think about the properties of the multiplication procedure but given multiple entry points (e.g. drawings, building with blocks) and multiple exit points (e.g. flexible procedures, critical thinking around multiplicative situations, development of properties). By observing children in problem-based activities, educators are better able to determine children's procedural flexibility through their entry and exit points.

Comparison Activities as Assessments

Yeh and colleagues (2017) also suggest that children compare two different procedures (one traditional and one child constructed), allowing children an opportunity to explain what they *do* when solving problems like this and *why*. This comparison-type task also allows children an opportunity to make connections between their own strategies and traditional procedures. For example, after children in third grade create area models to solve two-digit by two-digit multiplication tasks, similar to those constructed in Figure 6.2, they can then begin explaining the procedures that they constructed. At this point, unpacking what the children understand about how these procedures work the way they do would help Ms. Stone as she considers the degree of understanding the children in her classroom have with particular multiplication procedures. To do this, Ms. Stone places a child-constructed procedure that she observed in the swimming pool activity alongside the traditional procedure (see Figure 6.4).

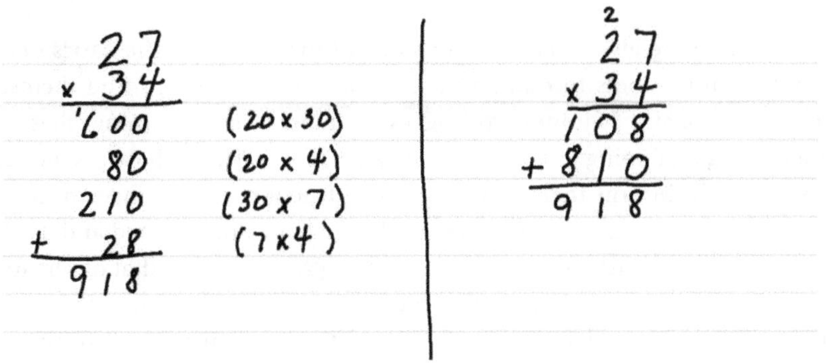

$$
\begin{array}{r}
27 \\
\times\,34 \\
\hline
600 \\
80 \\
210 \\
+\ 28 \\
\hline
918
\end{array}
\qquad
\begin{array}{l}
(20 \times 30) \\
(20 \times 4) \\
(30 \times 7) \\
(7 \times 4)
\end{array}
\qquad\qquad
\begin{array}{r}
2 \\
27 \\
\times\,34 \\
\hline
108 \\
+\ 810 \\
\hline
918
\end{array}
$$

Figure 6.4 A child-constructed and a traditional procedure

Note: Similarities and differences between partial products and traditional procedures

   Here, children in a whole-class discussion can talk about what they notice is the same and what is different between the two procedures. For example, Ms. Stone might hear the children in her class say, "I notice that 108 is the same as 80 + 28" and that "there are four products on the left-hand problem and two products on the right-hand problem." Ms. Stone can record the children's noticing to better help her connect her children's procedural development with their future procedural fluency. Moreover, the children begin to notice new things when they compare the similarities and differences between the procedures, providing new opportunities for mathematics learning. Again, these types of activities are meaningful because they simultaneously assess learning and allow for learning to occur, illustrating why formative assessments are *for* learning.

Examples of Formative Assessments for Conceptual Learning

When assessing children's conceptual learning in mathematics, educators can use a wider variety of assessment tools. For instance, these assessments might be in the form of interviews, observations, checklists, questions, number sorts, true–false tasks, or problem-based tasks. In the following section, these assessment tools will be explained in more detail with vignettes explaining how the tools can best be enacted.

Formative assessments for conceptual learning can be grouped into four different types of tools: observations, tasks, questions, and interviews (Van de Walle et al., 2019; Yeh et al., 2017). These tools have varying formats, outcomes, and purposes. By using a variety of formative assessments, educators are better able to draw more accurate inferences of children's mathematical understandings. In this section, we will explain these different tools in more detail and provide some vignettes to illustrate the varying formats, outcomes, and potential purposes.

Observations and Checklists as a Formative Assessment

Often, educators who are given insight in to some of the richest mathematics developments are simply not given the tools to capture them. In fact, educators will find themselves planning with colleagues or simply joining colleagues at a lunchtime, explaining what they noticed their children saying and doing during a mathematics lesson. How educators' noticing during observations can help inform their mathematics instruction is explained in more detail in Chapter 7. Here, we simply explain how observations can be documented and used to inform educators' instruction. For instance, Van de Walle et al. (2019) explain that observations can be formally documented with anecdotal notes and checklists. Anecdotal notes are first recorded by the educator walking around during small-group activities or sitting back during student-led whole-class discussions.

For instance, Mr. Johnson, a third grade teacher, engages the children in his class in the game, Four's a Winner (Wright et al., 2015, pp. 200–1). In this game, pairs of children are given an array of squares, each with a number representing a multiple. The goal of the game is for the children to take turns forming factor pairs so they can cover the associated product. The winner is the first player to cover four spaces in a row, column, or diagonal. The children cannot change both factors from the player before them, only one factor. Given this, there are ways to block an opponent from covering a particular product. As the children play in pairs, Mr. Johnson walks around the room observing the strategies children use to try and win the game. As Mr. Johnson approaches Brook and Carter playing, he takes note that both children are drawing flexibly from their relationships between factors 9, 8, 3, and 4 (see Figure 6.5). In fact, it seems that by having these flexible facts, both children are aggressively developing four in a column or diagonal while also trying to block each other's attempts to win.

Mr. Johnson walks over and observes Parker and Bailey playing the same game (see Figure 6.6). He notes in his observation that Parker and Bailey are struggling to use factors above five. In fact, Bailey, the child using factors above five, is only doing so by pairing them with factors 1 and 2. When pushed to consider three sets of six, Bailey counts on from 12, keeping track of six of his counts. This suggests to Mr. Johnson that these students may be engaging in Initial Number Sequence (INS) or Tacitly Nested Number Sequence (TNS) but not Explicitly Nested Number Sequence (ENS), preventing them from accessing the number of sophisticated and assertive strategies that Brook and Carter evidenced. These anecdotal notes are quite helpful as Mr. Johnson begins to plan activities for his next day's math lesson.

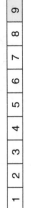

Figure 6.5 Mr. Johnson's observation of Brook and Carter's game play during the Four's a Winner game

First Turn

64	20	9	16	48	4	54	14	25
49	32	36	10	32	81	42	35	12
21	63	7	15	63	20	45	24	15
14	72	18	8	35	28	12	40	5
2	56	12	27	4	18	8	24	36
15	6	72	30	15	9	42	6	40
30	18	36	48	27	56	24	3	54
12	28	21	6	24	18	10	5	45

1	2	3	4	5	6	7	8	9

1	2	3	4	5	6	7	8	9

■ = Parker ■ = Bailey

Second Turn

64	20	9	16	48	4	54	14	25
49	32	36	10	32	81	42	35	12
21	63	7	15	63	20	45	24	15
14	72	18	8	35	28	12	40	5
2	56	12	27	4	18	8	24	36
15	6	72	30	15	9	42	6	40
30	18	36	48	27	56	24	3	54
12	28	21	6	24	18	10	5	45

1	2	3	4	5	6	7	8	9

1	2	3	4	5	6	7	8	9

■ = Parker ■ = Bailey

Third Turn

64	20	9	16	48	4	54	14	25
49	32	36	10	32	81	42	35	12
21	63	7	15	63	20	45	24	15
14	72	18	8	35	28	12	40	5
2	56	12	27	4	18	8	24	36
15	6	72	30	15	9	42	6	40
30	18	36	48	27	56	24	3	54
12	28	21	6	24	18	10	5	45

1	2	3	4	5	6	7	8	9

1	2	3	4	5	6	7	8	9

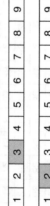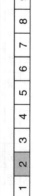

■ = Parker ■ = Bailey

Fourth Turn

64	20	9	16	48	4	54	14	25
49	32	36	10	32	81	42	35	12
21	63	7	15	63	20	45	24	15
14	72	18	8	35	28	12	40	5
2	56	12	27	4	18	8	24	36
15	6	72	30	15	9	42	6	40
30	18	36	48	27	56	24	3	54
12	28	21	6	24	18	10	5	45

1	2	3	4	5	6	7	8	9

1	2	3	4	5	6	7	8	9

■ = Parker ■ = Bailey

Figure 6.6 Mr. Johnson's observation of Parker and Bailey's game play during the Four's a Winner game

To capture and record observations of children's words, questions, gestures, actions, and drawings, Van de Walle et al. (2019) suggest using an electronic tablet. To better interpret these notes, it is helpful to first create a checklist to organize the notes. Checklists (like those in the white book – see pp. 40–8 and pp. 49–72) can be created with content standards, but to better examine it is advisable to use *Common Core* practice standards or NCTM *Process* standards (Van de Walle et al., 2019; Yeh et al., 2017). It is sometimes beneficial to create your own interview assessment. However, many educators can begin with those already created by the Math Recovery series and adapt them. By focusing on effective activity, educators are better able to make children's strategy development a primary focus for these formative assessment tools.

Another way to create a checklist is to create a scale of proficiency. This checklist could provide information for one student per checklist or information for several students per checklist. The former might have several content, process, and/or practice standards along the left-hand side with "not yet proficient," "proficient," "advanced proficient" along the top. By organizing a checklist for a whole class or several children in a class, an educator might place the students' name along the left-hand side of the checklist, with the three types of proficiency along the top of the checklist. This checklist would allow for one goal per checklist with some descriptions better illustrating what an educator might observe when categorizing children as "not yet proficient," "proficient," or "advanced proficient." By placing observable comments from the educators in the checklists, children, parents, and/or other educational stakeholders can directly connect how children's activity explains their degree of proficiency when constructing conceptual understandings.

Student Name ____Carter_____   Date ___4/19/2022___

	Not Yet Proficient	Proficient	Advanced Proficient	Comments
Multiply one-digit whole numbers by multiples of 10 in the range of 10–90.				N/A
Interpret products of whole numbers, as the total number of objects in 5 groups of 7 objects each.				N/A
Interpret whole-number quotients of whole numbers as a number of shares.				N/A
Use multiplication and division within 100 to solve word problems in situations.				N/A
Determine the unknown whole number in a multiplication or division equation.		✓	✓	Was able to move seamlessly between factors and products – OR quotients, divisors, and dividends.
Apply properties of operations (e.g. commutative, associative, distributive).				N/A
Understand division as an unknown factor problem.			✓	
Fluently multiply and divide within 100, using strategies such as the relationship between multiplication and division.			✓	

(Continued)

Figure 6.7   (Continued)

Student Name ____Bailey_____   Date ___4/19/2022___

	Not Yet Proficient	Proficient	Advanced Proficient	Comments
Multiply one-digit whole numbers by multiples of 10 in the range of 10–90.				N/A
Interpret products of whole numbers, as the total number of objects in 5 groups of 7 objects each.				N/A
Interpret whole-number quotients of whole numbers as a number of shares.				N/A
Use multiplication and division within 100 to solve word problems in situations.				N/A
Determine the unknown whole number in a multiplication or division equation.	✓			Was able to do this by relying on small factors or a counting sequence.
Apply properties of operations (e.g. commutative, associative, distributive).				N/A
Understand division as an unknown factor problem.	✓			
Fluently multiply and divide within 100, using strategies such as the relationship between multiplication and division.	✓	✓		Was proficient when factors were less than 5.

Figure 6.7   A checklist created by Mr. Johnson to better organize his observations of Carter and Bailey's mathematical proficiency

For instance, in the case of Mr. Johnson, after observing the different pairs, Mr. Johnson created a checklist that clearly stated the state standards related to multiplication. Each checklist could be used for one child (see Figure 6.7) but for multiple objectives. As you may notice, Mr. Johnson did not use all the objectives for this particular observation. However, he did note that Carter was "proficient" and "advanced proficient" on three different objectives and that Bailey was "not yet proficient" and "proficient" on three different objectives.

These checklists can also draw from more nuanced objectives, such as those delineated in the white book (Wright and Ellemor-Collins, 2018, Chapters 1–3). Moreover, an educator can provide details as to what is observed when determining if a child is performing at a different degree of proficiency. The more detailed the instrument, the more detailed the inferences one can make from these anecdotal notes. The less detailed the instrument, the more patterns and trends the educators can determine from multiple sets of anecdotal notes. Quite often, these observations can be developed to examine whole-class discussions or activity. However, observations can also be documented during small-group activity.

Interviews and Questions as a Formative Assessment

Often, formative assessments happen when children are solving mathematical problems but can be structured through educators' use of questions throughout a lesson or in a one-on-one interview. By providing more structure to a problem-based activity, educators can probe for particular conceptions children have or have not yet constructed.

The National Council of Teachers of Mathematics (NCTM, 2014) explains that when teachers design questions to encourage children to explain their reasoning, there are four main types of effective questions:

1. Information gathering
2. Student thinking
3. Mathematical structures, connections, and relationships
4. Reflection and justification

First, when gathering information children are asked broad questions about properties and mathematical conceptions. For instance, they may ask children to explain, "What does it mean to subtract?" or "Why is this a rectangle?" Second, when asking children to explain their thinking, educators can pose questions that encourage children to connect their strategies back to features of the original mathematics problem – for example, "How do your area models explain the two garden sizes?" or "How does this solution answer the story problem?" Third, when encouraging children to explain what they know about mathematical structures, connections, and relationships, educators should ask them questions focusing on these topics – for instance, to predict what the least common denominator might be, based on common factors, or why two different strategies might produce the same solution. Finally, when asking questions to reflect and/or justify their reasoning, educators can prompt children to compare their strategy to someone else's, explaining the similarities and differences. Another example might be to ask children, "How do you know these are all the possible solutions?"

By asking children questions like these, educators can focus on how children draw on mathematics to solve problems, make connections, anticipate effective reasoning, and reflect on their reasoning. Moreover, these questions challenge children to think more deeply about their mathematical engagement. To record these discussions, educators can video the discourse or use the aforementioned checklists. If video-recording children, be sure to reach out to your state/providence, district, and/or school leaders to establish the guidelines (i.e. storage, sharing, parent permissions) delineated for the video-recording of young children in a school setting.

When designing interviews, educators should already have a broad understanding of the child's mathematical conceptions. This will assist educators in determining the gaps in the child's knowledge and understanding. Next, when designing interviews educators should keep them short but give children opportunities to present their knowledge in multiple ways. For instance, an educator might ask a child if the following is true or false:

$$(60/3) + (60/3) = 60/6$$

To solve this, the child may need to use base-ten blocks to create an area model, draw an array, or write out some known mathematics facts. If a child is stuck, an educator can suggest they try using concrete, pictorial, or abstract representations. This allows the child an entry point to a problem she or he is unaware of in the moment. If a child simply says "true" or "false," follow-up questions that prompt a child to explain their reasoning can give an educator a lot more information about the child's strategy development. As with an observation, educators can capture a child's reasoning in an interview with a checklist. If the educator wants to capture the child's use of language or details of their reasoning, the interview can be audio or video recorded.

By structuring a formative assessment with questions and an interview, educators are probing for particular conceptions a child or children may have constructed. Educators often note the importance of such activity but believe these types of assessments take too much time. However, by embedding them in large- or small-group instruction and keeping them brief, educators can use assessments like these more regularly.

Formative Assessment Goals

To connect formative assessment designs with mathematical standards, we will conclude this chapter by describing (1) some formative assessment goals, and (2) how these goals relate to national standards. As stated before, the main goal of formative assessments should be to include children's conceptual understandings and mathematical reasoning. By drawing on practice standards, as developed by the *Common Core State Standards for Mathematics* (NGA Center and CCSSO, 2010), and the *Process* standards described by the National Council of Teachers of Mathematics (2000), educators can develop goals that focus on specific actions, which promote their children's conceptual understanding development in mathematics effectively. By delineating these in a rubric or a checklist, educators can more formally measure their children's mathematical competence along a continuum. By making these standards and practices primary in their assessment development, educators can elicit and use students' processes and practices in their instruction. Educators can also direct children's focus in their mathematics learning towards effective mathematical practices.

By looking across practices and processes, educators can develop meaningful foci for the learning experience they are assessing their children within and for assessment development. For instance, in Table 6.1, we can see that there are some broad connections between the CCSSM Practice standards (NGA Center and CCSSO, 2010) and NCTM Process standards (NCTM, 2000). By focusing on problem solving, an educator may want to borrow the language of the CCSSM practice standard by focusing on children's perseverance. In addition to the details in the practice standards, educators may note some details delineated on the NCTM website describing the process standards (www. nctm.org/Standards-and-Positions/Principles-and-Standards/Process). Under problem solving, there are specifically four aims of mathematics teaching (NCTM, 2000):

- Build new mathematical knowledge through problem solving
- Solve problems that arise in mathematics and in other contexts
- Apply and adapt a variety of appropriate strategies to solve problems
- Monitor and reflect on the process of mathematical problem solving

An educator may examine these details and determine that by focusing on children's perseverance when problem solving, they want to connect how children build new knowledge throughout their problem solving to perseverance. By making these mathematical processes and practices front and center, educators gather detailed information and design lessons about the processes their children develop when problem solving.

Table 6.1 Relationships between Practice and Process Standards

Practice Standards	Process Standards
Make sense of problems and persevere in solving them	Problem solving
Reason abstractly and quantitatively	Reasoning and proof
Construct viable arguments and critique the reasoning of others	Communications
Model with mathematics	Representations
Use appropriate tools strategically	Connections
Attend to precision	Communications
Look for and make use of structure	Connections
Look for and express regularity in repeated reasoning	Problem solving

Note: The Practice Standards are from the *Common Core State Standards* (www.corestandards.org/Math/Practice). The Process Standards are from the NCTM Process Standards (www.nctm.org/Standards-and-Positions/Principles-and-Standards/Process)

Source: NCTM Process standards: Reprinted with permission from Principles and Standards for School Mathematics, copyright 2000, by the National Council of Teachers of Mathematics. All rights reserved.; CCSSM Practice standards: © Copyright 2010. National Governors Association Center for Best Practices and Council of Chief State School Officers. All rights reserved.

In addition to mathematical practices and processes, it is important that educators focus on the dispositions children have when learning mathematics. For instance, research has found that children who are most successful in lifelong mathematics learning display perseverance when problem solving (Duckworth, 2016; Dweck, 2006). By collecting observational notes of their children's perseverance actions, educators can help determine how to challenge children in different ways in future mathematics instruction. For example, by noting how children revise their thinking or engage/disengage in a mathematics discussion, educators are able to intentionally include children's strategies in their instruction and future mathematics discussions. Educators can also share their observations with children in the classroom to help them reflect on their own strategies and engagement with other children's ideas in a mathematics discussion.

By developing mathematics goals in formative assessments, educators will be prepared to adjust their mathematics instruction to meet their children's mathematical needs. Rubrics can be created to formally establish particular goals for educators and children in elementary classrooms. By communicating these goals to children, educators can establish goals with children that position children as active learners of their own mathematics learning.

Connections to Other Math Recovery Books

Throughout this chapter, we have related many of the discussions to other books in the Math Recovery series. These connections are described explicitly below. This allows educators to draw on more detailed sets of assessment designs, rubrics, and checklists that this book is not intended to discuss.

The following books provide details of students' number strategies and tasks that teachers can use to distance the setting, extend the range of numbers, and increase the complexity of a task:

- The purple book, *Teaching Number in the Classroom with 4–8-Year-Olds* (Wright et al., 2015): Focus on p. 12, Figure 1.1, and pp. 24–6.
- The green book, *Teaching Number: Advancing Children's Skills and Strategies* (Wright et al., 2006): Focus on p. 26, Figure 2.1, pp. 52–3, Figure 3.3, and p. 60.
- The red book, *Developing Number Knowledge: Assessment, Teaching and Intervention with 7–11-Year-Olds* (Wright et al., 2012): Focus on Chapters 3–8.
- The blue book, *Early Numeracy: Assessment for Teaching and Intervention* (Wright et al., 2006): Focus on Chapters 1, 3, and 6.
- The orange book, *Developing Fractions Knowledge* (Hackenberg et al., 2016): Focus on Chapters 4–13.
- The white book, *The Learning Framework in Number: Pedagogical Tools for Assessment and Instruction* (Wright and Ellemor-Collins, 2018): Focus on Chapters 1–3.
- The brown book, *Numeracy for All Learners: Teaching Mathematics to Students with Special Needs* (Tabor et al., 2021): Focus on Chapter 5.
- The orange book, *Developing Fractions Knowledge* (Hackenberg et al., 2016): Focus on Chapter 3.

These books provide detailed assessments, discussions, questions, rubrics, checklists, and goals, which can be used to design and enact meaningful assessments.

Questions for Reflection

To wrap up this chapter on assessments, we find it useful to reflect on a few questions that might guide your design and use of formative assessments. By posing these questions, we want to challenge you to consider how assessments can be used in multiple contexts and with multiple populations. Our goal is also to develop some collegial discussions amongst your school community as you enact many of these assessments.

- How do the assessments you are designing allow for multiple entry points, strategy development, and exit points?
- How can the assessments created in the Math Recovery series be used to inform your development of meaningful assessments? Which books are most helpful and why?
- How can you build on the strengths your curriculum already provides? If you do not have a lot of curriculum strengths to draw on, how might you design formative assessments that run parallel with the topics and goals you are working towards? If you do have a lot of curriculum strengths, how might you further refine these assessments?
- What role or position do you take up when enacting assessments in your classroom? What role or position do the children in your classroom take on when providing feedback for assessments?
- When designing assessments, how do you ensure all of your students have access to the mathematical ideas you are assessing? If access is an issue, how do you refine your assessments to allow greater access?
- How do assessments change when working with students with different learning needs? Is the goal to progress monitor and if so, what are the learning goals for these more nuanced assessments?

References

Black, P. and Wiliam, D. (1998). Assessment and classroom learning. *Assessment in Education: Principles, Policy & Practice, 5*(1), 7–74.

Duckworth, A. (2016). *Grit: The Power of Passion and Perseverance* (Vol. *234*). New York: Scribner.

Dweck, C.S. (2006). *Mindset: The New Psychology of Success*. New York: Ballantine Books.

Lee, H., Chung, H.Q., Zhang, Y., Abedi, J. and Warschauer, M. (2020). The effectiveness and features of formative assessment in US K-12 education: A systematic review. *Applied Measurement in Education, 33*(2), 124–40.

National Council of Teachers of Mathematics (NCTM) (2000). *Principles and Standards for School Mathematics*. Reston, VA: National Council of Teachers of Mathematics.

National Council of Teachers of Mathematics (NCTM) (2014). *Principles to Action: Ensuring Mathematical Success for All*. Reston, VA: NCTM.

National Governors Association Center for Best Practices and Council of Chief State School Officers (NGA Center and CCSSO) (2010). *Common Core State Standards for Mathematics*. Washington, DC: Authors.

Van de Walle, J., Karp, K. and Bay-Williams, J.M. (2019). *Elementary and Middle Years Mathematics: Teaching Developmentally*. New York: Pearson.

Wiliam, D. (2010). The role of formative assessment in effective learning environments. In H. Dumont, D. Istance and F. Benavides (Eds), *The Nature of Learning: Using Research to Inspire Practice* (pp. 135–55). Paris: OECD.

Wiliam, D. (2018). Feedback: At the heart of – but definitely not all of – formative assessment. In A.A. Lipnevich and J.K. Smith (Eds), *The Cambridge Handbook of Instructional Feedback* (pp. 3–28). New York: Cambridge University Press.

Wright, R.J. and Ellemor-Collins, D. (2018). *The Learning Framework in Number: Pedagogical Tools for Assessment and Instruction*. London: Sage.

Wright, R.J., Martland, J., Stafford, A.K. and Stanger, G. (2006). *Teaching Number: Advancing Children's Skill and Strategies*, 2nd edition. London: Sage.

Wright, R.J., Stanger, G., Stafford, A.K. and Martland, J. (2015). *Teaching Number in the Classroom with 4–8-Year-Olds*, 2nd edition. London: Sage.

Yeh, C., Ellis, M.W. and Hurtado, C.K. (2017). *Reimagining the Mathematics Classroom*. Reston, VA: National Council of Teachers of Mathematics.

7

Monitoring Mathematics Learning

Guiding Principle: Observing the child and fine-tuning teaching

"Teaching involves intensive, ongoing observation by the teacher and continual micro-adjusting or fine-tuning of teaching on the basis of [their] observation." (Wright et al., 2006, p. 27)

Introduction

Close observation of students and responsive adjustment of instruction are instrumental in productive mathematics teaching. This chapter will focus on how teachers' observations of students' mathematical activity shape interpretations of such activities as well as subsequent instructional decisions. We will situate this aspect of practice in the research literature and examine different ways of noticing students' mathematical thinking. Lastly, we will explore practical examples and connect this way of responsive teaching to other ideals of mathematics teaching and learning.

Diving in with an Example

Before diving into the research behind the ways that teachers observe, or notice, students' mathematical thinking and activity, let's examine a brief exchange between a student and a teacher. In this exchange, the student has been tasked with determining two numbers that add up to 14 (see Figure 7.1).

> **Teacher:** Can you tell me two numbers that make 14?
> **Student:** [*Raises ten fingers sequentially and whispers*] One, two, three … nine, ten. [*Points four times to the side of right hand and whispers*] Eleven, twelve, thirteen, fourteen … Ten and four!
> **Teacher:** How do you know ten and four?
> **Student:** I counted up ten on my fingers and then imagined four more fingers.

Figure 7.1　Two numbers that add up to 14

First, let's identify some key details of the student's mathematical activity and talk. In this instance, we see the student enact a verbal counting sequence (i.e. whispering "one, two, three …") in conjunction with her creation of a finger pattern. We also observe her continue that sequence (from 11–14) via the counting of "imaginary fingers." Lastly, she separates those two counting sequences to announce an answer of "ten and four." Next, having observed these details of the students' activity, we ask ourselves what it means with respect to her mathematical thinking. From this exchange, we may determine that the student has a stable forward number word sequence (FNWS) to at least 14, although strictly speaking, we may not be able to determine a particular level as we did not observe her verbalizing number words before or after a given number (Wright and Ellemor-Collins, 2018). Perhaps, more importantly, we see the student continue a count from one via the creation of imaginary fingers. This activity could be interpreted as being consistent with a figurative counting scheme (Steffe et al., 1988; Wright et al., 2006). Lastly, from this interpretation (which itself is based on our specific observations), we may decide upon a next move. Perhaps this next step is more diagnostic in nature. For example, we might probe her number word sequence a bit (e.g. "Tell me the number that comes after 14") or we might change the instructional setting to examine her figurative counting activity in another context (e.g. present two covered collections of counters, nine and six, and ask, "How many altogether?"). Perhaps our next step, or task micro-adjustment, is more instructional in nature and we engage the student in naming and visualizing ten-wise patterns for 15–20 using an arithmetic rack (Wright et al., 2006). In any event, we see how a next step or decision may naturally flow from our interpretation of a moment which itself springs from the key aspects of activity to which we attended.

Noticing Children's Mathematical Thinking

The type of coherent, responsive teaching practice described above is often referred to as *teacher noticing* or *professional noticing*. While not quite synonymous, teacher noticing and professional noticing both describe a teaching practice grounded in observation and the interpretation of what is being observed. Throughout this chapter, for simplicity's sake, we will hereafter refer to this practice as *noticing*. While noticing has been the focus of considerable scholarly attention over the past decade (Schack et al., 2017; Sherin et al., 2011a), the foundations of such noticing may be traced back to the psychological examinations of attention and processing (Shiffrin and Schneider, 1977) and what is seen and not seen by individuals (Simons and Chabris, 1999). Delving into the nature of noticing, the practice is often organized around at least two components: "attending to particular events in an instructional setting" and "making sense of events in an instructional setting"; further, these two processes are typically described as being interrelated (Sherin et al., 2011b, p. 5). In their highly influential work, Jacobs et al. (2010) referred to these component processes as *attending* and *interpreting*. In that same publication, they also describe a third component, *deciding*, which refers to a teacher's intended action or response. It is this deciding component that directly relates to the micro-adjustment of our instruction referenced in the Guiding Principle. Specifically, the moment-by-moment decisions we make in an instructional space are very often oriented around adjusting the task or learning experience in some manner. Taking these component processes in concert, Fisher et al. (2018) describe the component processes of noticing thusly:

> [a]ttending involves concentrating one's attention on the students' actions and verbalizations within a mathematical moment. For example, details worthy of attention might include a student's movement of manipulatives, finger counting, or voice level. Interpreting involves an analysis of the observed behaviors or verbalizations with the aim of making some determination regarding the mathematical understanding of a student. Deciding refers to the teacher's leveraging a particular interpretation to plan and enact a sound instructional or diagnostic course of action. (p. 211)

This is precisely the noticing approach (attending, interpreting, deciding) that we took in our examination of the mathematical moment in the previous section, and such noticing provides both a lens and language for responsive teaching practices founded on observation and instructional micro-adjustment. Further, implicit in this process is that the component processes of attending, interpreting, and deciding are thematically connected in some manner (Thomas et al., 2021). Or, in other words, that to which we attend links to our interpretations which, in turn, link to our decisions. Using this basic approach, in the coming sections, we will explore different ways we might notice a moment, engage in some practical applications, and conclude with some reflective questions to shape our practice moving forward.

Ways of Noticing

In our earlier example, we engaged in the noticing (attending, interpreting, deciding) of a mathematical moment centered on an exchange between a student and a teacher. While such moments often provide rich contexts and opportunities to notice students' activity and thinking, there are several distinct ways of noticing that can guide our practice in this area. First, there is what we might call the *comprehensive capture* way of noticing (see Thomas et al., 2015 for examples). In this mode, the goal of noticing is to attend to as much detail as possible from a given moment and use that detail to form as rich or nuanced interpretation as possible. Our noticing work in the prior example typifies this perspective in that we focused intently on gathering and considering details of the students' activity (e.g. finger movements, verbal sequences) to construct a conceptual interpretation of the child's capacity to construct units. In this example, we sought to gather as much information from a moment as possible and leverage that information in our interpretation.

Another way of noticing is what we might call *opportunity capture*. Noticing in this manner is organized around attending to and interpreting key aspects of a moment, or opportunities, for furthering a mathematical goal (Leatham et al., 2015). Whereas noticing for comprehensive capture is focused on casting a net around every aspect of a moment, opportunity capture is about filtering such moments such that the teacher may discern points of mathematical opportunity to be interpreted and guide subsequent decisions, and this way of noticing is often quite useful in complex interactions amongst the teacher and multiple students – managing the "blooming, buzzing, confusion of sensory data" that teachers face in the mathematics classroom (Sherin et al., 2011b, p. 5). Interestingly, in this way of noticing, there are some open questions regarding the relationship between attending and interpreting. From a comprehensive capture perspective, one first attends to a moment and then interprets all of the captured details. If one is noticing to capture opportunity, then some manner of initial interpretation of a moment is necessary before focusing attention on a specific aspect. This sort of 'chicken and egg' relationship has been explored by researchers, and some have described the relationship between attending and interpreting as reflexive in that they occur in concert with one another and shape one another (Castro-Superfine et al., 2017).

As a way to envision noticing for opportunity capture, consider the following exchange (see Figure 7.2).

TEACHER: So what about eight plus eight equals blank plus four? [*Writes 8 + 8 = ___ + 4 on the board*] What do you think the answer would be? Jaden?

JADEN: Twelve.

TEACHER: Why twelve?

JADEN: Because if you add the eights, that's sixteen. So, twelve has to go with the four.

TEACHER: [*Records 12 on the board*] OK, other thoughts? Shan?

SHAN: It has to be four, because if you add four, four times, then that gives you sixteen.

TEACHER: Interesting, four, huh? [*Records 4 on the board*] How about you, Aubrey?

AUBREY: I kind of thought sixteen at first, but I think it's twelve. You have to balance the eights with twelve and four.

TEACHER: Interesting stuff.

Figure 7.2   Small-group working on 8 + 8 = ___ + 4

In this moment, there are multiple students sharing different avenues of thought regarding the task at hand, and the teacher must be selective with respect to noticing. While it is advantageous for us to try and capture as much detail as possible in any given moment, noticing for opportunity primes us to pay particular attention to the potential openings that might provide some lift or extension of the mathematics. In the example above, the task is ostensibly aimed at developing a relational understanding of equality (Leavy et al., 2013), and both Jaden and Aubrey's responses appear organized around that concept (e.g. equality as balance). While Aubrey's response provides a bit of opportunity to explore a typical, operational misconception of equality, Shan's response of "four" is perhaps the most intriguing. Indeed, there appears to be some manner of operational misunderstanding (e.g. repeated addition); however, there is an aspect of Shan's response that is true in a sense: $4 + 4 + 4 + 4$ does equal sixteen which, in turn, does balance $8 + 8$. Perhaps one productive decision might be to ask Shan what she thinks the equal sign in this problem means. Or perhaps we might ask Shan to compare one side of the equation ($8 + 8$) to the other ($\_ + 4$) and ask what she thinks is happening arithmetically. It is important to note that there is rarely, if ever, a singular "correct" decision for a given moment, but rather a range of decisions at one's disposal, with some being more productive than others. Returning to ways of noticing when engaging in such noticing to capture opportunity, Shan's response in this moment provides an opening to dive a bit deeper into her thinking as well as the demands of the task and the nature of equality. If we want to consider our decisions in terms of task micro-adjustment, perhaps we might augment the symbolic task portrayal with a visual or representation (e.g. balance scale) of some sort. We could even introduce a physical tool to illustrate how equality is mediating this mathematical space. In any event, there are a number of decisions, or instructional micro-adjustments, we could make to fine tune this task space to these student participants.

Objects of Noticing

First among these variants is noticing in the context of written work or some other produced artifact. Insofar as we can attend, interpret, and base our decisions upon a mathematical moment, we may also follow the same process for artifacts (e.g. written or digital work) that students produce in a mathematical moment. Indeed, these artifacts signify some manner of mathematical activity that, in turn, features embedded reasoning which may be unearthed. Continuing with the mathematical topic of equality, consider two examples of student written work (see Figure 7.3).

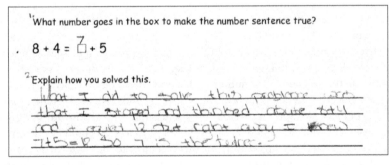

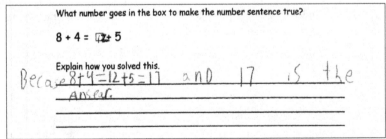

Figure 7.3   Written work examples

Beginning with the first student's work (top example), we may attend to the correct answer (7), but also to aspects of the written response. The student writes, "I stopped and thought about 8 + 4 and it equals 12, but right away I knew 7 + 5 = 12 ..." This portion of the response appears most noteworthy, and interpreting these words, one might conclude that, to some extent, the student is considering both portions of the equation in concert. Thus, the student is manifesting a relational understanding of equality – equality as balance (Leavy et al., 2013). One productive decision, in this instance, might be to increase the task demand and present the student with problems such as ___ + 6 = 9 + __. For this type of problem, there is no longer a fixed "target number" on one side of the equation to which the other side must balance. Rather, the student must consider both sides of the equation simultaneously when deciding upon viable solutions.

Turning to the second student's work (bottom example), again, we may attend to an incorrect answer (12), but also to the student's written rationale. In this instance, the student writes, "8 + 4 = 12 + 5 = 17 and seventeen is the answer." Here, we see a fairly representative example of operational understanding of equality – that the function of the equal sign is to trigger the answer. Indeed, we might interpret the student's response as not considering the different components of the equation in concert and with any attention to balance. Thus, a productive decision might be to introduce a balance scale and model this task directly using that tool. Or, perhaps, to work with the student to simplify portions of the equation (8 + 4; 12 + 5) and then rewrite and evaluate. In any event, noticing the written work of both students provides ample terrain to attend, interpret, and decide productively regarding their mathematical development.

Moving a bit afield of the Guiding Principle (e.g. intensive, ongoing observation of students and refinement of instruction accordingly), it is worth mentioning that the lens of noticing may also be applied to other adjacent structures and participants, including ourselves. For example, we may attend to and interpret aspects of our instructional plans with the intent to decide upon produc-tive refinements to such plans (Santagata, 2011). Or, for example, in a review of a video-recorded intervention lesson, we may choose to attend to and interpret our own actions as teachers in that moment and make decisions about how we might lead that bit of instruction more productively in future iterations. On this last point, one author of this book had a recent experience of self-noticing when reviewing a video-recorded lesson of his own teaching with fifth grade students around func-tions and graphs of functions. Specifically, the video revealed the author unwittingly gesturing with his hands and essentially providing students with the shape of a given graph (see Thomas, 2018 for more description of gesture and suggestion). In this instance, attending to these teacher gestures provided useful context to interpret the subsequent student responses and to guide the instructional decisions that followed. Indeed, noticing provides us with a wide lens that may be used across a range of settings, including those beyond students themselves.

Noticing for Equity

Another way of noticing that is arguably deserving of its own section is noticing for equity. This type of noticing blends focus upon aspects of a mathematical moment with key equity considerations such as access, achievement, power, and identity (Gutiérrez, 2009). While equity is an expansive area that may range from ways of rehumanizing mathematics for historically marginalized groups to vivid societal critique embedded within mathematical activity, the broad dimensions of access, achievement, power, and identity provide useful lenses through which we might focus our notic-ing. While these dimensions and other perspectives of equitable teaching of mathematics will be discussed in detail in Chapter 11, it is useful to briefly operationalize some broad categories in this area as they relate to noticing. Thus, taking these dimensions in turn, access refers to an individu-al's capacity to participate mathematically and to how teachers may deploy different instructional design elements (e.g. tools, differentiation) to maximize such participation. Achievement refers, at the macro level, to course-taking patterns, standardized test scores, and students' progress through a mathematical pipeline. In moments of our teaching that are so valuable for noticing, though, this distills down to some foundational value of right and wrong regarding students' thinking and abilities. What manner of thinking is deemed correct, valued, or lifted up in some way (and what thinking is not) connects to this dimension of achievement. Identity refers to the manner in which an individual's lived experience connects to a mathematical moment or activity and also whether or not one feels valued, represented, and mathematically capable in that moment. Lastly, power refers to the assignment of authority within a particular learning space. Who gets to make decisions and have a voice in a particular moment are manifestations of power.

Now that we have a general idea of some broad categories, or lenses, for equitable noticing, let's examine a particular moment and put these ideas into practice. Toward that end, consider this exchange around the task 60 – 29 (see Figure 7.4).

TEACHER: So before we talk answers to sixty minus twenty-nine, I want to hear about favorite strategies. Who wants to tell me about their favorite?

JOSIAH: I can just count back. Like, I start at sixty and go back to twenty-nine. I get thirty-two, I think. It takes a while, but it's the easiest.

KABREY: I don't like that way. It takes forever, and it's easy to forget where you are.

TEACHER: OK, so what do you like, Kabrey? What makes sense to you?

KABREY: It's easier to just think about a line. And start at sixty. Then you jump back to thirty, but that's too far, so you have to put one back, so the answer is thirty-one.

MARC: That's not easier, Kabrey. It's subtraction, and I don't get why you go forward and backward. The right way to do this is like subtraction [*points to base-10 blocks on table*]. Like, you get six of these long ones and then take away two and then nine more of the littles. The blocks aren't perfect because they should come apart like Lego, but they work. That's the right way. I mean, it's the way we are supposed to.

TEACHER: Well, let's hold up on any one way being the right way. Kabrey, I think maybe Marc is having trouble seeing how your strategy works. Would you mind taking over as teacher and walking us through your thinking again?

Figure 7.4   Small-group work on 60 – 29

Noticing the exchange above with strict attention to students' mathematical thinking, we might attend to Josiah's preference of a long count by ones and interpret that as an indicator of a more unitary (by ones) arithmetic perspective. We might attend to Kabrey's description of a number line and a "jump" backwards of 30 and interpret that as an indicator of her capacity to construct composite units. These interpretations could then lead us to certain decisions aimed at advancing their arithmetic reasoning. Noticing this moment through a lens of equity, however, opens up additional terrain for consideration. For example, attending to Marc's assertion that the base-10 blocks are the "correct" way to approach this problem, we might interpret some connection to the equity dimension of achievement, thus opening space for the teacher's decision to push back a bit on ascriptions of right/wrong regarding students' strategies at that point. Attending to and interpreting Kabrey's remarks, the teacher decides to position her as the teacher, thus connecting to the dimension of identity by signaling her mathematical capability to other students. Certainly, noticing for equity (using these particular dimensions) may involve multiple dimensions in a given moment as well as overlap or blurring of category lines with respect to particular dimensions (e.g. an interplay between identity and power). However, this example serves merely to illustrate how a lens of equity may inform teachers' noticing of a mathematical moment. Lastly, we also note that noticing, as a human practice, opens the potential for bias. What we choose to attend to, and how we interpret a moment, is uniquely shaped by our own lived experiences, ideas, attitudes, and biases. For example, researchers have observed manifestations of bias in the form of asset-oriented and deficit-oriented perspectives with respect to students' gender and race within the interpreting component (Thomas et al., 2020). As such, it is important to remain cognizant of our own positioning, power, and worldview as we engage in noticing students' mathematical thinking, such that we reduce the potential for hidden biases to unduly influence our practice. While we may never be able to fully mitigate our own biases, particularly our unconscious biases, being mindful of ourselves and questioning our focal points for attending, our interpretations, and our subsequent decisions allow us to operate more critically and thoughtfully in the moment.

Noticing in Practice

Thus far, we have explored different ways of noticing, objects for noticing, and how one might couple notions of equity and the practice of noticing. Along the way, we have used various mathematical moments and exchanges to illustrate these ideas. In this section, we will, again, engage you in noticing another mathematical moment. Thus far, though, we have presented individual or small-group interactions. In this instance, however, we will present a segment of a number talk involving an entire classroom of students. Further, we will challenge you to consider your own noticing before we discuss our perspectives. With that in mind, consider the following exchange around a patterning task (see Figure 7.5).

In this moment, there is a lot of mathematical reasoning packed into a relatively brief sequence of events. As such, perhaps we might notice to capture opportunities where we can build upon ideas or encourage students to consider their own reasoning. With this in mind, review the exchange and attend to particular comments (made either by a student or the teacher) that stand out to you in some way – comments that could, perhaps, open the door for building or further examination in some way. Having attended to certain aspects of the moment, then interpret those aspects by asking yourself what you think they mean. In this space, you might consider different lenses. For example, you might interpret a student's remark with a particular progression in mind (Wright and Ellemor-Collins, 2018). Or maybe you are interpreting something a student said with an equity emphasis – how, for example, achievement (right/wrong) connects to what is being said. In any event, a key goal of interpreting is to generate meaning of some sort to that which has been attended. Lastly, based on our interpretation, we formulate a decision. If what we have interpreted takes place at the end of the sequence, perhaps we can envision some productive action, task, or question the teacher might take or pose. Or, if our focus is earlier in the sequence, perhaps we might consider decisions that differ from those made by the teacher. Regardless of the decision, our goal with this practice is to be mindful of linkages across each of the components (Thomas et al., 2021). Or, in other words, our decisions relate to our interpretations which, in turn, spring from our attending to key aspects of a moment.

By this time, we hope you have engaged in some productive noticing of the moment above and have imagined some possible decisions that advance these students' understanding or patterning in

TEACHER:	So I am going to write a pattern up here on the board, and then I am going to ask you to tell me what you notice about the pattern. [*Teacher draws the pattern* □□△□□△□□△□□△]
TEACHER:	OK, so what do you all notice about that pattern?
EMILY:	Shapes.
JESS:	Squares and triangles.
REMY:	A triangle comes after the squares.
JULES:	There's twelve things in it.
TEACHER:	OK, good stuff, you all. Let's say the pattern aloud, say it with me. Square, square, triangle [*students repeating in unison*], square, square, triangle. Square, square, triangle. Square, square, triangle. Nice work. What do you notice about the pattern?
JESS:	Two squares and a triangle.
KADEN:	Yeah, you say square, square, triangle, like a rhythm.
SHAQUAN:	Every third one is a triangle. That's why it has rhythm.
REMY:	Yeah, but every fifth one is a square.
TEACHER:	Interesting, I like the way you are noticing things about this pattern. Remy, I want to come back to your idea in a minute, but let's focus on the idea that we can number these shapes … like the first one, the third one, the fifth one, and so on. We have twelve shapes in our pattern, and I want you to take a second and think about what the fifteenth shape would look like. Think for ten seconds and then I will ask folks to share. [Waits 10 seconds] OK, Remy, what do you think fifteen will be?
REMY:	Square because if the fifth one is a square, the tenth one is a square, so every five shapes it's going to be a square.
MARTA:	That's wrong. Number twelve is a triangle, so thirteen is square, fourteen is square, and fifteen is triangle. Square square triangle.
SHAQUAN:	Yeah, Marta's right on that.
CHERIE:	Eighteen is a triangle. So is twenty-one.
JESS:	No, Remy is right. Five is a square, and ten is a square. That's right.
TEACHER:	OK, let's come back together for a second. Setting aside who is right or wrong, let's focus back on the pattern. What we want to know is what the fifteenth shape will be. Marta, take over the marker and tell me how you see this working. Then, Remy and Jess, I want you to tell me what you think Marta did. Cherie, here in a second, I want to hear more about that eighteen and twenty-one, but for now, let's focus on sorting fifteen.

Figure 7.5   Whole-class number talk – patterning task

some key way or open up more equitable and inclusive spaces for participation. Now that you have developed your own ideas about the moment, we will briefly share a bit of our own noticing. Again, as this is a complex moment, we might focus on capturing the opportunity presented by Cherie ("eighteen is a triangle, so is twenty-one"). In that portion of the exchange, the teacher ostensibly is attending to Marta's building of the pattern beyond the provided terms (i.e. "thirteen-square, fourteen-square, fifteen-triangle") and interpreting that as some sequential understanding of the AAB nature of the pattern. This in and of itself is fruitful terrain to test Remy's notion that every fifth shape is a square. As such, the teacher's decision to empower Marta to share her thinking is productive. Moving forward from there, however, attending to Cherie's brief comment, we might interpret that she has gathered some additional insight into this pattern and is able to extrapolate terms without having to build the sequence as Marta does. As such, we might decide to invite Cherie to share her thinking in more detail and how she is able to make those determinations (e.g. "Cherie, tell me about your thinking and how you were able to come up with eighteen and twenty one?"). As with the teacher's empowering of Marta and positioning her as mathematically capable, we might also consider decisions to foreground Cherie's thinking through equity lenses such as power and identity. This is but one possible pathway to productively monitor and respond (via noticing) to a complex mathematical moment. There are likely many other ways we could navigate this exchange to further students' thinking and create equitable spaces for mathematical practice. Nevertheless, our hope is that this example provides some guidance on how to mindfully notice in the moment.

Connecting and Reflecting

Connecting to Other Practices

Noticing is deeply connected to other practices put forth in this book, and it is useful to consider how such noticing works in concert with ideas and concepts from other chapters. While we could draw meaningful connections to each of these chapters, we find it useful to highlight some of the more meaningful linkages with respect to monitoring and responding to (or noticing) students' mathematical thinking. Beginning with the importance of inquiry-based instruction and the role that inquiry plays with respect to students' mathematical construction (Chapter 2), we note a core, dispositional aspect of noticing that is important to habituate – that our attending, interpreting, and deciding should always aim to examine and create spaces for inquiry. While we may focus on varying aspects of a moment (e.g. tasks, tools, our own teaching), fundamental to this noticing should be how those aspects relate to students' experience of that moment and the extent to which that experience provides meaningful terrain to mathematically explore and construct ideas.

Progressions of mathematical learning (Chapter 3) are mentioned frequently in our discussion of noticing as they provide structures through which we may interpret a student's activities in a given moment. For example, having attended to a student's counting of fingers, our understanding of a unit's construction progression (emergent, perceptual, figurative, etc.) allows us to interpret such counting with sophistication and nuance, thus resulting in a decision that is much more productive than one without this interpretive lens. These progressions of mathematical development should always be at or near the forefront of one's mind when noticing students' activities in the classroom as they ground our noticing in knowledge of development around a particular concept and also provide something of a roadmap for what might come next conceptually, and inform our decisions in that direction.

Turning to practices around providing feedback and structuring discourse (Chapter 8), noticing is an absolutely essential skill in that area. To the extent that we aim to provide meaningful comment or evaluation of a student's thinking, we must first attend to and interpret aspects of that thinking. Moreover, when creating spaces for productive discourse, the practices of monitoring, selecting, sequencing, and connecting (Smith and Stein, 2011) are deeply connected to and reliant upon astute attending, interpreting, and deciding in the moment. Similarly, choices made regarding the promotion of productive struggle (Chapter 9) are also predicated on close attending to and interpreting students' mathematical activity in the moment, and on devising decisions that create space for challenging problem-solving experiences which provoke disequilibrium.

Lastly, as we have discussed in earlier sections of this chapter, noticing has deep implications for the equitable teaching of mathematics (Chapter 11). What we notice in a given moment has profound implications for how students experience that moment. Our decisions, which are themselves products of our attending and interpreting, shape the manner in which such moments are accessible to students, empower them as learners, or connect to some aspect of their identity to name but a few aspects. When we look deeply into our moments of teaching, we begin a process where we can open doors for students, create support, rethink the nature of correctness, and balance power productively such that students, particularly those who have been historically marginalized, see such moments as relevant and see themselves as capable mathematical thinkers. In summary, noticing is a core practice of teaching that, when done well, provides the moment-by-moment conduit through which all of our knowledge and capability may flow.

Questions for Reflection

To conclude this examination of monitoring and responding to students' mathematical thinking via the core practice of noticing, perhaps it is useful to consider some key questions that might guide us in this area. Note that these questions are designed, we hope, to challenge you and, as such, may not be easily answered. Nevertheless, we offer them as lingering points of reflection for you to ponder as you put these ideas into practice.

Attending

- What is your mathematical goal in a given moment? What sorts of activities, actions, and words do you anticipate from students? What do you hope to see? What might signal mathematical struggle?
- How complex is the mathematical moment at hand? Are you able to detect lots of detail from all participants, or do you need to look for moments of opportunity? If it is the latter, what might you imagine students saying or doing that would present opportunities?
- Where is the most productive place to focus your attending? Are there particular students who would benefit from additional focus? How did you select these students and what might you be looking for? Are you interested in examining an artifact, tool, or perhaps your own teaching? In these areas, what might you be looking for?

Interpreting

- What mathematical lens is shaping your interpretation? Are you considering a particular progression or trajectory? Are there multiple progressions or trajectories that could inform what you saw in a moment?
- What other lenses might influence your interpretation of a moment? How might access, achievement, power, and identity impact your interpretation?

- What are my own attitudes, beliefs, and perspectives of a moment? Are my interpretations negative, more often than not, for certain students and their capabilities? Are they positive, more often than not, for other students and their capabilities? What is guiding this and what biases might I have regarding students' mathematical thinking?
- How might I consider and highlight students' strengths in addition to their struggles in a particular moment?

Deciding

- What is my goal for this moment and what are the possible decisions at my disposal? What action might I take that will result in progress toward my goal?
- To what extent is my decision consistent with inquiry-oriented learning and the promotion of productive struggle?
- How does my decision enhance or constrain students' access to the mathematics of a moment? To what extent am I signaling correctness and acting as the keeper of right and wrong? Does my decision connect, in a relevant way, to the unique, lived experiences of my students and does it empower them as mathematical thinkers?
- How will I know if my decision was productive? What sorts of things might I attend to and interpret in the aftermath of my decision to gain a sense of its value or effectiveness?

Noticing Coherence

- To what extent is my noticing connected and coherent? Can I link my decision to an interpretation of a moment which, itself, may be linked to students' mathematical activity to which I attended?
- Is there a particular theme or idea that guides my thinking through attending, interpreting, and deciding?

References

Castro-Superfine, A., Fisher, A., Bragelman, J. and Amador, J.M. (2017). Shifting perspectives on pre-service teachers' noticing of children's mathematical thinking. In E.O. Schack, M.H. Fisher and J.A. Wilhelm (Eds), *Teacher Noticing: Bridging and Broadening Perspectives, Contexts, and Frameworks* (pp. 409–26). New York: Springer.

Fisher, M.H., Thomas, J., Jong, C., Schack, E.O. and Tassell, J. (2018). Noticing numeracy now! Examining changes in preservice teachers' noticing, knowledge, and attitudes. *Mathematics Education Research Journal*, 30(2), 209–32.

Gutiérrez, R. (2009). Framing equity: Helping students "play the game" and "change the game." *Teaching for Excellence and Equity in Mathematics*, 1(1), 4–8.

Jacobs, V.R., Lamb, L.L.C. and Philipp, R.A. (2010). Professional noticing of children's mathematical thinking. *Journal for Research in Mathematics Education*, 41(2), 169–202.

Leatham, K.R., Peterson, B.E., Stockero, S.L. and Van Zoest, L.R. (2015). Conceptualizing mathematically significant pedagogical opportunities to build on student thinking. *Journal for Research in Mathematics Education*, 46(1), 88–124.

Leavy, A., Hourigan, M. and McMahon, A. (2013). Early understanding of equality. *Teaching Children Mathematics, 20*(4), 246–52.

Santagata, R. (2011). From teacher noticing to a framework for analyzing and improving classroom lessons. In M.G. Sherin, V.R. Jacobs and R.A. Philipp (Eds), *Mathematics Teacher Noticing: Seeing through Teachers' Eyes* (pp. 152–68). New York: Routledge.

Schack, E.O., Fisher, M.H. and Wilhelm, J. (Eds) (2017). *Teacher Noticing: Bridging and Broadening Perspectives, Contexts, and Frameworks.* New York: Springer.

Sherin, M.G., Jacobs, V.R. and Philipp, R.A. (Eds) (2011a). *Mathematics Teacher Noticing: Seeing through Teachers' Eyes.* New York: Routledge.

Sherin, M.G., Jacobs, V.R. and Philipp, R.A. (2011b). Situating the study of teacher noticing. In M.G. Sherin, V.R. Jacobs and R.A. Philipp (Eds), *Mathematics Teacher Noticing: Seeing through Teachers' Eyes* (pp. 3–13). New York: Routledge.

Shiffrin, R.M. and Schneider, W. (1977). Controlled and automatic human information processing: II. Perceptual learning, automatic attending and a general theory. *Psychological Review, 84*(2), 127–90.

Simons, D.J. and Chabris, C.F. (1999). Gorillas in our midst: Sustained inattentional blindness for dynamic events. *Perception, 28,* 1059–74.

Smith, M.S. and Stein, M.K. (2011). *5 Practices for Orchestrating Productive Mathematics Discussions.* Reston, VA: National Council of Teachers of Mathematics.

Steffe, L.P., Cobb, P. and von Glasersfeld, E. (1988). *Construction of Arithmetical Meanings and Strategies.* New York: Springer.

Thomas, J. (2018). Talking with our hands. *Teaching Children Mathematics, 24*(5), 308–14.

Thomas, J., Dueber, D., Fisher, M.H., Jong, C. and Schack, E.O. (2021). Professional noticing coherence: Exploring relationships between component processes. *Mathematical Thinking and Learning,* https://doi.org/10.1080/10986065.2021.1977086

Thomas, J., Fisher, M., Eisenhardt, S., Schack, E., Tassell, J. and Yoder, M. (2015). Professional noticing: Developing responsive mathematics teaching. *Teaching Children Mathematics, 21,* 295–303.

Thomas, J., Sawyer, B., Marzilli, T., Jong, C., Schack, E.O. and Fisher, M.H. (2020). Investigating the manifestations of bias in professional noticing of mathematical thinking among preservice teachers. *Journal of Mathematics Education at Teachers College, 11*(1), 1–11.

Wright, R.J. and Ellemor-Collins, D. (2018). *The Learning Framework in Number: Pedagogical Tools for Assessment and Instruction.* London: Sage.

Wright, R.J., Martland, J. and Stafford, A.K. (2006). *Early Numeracy: Assessment for Teaching and Intervention,* 2nd edition. London: Sage.

Wright, R.J., Stanger, G., Stafford, A.K. and Martland, J. (2015). *Teaching Number in the Classroom with 4–8-Year-Olds,* 2nd edition. London: Sage.

8

Feedback and Discourse in Mathematics Instruction

Introduction

While the activity of mathematics almost always centers on some problem or challenge, the reasons that people engage in such activity are often much deeper. Certainly, in school contexts, we often compel students to think and act mathematically, but a more optimistic view of practice must be organized around intrinsic satisfaction. This satisfaction may come from achieving some mathematical goal. Satisfaction might be the result of a rich interaction with peers that involves healthy discussion and disagreement. Or, perhaps, satisfaction is derived from the act of doing mathematics, the sustained hard thinking, even if a goal is not accomplished. Our point is that mathematical satisfaction can spring from a variety of sources, and self-recognition of one's progress, broadly construed, in mathematical spaces is a key part of realizing and experiencing such satisfaction.

This chapter will focus on the nature and importance of intrinsic satisfaction in mathematical activity and how, as teachers, we might create experiences that promote satisfaction and the recognition of such satisfaction amongst our students. We will examine different wellsprings from which mathematical satisfaction may arise. We will explore how self-reflective opportunities with respect to one's practice and progress serve as a catalyst for the realization of intrinsic satisfaction. Lastly, we will delve into some practical examples of mathematics teaching and learning that enhance or constrain opportunities for students to realize and reflect upon their satisfaction and this practice to other Guiding Principles in this book.

Diving Deep into Satisfaction

In this section, we will examine the nature of intrinsic mathematical satisfaction, and the different sources that might fuel such satisfaction. Note, many of the ideas throughout this section (and this chapter) are predicated on rich, inquiry-oriented problem experiences of the type described in Chapter 2. Indeed, inquiry and mathematical meaning are fundamental ideas with respect to the creation of mathematical satisfaction, and we encourage the reader to revisit the ideas of Chapter 2 prior to pressing forward. Before diving deeper into the nature of satisfaction, let's consider an example involving a small group of early primary students working on individual artwork in the style of Piet Mondrian (Chandler, 1972). For those not familiar with Mondrian's artwork, it is eminently recognizable in that each work is an assemblage of shapes (squares, rectangles, and lines most often) with sparing use of bold color. The students' works (Figure 8.1) capture this style quite well. In these examples, the students have been tasked with creating their own artwork, inspired by Mondrian and taking note of any mathematical ideas they see in their creations. Consider the following exchange (see Figure 8.2).

Kai   Amara   Zooey

Figure 8.1   Student artwork inspired by Mondrian

TEACHER: So take a few moments, people, and share with each other about your creations. Where do you see math in your artwork? Kai, why don't you kick things off.

KAI: I noticed in the Mondrian art, he used squares and rectangles, so I made my drawing with squares and rectangles … and lines. So that's the math I see.

ZOOEY: Yeah, yours [*Kai*] looks a lot like his artwork. It could almost be the same thing. I kinda thought about it like Mondrian future style. Like, when I see his artwork, I kinda saw a computer brain or something. You know, like the parts inside a computer. So, I used shapes and lines to make that. And technology is math, too.

TEACHER: Interesting, like a circuit board inside a computer or tablet or smartphone, huh? That's very creative. What did you mean by technology is math?

ZOOEY: All of the programs on computers are like a math problem. It's like math codes they have to make up to make them work.

AMARA: But it's not really Mondrian, Zooey. The shapes have to touch for it to be Mondrian.

TEACHER: You know, a good word for that, when shapes and lines touch. When lines meet, they intersect. When shapes share a border, we could say they are contiguous.

KAI: [*whispers*] Contiguous, contiguous.

ZOOEY: Yeah, Mondrian's stuff was contiguous, but we were doing our own thing inspired by Mondrian. That's art, right?

TEACHER: Sure thing, Zooey. Part of making art is making it your own. Amara, I noticed you used some triangles and Mondrian doesn't do a whole lot of that.

AMARA: Yeah, I mean, Mondrian is OK, but I feel like he gets repetitive, and I thought about adding in some new shapes. But mine all do touch … are contiguous.

KAI: You did all the triangles yellow.

AMARA: I wanted them to stand out because they are different. Triangles have math stuff, too, like the other shapes.

TEACHER: I like that idea of standing out. What's the math stuff in a triangle?

AMARA: Yeah, Zooey is kinda right in a way. I did make it my own a little which made it more fun to draw. But there are different triangles, and I wanted to use the ones that matched with Mondrian the best. The triangle side is the longest side of the triangle that basically just cuts a rectangle in half.

TEACHER: Interesting. How did you know that diagonal, or triangle side as you call it, is the longest side?

AMARA: Because you have to go all the way from one corner of the rectangle to the other. The other two sides don't have to go that far.

KAI: But it's a straight line from end to end. It's the shortest distance. The other sides have to go all the way around the rectangle.

AMARA: Look at it Kai, it's definitely longer than the other sides.

KAI: Maybe for those yellow ones, but if you drew a triangle in one of your red ones, it would be the same. Maybe shorter. I still think the most fun way is to think of it like a grid and you can make some of the squares and rectangles bigger or smaller. But I didn't just draw rectangles and squares. I did lines and made them all different lengths and let them just kinda touch where they did. And then the rectangles and squares were just there.

TEACHER: How did you decide which ones needed color?

KAI: I thought of it like a little city. The lines are like roads and the black boxes are buildings. The blue boxes are swimming pools or lakes, and the green are parks.

TEACHER: Interesting. I definitely see it. I notice that the parks and swimming pools are next to each other.

KAI: Yeah, I thought that's how a city designer would think. I wonder if Mondrian saw stuff in his drawings or if they were like, just drawings.

Figure 8.2 Student artwork exchange

In this task, the students are presented with a creative avenue to identify and consider mathematical connections with little regulation on where their thinking may travel. Further, two of the students explore adaptation of the artistic style itself. For example, Zooey describes art as "doing our own thing" and Amara introduces triangles to her work as a means to improve upon perceived repetition of squares and rectangles within Mondrian's work. Regarding connections to mathematical ideas, Kai identifies certain polygons within his work and imagines a city design while Amara describes the triangles in her work and explores the differences in side lengths. Zooey posits a connection to technology (i.e. "Mondrian future style") in her work and connects mathematics to coding processes. In each instance, the student is working to see something mathematical within their own work – to focus inward rather than outward. Additionally, the teacher creates space for mathematical discourse. Amara and Kai have an interesting exchange around the differing lengths of triangle sides and informally explore the concept of hypotenuse and, by extension, the Pythagorean theorem. Throughout this exchange, there are different opportunities for students to gain satisfaction, whether it is in the creation and exploration of their own mathematical art, the engagement in spirited discussion with a peer, or even just learning and repeating a pleasing new word (i.e. Kai: [whispers] "contiguous, contiguous"). We recognize that this example presented a fairly unstructured task and that, often, learning goals and curricular materials impose a greater degree of structure upon a mathematical experience. Here students were asked to connect to any mathematical idea of their choosing; however, the overlay of Mondrian for artistic inspiration tilts the activity in a geometric direction (and towards lines and polygons in particular). All of this is to say that thoughtful instructional design intends to balance exploration and goal-oriented activity (see Chapter 5 for an explication of these ideas).

We are also careful to note that this exchange is presented in the context of opportunity rather than confirmation of student satisfaction. By definition, intrinsic satisfaction is an internal experience that is primarily veiled to the outside observer. Manifestation of such satisfaction has varying degrees of affirmative clarity. For example, a student who exclaims, "Wow, this activity is so much fun!" is explicitly signaling satisfaction. However, another student who exhibits a smile as she works mathematically is, perhaps, experiencing satisfaction related to that activity (or perhaps the smile is unrelated). In other instances, satisfaction may manifest as a more engaged and spirited dialogue with colleagues and/or a teacher. This is not to discount the more subtle signs of student satisfaction. Indeed, for teachers, these cues are important in interpreting how students are experiencing a mathematical moment. However, had the teacher in this example explicitly posed the question aimed at satisfaction (e.g. "How satisfying was this activity? What parts of this did you enjoy? Which parts didn't you enjoy and why?"), we likely would gain more insight into the extent to which Kai, Amara, and Zooey found satisfaction within the activity and whether or not that satisfaction had mathematical connections.

Achievement, Fulfillment, Flourishing, and Virtue

Given the elusiveness of determining the intrinsic satisfaction of another, it is worthwhile to examine the nature of satisfaction and how it may be formed, fueled, and felt in the mathematics classroom. Beginning with the nature of satisfaction itself, scanning the research literature reveals that satisfaction may be examined in very particular contexts such as being a consumer (Giese and Cote, 2000) or within one's job (Aziri, 2011), and that these forms of satisfaction are linked to certain situational features. However, there do seem to be more elemental aspects of satisfaction that transcend context.

Satisfaction is defined, in part, as "achieving something" as well as "fulfilling a need or desire" (Oxford Learner's Dictionary, n.d.). These notions of *achievement* (of some goal) and *fulfillment* (of some need) provide a foundation by which we may begin to understand how such satisfaction might be created and felt in a mathematics classroom.

Achievement

Progress toward and achievement of a mathematical goal can take many different forms, ranging from earning a good score on a test to gaining insight into a particularly vexing problem. Certainly, each instance of achievement may bring satisfaction of some sort; however, our aim is to explore achievements that lead to intrinsic satisfaction that is meaningful and durable. In his portrayal of mathematics learning principles, Polya (1963) writes, "the pleasure of the mental activity should be the best reward for such activity" which he terms the learning principle of "best motivation" (p. 608). Here, Polya describes a type of satisfaction whereas sustained mathematical activity is an achievement in and of itself, and a driver of intrinsic satisfaction. Relatedly, one element of Self-Determination Theory, *competence*, refers to the need to feel that one's efforts are productive toward achieving a desired outcome, and that such competence is an essential element for psychological growth and satisfaction (Deci and Ryan, 2000). Coordinating these two perspectives moves mathematical learning away from merely arriving at correct answers and toward a landscape organized around elevating sustained hard thinking as an essential element of that process. Consider the following example involving a first grade student working with an interventionist on a missing-subtrahend task (see Figure 8.3).

TEACHER: So we've got twenty-one [*taps the concealed collection of 21 counters on left*]. I am going to sneak some away. [*removes 6 counters from the collection and slides them beneath his hand across the table and covers them*] Now, there's fifteen left. How many did I slide across over here? [*taps the collection of 6 counters*]

WILLIAM: Started with twenty-one and now there's fifteen [*looks at the table for some time ... slowly raises six fingers sequentially*] [*whispers*] sixteen, seventeen, eighteen, nineteen, twenty, twenty-one. [*exclaims*] You took six! Didn't think I was going to get that one, did you? [*smiles*]

TEACHER: How do you know I took six?

WILLIAM: I started with fifteen and counted until I got to twenty-one. I was counting on my hand so I wouldn't lose my place, and it's six. I know it's six. [*holds up six fingers*]

TEACHER: [*lifts cover on collection of six counters*]

WILLIAM: I knew it! I got that one! [*smiles*]

TEACHER: How does that make you feel?

WILLIAM: Good! That was one of those hard ones that I hate, but I liked it this time.

$$21 - \underline{} = 15$$

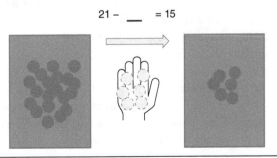

Figure 8.3 Missing subtrahend satisfaction

This exchange, drawn from an intervention lesson conducted by one of the authors of this book, illustrates how achievement, springing from sustained mathematical thinking on a challenging task, creates intrinsic and deeply felt satisfaction. William had, thus far, struggled with concealed collections, and on a few occasions, wondered aloud if he could ever work with materials which were not perceptually available to him. In this instance, though, after some contemplation (i.e. staring at the table), William re-presents the screened collection with his fingers (Steffe et al., 1988) and arrives at the response of "six". Germane to this discussion, though, is William's visceral reaction to *his own achievement* evidenced in his smiling, gentle taunt of the teacher ("didn't think I was going to get that one, did you?") and his explicit affinity for this task ("I liked it this time"). Indeed, on this last point, William describes the task as "one of those hard ones" and he found intrinsic satisfaction in achieving a viable strategy through his own sustained efforts. This is in keeping with Polya's (1963) description of pleasure stemming from mental activity and how the experience of such pleasure is, indeed, the "best motivation" with respect to mathematics learning, and William's perceptions of his own competence were derived not only from his response, but also from the effort he expended to achieve that response.

Fulfillment and Virtue

Considering progress in a deeper and more humanistic way leads us to the notion of fulfillment. How am I making progress toward fulfilling my needs as a human being? This type of fulfillment, sometimes referred to as eudaimonia [living a complete life], may be traced back to the earliest of scholarly work. Indeed, Aristotle (2002), commenting in *Nicomachean Ethics*, distinguishes between hedonic happiness derived from fleeting pleasures and deeper fulfillment stemming from a life lived more completely by "actively pursuing virtues and excellences" (Ryan et al., 2008, p. 143). Connecting lofty notions such as virtues to mathematics teaching and learning, however, may appear tricky at best. Who defines such virtues with respect to a mathematical activity or concept? How does one engage in virtuous mathematics anyhow?

Referenced earlier in Chapter 2, Francis Su's (2020) *Mathematics for Human Flourishing* tackles these heady questions by presenting a case for fulfillment, or flourishing as he describes it, through virtuous mathematical activity. Su writes:

[T]he proper practice of mathematics cultivates virtues that help people flourish. These virtues serve you well no matter what profession you choose or where your life takes you. And the movement toward virtue is aroused by basic human desires – the universal longings that we all have – which fundamentally motivate everything we do. These desires can be channeled into the pursuit of mathematics. (pp. 10–11)

Su goes on to illustrate how mathematical activity in classrooms and beyond connects to virtues such as play, justice, freedom, love, truth, and many others. In this section, though, we will explore a few examples of how mathematical teaching and learning, steeped in virtue, are a catalyst for deep fulfillment and the intrinsic satisfaction described in the Guiding Principle of this chapter.

Freedom

Freedom, as a human desire, has been a central pursuit of societies throughout history. The virtue of freedom in mathematics learning can come in many forms. For example, knowledge of multiple strategies provides a freedom of choice with respect to a particular problem. Another type of freedom relates to one's acceptance as a mathematical thinker and how freely students may become a part of a community of learners. Su (2020) refers to this as *freedom of welcome*. In the work of mathematics teaching and learning, we might consider the freedom to explore as a way of tapping into this virtue. Consider an excerpt from an earlier exchange involving students' creation of Mondrian-inspired artwork (see Figure 8.4).

ZOOEY:	Yeah, yours [*Kai*] looks a lot like his artwork. It could almost be the same thing. I kinda thought about it like Mondrian future style. Like, when I see his artwork, I kinda saw a computer brain or something. You know, like the parts inside a computer. So, I used shapes and lines to make that. And technology is math, too.
TEACHER:	Interesting, like a circuit board inside a computer or tablet or smartphone, huh? That's very creative. What did you mean by technology is math?
ZOOEY:	All of the programs on computers are like a math problem. It's like math codes they have to make up to make them work.
AMARA:	But it's not really Mondrian, Zooey. The shapes have to touch for it to be Mondrian.
TEACHER:	You know, a good word for that, when shapes and lines touch. When lines meet, they intersect. When shapes share a border, we could say they are contiguous.
KAI:	[*whispers*] Contiguous, contiguous.
ZOOEY:	Yeah, Mondrian's stuff was contiguous, but we were doing our own thing inspired by Mondrian. That's art, right?
TEACHER:	Sure thing, Zooey. Part of making art is making it your own. Amara, I noticed you used some triangles and Mondrian doesn't do a whole lot of that.
AMARA:	Yeah, I mean, Mondrian is OK, but I feel like he gets repetitive, and I thought about adding in some new shapes. But mine all do touch … are contiguous.
KAI:	You did all the triangles yellow.

Figure 8.4   Artwork exchange excerpt

In this excerpt, we see how the task parameters provide students with considerable freedom to explore their own connections to Mondrian, interpret those connections, and create something mathematical of their own designs. For example, Amara determined that Mondrian was limited by his use of lines/rectangles and elected to introduce a new form: triangles. Zooey saw computer circuitry in the work of Mondrian and expanded upon that idea in her own work. Indeed, at one point, she muses on the nature of artwork as "doing our own thing," which explicitly denotes a freedom to explore. While, perhaps, not every task can be as open-ended as this example, we do well as teachers to consider the extent to which the virtue of freedom is embodied in our classroom experiences and how such freedom contributes to one's intrinsic satisfaction and progress towards fulfillment.

Beauty

There is a deep human attraction to beauty and pursuit of this virtue may be found across societies. Su (2020) writes:

The desire for beauty is universal. Who among us does not enjoy beautiful things? A striking sunset. A sublime sonata. A profound poem. An illuminating idea. We are drawn to beauty. We are enamored of it. We dwell on it. We seek to create it. Beauty is a basic human desire, and expressions of beauty are marks of human flourishing. Beauty appears in mathematics, too – in many forms – though it is less appreciated there because many have not had the chance to experience it, or if they have experienced it, they have not recognized the experience as mathematical. (p. 69)

Beauty can take on many varied forms including experiences involving the physical senses such as sight, sound, and touch. Su refers to this as sensory beauty. However, beauty may also be found in the *wonder* we feel as we experience the relentless curiosity that comes with exploring something new and interesting. "While sensory beauty usually concerns itself with physical objects, wondrous mathematical beauty always invites a dialogue with ideas" (Su, 2020, p. 73). Consider the following exchange amongst a small group of middle-level students and their teacher (see Figure 8.5).

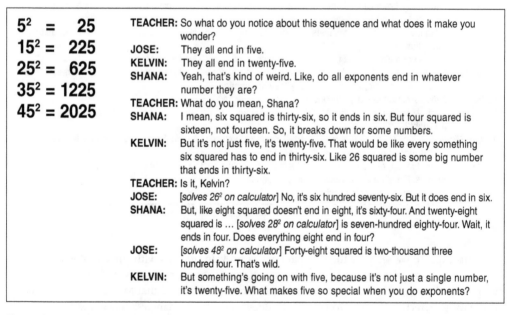

$$5^2 = 25$$
$$15^2 = 225$$
$$25^2 = 625$$
$$35^2 = 1225$$
$$45^2 = 2025$$

TEACHER: So what do you notice about this sequence and what does it make you wonder?

JOSE: They all end in five.

KELVIN: They all end in twenty-five.

SHANA: Yeah, that's kind of weird. Like, do all exponents end in whatever number they are?

TEACHER: What do you mean, Shana?

SHANA: I mean, six squared is thirty-six, so it ends in six. But four squared is sixteen, not fourteen. So, it breaks down for some numbers.

KELVIN: But it's not just five, it's twenty-five. That would be like every something six squared has to end in thirty-six. Like 26 squared is some big number that ends in thirty-six.

TEACHER: Is it, Kelvin?

JOSE: [*solves 26² on calculator*] No, it's six hundred seventy-six. But it does end in six.

SHANA: But, like eight squared doesn't end in eight, it's sixty-four. And twenty-eight squared is … [*solves 28² on calculator*] is seven-hundred eighty-four. Wait, it ends in four. Does everything eight end in four?

JOSE: [*solves 48² on calculator*] Forty-eight squared is two-thousand three hundred four. That's wild.

KELVIN: But something's going on with five, because it's not just a single number, it's twenty-five. What makes five so special when you do exponents?

Figure 8.5   Squaring numbers

In this exchange, students are tasked with noticing aspects of a sequence and describing where such noticing takes their thinking, or, in other words, *What does it make you wonder?* Quickly, Jose and Kelvin note a pattern (i.e. end in 5; end in 25), which quickly leads the group to consider other such sequences. For example, Shana notes that, for some sequences, the solution ends in the number which was squared (i.e. $6^2 = 36$) but for others the solution ends in a different number (i.e. $4^2 = 16$). After some exploration, though, Shana and Jose conjecture that each sequence ends in some specified number (i.e. $8^2 = 64$; $28^2 = 784$; $48^2 = 2304$). Jose exclaims, "That's wild!", suggesting wonder with this discovery. Kelvin continues in this direction as he ponders why five is special in that it results in not a single ending number, but a two-digit ending number (i.e. 25). In this moment, Kelvin is literally engaged in a state of wonder stemming from his dialogue with the mathematical idea at hand.

Another type of beauty exists in one's ability to see into an idea and draw new meaning. Described as *insightful beauty*, "[t]his is the beauty of understanding … Insightful mathematical beauty is like a feeling when you're shopping, on stumbling on a sale for an item you never knew you needed that meets desires you never knew you had" (Su, 2020, pp. 76–8). Consider the following exchange involving an early primary grades student's use of a balance scale to consider the task: 7 = _ + _ (see Figure 8.6).

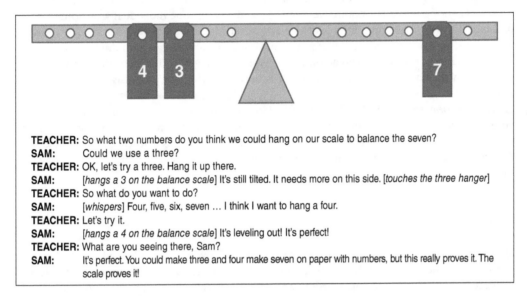

TEACHER: So what two numbers do you think we could hang on our scale to balance the seven?
SAM: Could we use a three?
TEACHER: OK, let's try a three. Hang it up there.
SAM: [*hangs a 3 on the balance scale*] It's still tilted. It needs more on this side. [*touches the three hanger*]
TEACHER: So what do you want to do?
SAM: [*whispers*] Four, five, six, seven … I think I want to hang a four.
TEACHER: Let's try it.
SAM: [*hangs a 4 on the balance scale*] It's leveling out! It's perfect!
TEACHER: What are you seeing there, Sam?
SAM: It's perfect. You could make three and four make seven on paper with numbers, but this really proves it. The scale proves it!

Figure 8.6 Balance scale exchange

Of particular note in this exchange is the aftermath of Sam's selection of 3 and 4 to balance the 7 placed by the teacher on the scale. Sam describes the "leveling out" of the scale as "perfect" and goes on to affirm the power of this model and how it embodies proof in a way that other forms of the task don't. As Sam puts it, "You could make three and four make seven on paper with numbers, but this really proves it. The scale proves it." This verbalization embodies the beauty that comes with understanding an idea deeply and engaging with something (the balance scale in this instance) that captures your thinking in some transcendent way. Indeed, referring to Sam yet again, "it's perfect!"

Community

Community refers to the deep human desire to connect with those around us in meaningful ways and is a cornerstone virtue upon which most societies rest. Togetherness and camaraderie with family, relatives, friends, and classmates provide a specific kind of intrinsic satisfaction. Su (2020) writes:

> [Community] serves as an entryway for many people to flourish in mathematical pursuits whether recreational, educational, or professional, or in the home. By 'mathematical community,' I mean any group of people who gather together over common mathematical experiences. You are forming a mathematical community … when you share math jokes, show enthusiasm for mathematics, make geometric objects, read stories together that involve math. (p. 188)

Central to the idea of a mathematical community (and to the virtue of community itself) is that individuals are working and thinking together. In many of the examples in this chapter (and in this book), we see students and teachers thinking with one another. They are sharing their ideas and affirming or critiquing the ideas of others. They are operating as a mathematical community and, in many examples, the teacher is deliberately working to foster community through rich task selection and facilitation of discourse. At times, mathematics in schools is organized around the individual student. Glancing into a classroom, we often see students working individually on some task or problem. The virtue of community leads us, as teachers, to build a mathematical society within our classroom. We aim to create a community of young mathematicians who think hard with one another, challenge each other, and accomplish shared goals together. The intrinsic satisfaction that comes from such a mathematical community is both powerful and propulsive for students and teachers alike.

In this section, we have explored three virtues (Freedom, Beauty, and Community) and how these virtues intersect with mathematics teaching and learning. There are many other virtuous aims for mathematical activity, but these serve as examples of how our work as teachers can be grounded in deeper human spaces which drive fulfillment among our students and lead to intrinsic satisfaction for all involved.

Metacognition and Self-Assessment

Having spent some time examining intrinsic satisfaction derived from mathematical learning, let's consider the other portion of the Guiding Principle at hand – students' realization of progress and verification of their own thinking, practices, and strategies. Central to this portion of the principle is the idea of metacognition, or the ability to think about one's own thinking. Metacognition has been the subject of considerable study for decades (Flavell, 1976; Schoenfeld, 1992). While researchers may operationalize metacognition somewhat differently, there are two key elements central to the construct. Specifically, metacognition may be thought of as (1) knowledge about cognition and (2) self-regulation of cognition (Brown, 1987). More recently, these two elements have been used to refer to "the awareness individuals have of their own thinking, their evaluation of that thinking, and their regulation of that thinking" (Wilson and Clarke, 2004, p. 26). While each aspect of metacognition is germane to this discussion, evaluation of one's thinking is particularly resonant with respect to the Guiding Principle of this chapter. On this point, Wilson and Clarke write:

> [m]etacognitive evaluation refers to judgments made regarding one's thinking processes, capacities, and limitations as these are employed in a particular situation or as self-attributes. For example, individuals could be making a judgment regarding the effectiveness of their thinking or of their strategy choice. Such an evaluative function assumes some awareness of the individual's thinking processes and anticipates the possible regulation of those processes. (p. 27)

What Wilson and Clarke are describing is precisely the capacity for students to realize their progress and verify their thinking via evaluative metacognition. Returning to the ideas of the previous section, we note that the aim is for students to generate intrinsic satisfaction and that realizing progress and verification of thinking is best connected to meaningful achievement and fulfillment of human needs (i.e. virtues).

In the mathematics classroom, evaluative metacognition is the mental engine that drives the activity of self-assessment. In *Principles to Action*, the National Council of Teachers of Mathematics (2014) write:

> At the center of the assessment process is the student. An important goal of assessment should be to make the students effective self-assessors, teaching them how to recognize the strengths and weaknesses of past performance and use them to improve their future work. (p. 95)

Central to this process of recognizing one's own strengths and weaknesses is the capacity to engage in metacognitive evaluation; however, as teachers, we know that such metacognition must be cultivated and supported amongst our students. As we think about how to support this sort of assessment, there are several preconditions that set the stage for students to engage in this work (Andrade and Goodrich, 1996). First, students must affirm the value of self-assessment. Again, if we are grounding our mathematical work in pursuit of meaningful achievement and the fulfillment of human needs, creating a sense of value for appraising one's progress towards those ends is much easier. Second, there must be a specific task, activity, or practice to anchor one's self-assessment. Having some central focus upon which students' can ground their self-assessment helps them realize the process and make the results more actionable regarding teaching and learning. Third, teachers should provide explicit cues for students regarding their enactment of self-assessment. While continuous assessment of one's mathematical thinking is certainly a desirable goal, supporting students toward this goal involves providing explicit signals and guidance regarding their engagement in such self-assessment. Fourth, and lastly, self-assessment assumes the opportunity for growth and improvement of one's thinking and practice. In other words, teachers must provide opportunities for students, post self-assessment, to continue their thinking and activity on a topic or concept. With these ideas in mind, consider the following exchange (see Figure 8.7).

$4 \div \frac{1}{2}$

TEACHER: So I saw you all doing some good thinking on this one, and I liked how you described your strategies, but let's think on it again. I want you to think about your strategy and each other's strategies and tell me things you notice, like or don't like. Let's think about our thinking. What worked, maybe what didn't work so well?

SOFIA: So, I thought it was two at first. Like, you cut four in half, and thinking about it that way made so much sense. But then Matias shared, and I was like, whoah!

TEACHER: What made you say whoah?

SOFIA: Well, he was talking about how many halves fit inside of four, which is a totally different way of looking at it, and something clicked in my head.

MATIAS: I know what you mean, Sofia, because I landed on two first, too. Like, if you don't really think about it, or I mean, just sort of go fast, two makes sense. But then, I was, like, four divided by two equals two, so four divided by one half can't be two, too.

SOFIA: But how did you come up with that halves fit into four thing? I don't think I was thinking like that. I was thinking about, you know, how you divide up a candy bar – like if you split it between people or something.

TEACHER: So, Matias, I hear that you can relate to Sofia's thinking and that was your starting point too. Sofia, tell me how you are thinking about your thinking now?

SOFIA: Well, I think the how many halves fit into four works good for this one. Like, I can fit eight halves inside of four. That really clicks, and I could even draw a picture of that if I wanted to. But I don't know why the sharing, you know, the candy bar sharing idea doesn't work like that. It's like my first idea didn't work, so I needed a new way to think or something. I'm still not sure I know how division by a half works, though. Like if I had to make a story about dividing by a half, what does it even mean to divide by a half?

Figure 8.7   Informal self-assessment

Self-assessment can be enacted with varying degrees of structure and formality. In this instance, students are cued to engage in self-assessment (via metacognitive evaluation) somewhat informally at the conclusion of a task. Having completed and shared their strategies, students are asked to think again on their mathematical activity. In their chapter on mental management, Perkins et al. (1994) refer to this type of double processing (e.g. the first thinking on the task, then thinking on their thinking) as a *thinking sandwich*, and it's in this second round of thinking that Sofia and Matias enact some evaluative metacognition to consider their own thinking, how their thinking connects, and in Sofia's case, what remains missing in her conceptions of fraction division. Harkening back to earlier ideas in this chapter, we may also see an instance of Sophia experiencing *insightful beauty* as she considered Matias's quotative (measurement) strategy in relation to her own partitive (sharing) strategy (i.e. "and I was like, whoah!"). Further, Sofia, Matias, and the teacher are operating as a community – sharing ideas and connecting with one another. This is the sort of activity that supports the development of intrinsic satisfaction derived from a problem-solving experience (i.e. "it just clicks"). Lastly, we note that Sofia's self-assessment also contains a critical valence in that she purports some limits in her understanding of fraction division. Specifically, even though she understands this task with respect to a quotative model for division, she is still unable to generate a context for 4 divided by 1/2. This combination of virtue-embedded experience and self-assessment through evaluative metacognition is a powerful mixture for intrinsic satisfaction as well as a springboard for honest appraisal of where one may travel next with that thinking. Whoah, indeed!

Connecting and Reflecting

Intrinsic mathematical satisfaction and awareness of such satisfaction are fundamentally connected to each chapter in this book. Indeed, helping students construct, realize, and build upon the satisfaction that comes from engaging in mathematical thinking and activity is at the center of each guiding practice that we explore. In this section, we will highlight and briefly explore a few connections we feel are especially important such that your reading experience will, perhaps, be more coherent and fulfilling. Undoubtedly, having read thus far, you have made many connections of your own, and maybe some of your ideas will arise in the following paragraphs.

Beginning with our exploration, in Chapter 2, of teaching approaches that are inquiry based and organized around mathematical meaning, we dove deeply into the nature and importance of the mathematical tasks and problems we select for our students. At the onset of this chapter, we examined the importance of meaning and considered how striving for meaning is a deeply felt human need – a virtue in the parlance of this chapter. Further, the extent to which we choose rich problems, leverage realistic contexts, and open tasks for exploration and creativity directly impacts the potential for such tasks to act as catalysts for mathematical satisfaction amongst students as well as for reflection (i.e. evaluative metacognition) upon their activity and thinking. Extending this connection a little moves us into the realm of instructional design, which we examined in Chapter 5. Indeed, thoughtfully setting the stage and creating space for rich mathematics to be discovered and discussed are part and parcel of helping students to create and evaluate their own progress and satisfaction.

In Chapter 4, we described the importance of deeply understanding our students' mathematical thinking and working to develop their thinking in more sophisticated directions. In particular, we examined how our own knowledge as teachers and the enactment of effective teaching practices help propel students towards more enriching mathematical destinations. These ideas are closely related to the fulfillment and satisfaction that come from one's achievement described earlier in this chapter.

Lastly, grounding intrinsic satisfaction in virtue and one's sense of progress toward something real and meaningful necessarily guides us towards the ideas of equity examined in Chapter 11. Freedom, beauty, and community (along with other virtues) have deep grounding in conceptions of equitable teaching and learning. Viewed through more critical equity lenses, freedom, for example, implores us to consider to whom such freedom is afforded. When and how is freedom experienced and felt amongst student constituencies – particularly those who have been historically marginalized in mathematical spaces. Similarly, community provokes critical examination with respect to the composition of our mathematical groups. Who is inside the community? Who is outside and why? Beauty allows us to ponder what forms we elevate as beautiful. From where do we draw mathematical inspiration for our tasks and lessons? What cultural practices are we lifting up as desirable and what practices are left undiscovered? One virtue that we didn't explore in this chapter, but Su (2020) examines in great detail, is *justice*. Specifically, how might our mathematical experiences in classrooms be used to shine light upon just and unjust treatment of humans, and how might we leverage mathematics to make the world a better and more just place around us? Fundamental to this discussion is the affordance of opportunities to create, examine, and evaluate deep intrinsic satisfaction as a result of engaging in mathematical thought and action. Considering this principle through the lens of equity forces us to consider the extent to which such pursuit of satisfaction is open to all of our students.

Questions for Reflection

To conclude this examination of intrinsic satisfaction and realization of mathematical progress, we find it useful to consider a few key questions that might guide us in this area. Note, these questions are designed to, perhaps, carry your thinking further and help you envision how you might act upon these ideas in your own practice.

- If someone were to observe your mathematics teaching and the experiences of your students, what virtues might they identify?
- How would you describe the mathematical experiences in your classroom with respect to the opportunities for students to realize satisfaction and fulfillment?
- How and how often do you provide opportunities for students to critically examine their own mathematical thinking?
- How and to what extent do you model and support evaluative metacognition amongst students?
- How is mathematical progress defined in your classroom and to what extent is such progress connected to deeper human satisfaction and fulfillment?

References

Andrade, H.G. and Goodrich, H. (1996). Student self-assessment: At the intersection of metacognition and authentic assessment. Unpublished doctoral dissertation, Harvard University, Cambridge, MA.

Aristotle (2002). *Nicomachean Ethics* (S. Broadie and C. Rowe, translators and commentary). New York: Oxford.

Aziri, B. (2011). Job satisfaction: A literature review. *Management Research and Practice, 3*(4), 77–86.

Brown, A. (1987). Metacognition, executive control, self regulation and mysterious mechanisms. In F. Weinert and R. Klume (Eds), *Metacognition, Motivation and Understanding* (pp. 65–117). Hillsdale, NJ: Erlbaum.

Chandler, A. (1972). *The Aesthetics of Piet Mondrian*. New York: MSS Information.

Deci, E.L. and Ryan, R.M. (2000). The "what" and "why" of goal pursuits: Human needs and the self-determination of behavior. *Psychological Inquiry, 11*(4), 227–68.

Flavell, J. (1976). Metacognitive aspects of problem solving. In L. Resnick (Ed.), *The Nature of Intelligence* (pp. 231–5). Hillsdale, NJ: Erlbaum.

Giese, J.L. and Cote, J.A. (2000). Defining consumer satisfaction. *Academy of Marketing Sciences Review, 2000*(1), 1–26.

National Council of Teachers of Mathematics (NCTM) (2014). *Principles to Action: Ensuring Mathematical Success for All*. Reston, VA: NCTM.

Oxford Learners Dictionary (n.d.). "Satisfaction." Retrieved March 14, 2022, from www.oxfordlearners-dictionaries.com/us/definition/american_english/satisfaction

Perkins, D.N., Goodrich, H., Tishman, S. and Owen, J.M. (1994). *Thinking Connections: Learning to Think, Thinking to Learn, Grades 4–8*. Menlo Park, CA: Addison-Wesley.

Polya, G. (1963). On learning, teaching, and learning teaching. *The American Mathematical Monthly, 70*(6), 605–19.

Ryan, R.M., Huta, V. and Deci, E.L. (2008). Living well: A self-determination theory perspective on eudaimonia. *Journal of Happiness Studies, 9*(1), 139–70.

Schoenfeld, A. (1992). Learning to think mathematically: Problem solving, metacognition and sense making in mathematics. In D. Grouws (Ed.), *Handbook of Research on Mathematics Teaching and Learning*, pp. 189–215. New York: Macmillan.

Steffe, L.P., Cobb, P. and von Glasersfeld, E. (1988). *Construction of Arithmetical Meanings and Strategies*. New York: Springer.

Su, F. (2020). *Mathematics for Human Flourishing*. New Haven, CT: Yale University Press.

Wilson, J. and Clarke, D. (2004). Towards the modeling of mathematical metacognition. *Mathematics Education Research Journal, 16*(2), 25–48.

Wright, R.J., Martland, J., Stafford, A.K. and Stanger, G. (2006). *Teaching Number: Advancing Children's Skill and Strategies*, 2nd edition. London: Sage.

9

Grouping Students to Promote a Productive Struggle in Mathematics Instruction

Guiding Principle: Teaching just beyond the cutting edge (ZPD)

"Teaching is focused just beyond the 'cutting-edge' of the child's current knowledge." (Wright et al., 2006b, p. 26)

Introduction

A key feature of any productive learning experience is that it is just beyond what is comfortable to us at a given time. In Chapter 2, we examined the nature of mathematical problems. Fundamentally, what makes something a problem is that it is just beyond the "cutting edge" of our current knowledge and thus problematic for us to approach. That is, we don't have a reflexive solution or strategy to apply and have to engage in some sustained hard thinking to make our way through. However, at times, some problems may prove too challenging for us. These problems are too distant from our current knowledge; thus, they may frustrate us because even our best thinking doesn't propel us through (or even deeper into) the task. Indeed, at any given moment and for any area of knowledge, we each have a cutting edge where thinking and activity are optimized for our development.

This chapter will focus on the nature of conceptual development in mathematics with respect to this optimal space for development. We will explore the theoretical foundations for optimizing our teaching opportunities and why a certain amount of struggle in the mathematics classroom is healthy and desirable. Further, we will learn to identify experiences that exist too far within and too far beyond our students' cutting edge for mathematical growth and how to adjust our instruction for optimal development. Lastly, we will dig into a few practical examples of instruction and evaluate the extent to which this instruction allows for supportive growth among students.

Instruction at the Cutting Edge?

Before we delve into the foundations of well-positioned instruction with respect to students, let's consider two examples from an intensive intervention lesson involving a teacher and individual first grade students (William and Sarama) working on addition and subtraction using number cubes (i.e. dice) to generate the tasks (see Figure 9.1).

TEACHER AND WILLIAM

TEACHER: [rolls a numeral-die and a dot-die] OK, so we rolled a five (numeral) and a three (dot) and the plus sign. How much altogether?

WILLIAM: [touches the three dots] One, two, three.

TEACHER: Three, good, what about the five?

WILLIAM: [touches the 5-die] I don't know. It's more. It goes with the three. It's probably like ten or eleven?

TEACHER: How could you tell for sure?

WILLIAM: Probably counting or something but you need the dots. Can we do something else? [slides chair away from table]

TEACHER AND SARAMA

TEACHER: [rolls a numeral-die and a dot-die] OK, so we rolled a seventeen (numeral) and a two (dot) and the plus sign. How much altogether?

SARAMA: [approx. 10 second pause] Seventeen … eighteen, nineteen, twenty, twenty-one. Wait, seventeen, eighteen, nineteen [raises two fingers sequentially as she counts], nineteen? I think it's nineteen, right?

TEACHER: Good deal. Nineteen! Seventeen, jump one is eighteen, jump one more is nineteen.

Figure 9.1   Arithmetic interactions with William and Sarama

Using our noticing skills (see Chapter 7), we might attend to William's favoring of the dot-die and his touching of those dots to count them. From this, we might interpret William's activity to be consistent with a perceptual counting scheme (Wright and Ellemor-Collins, 2018). Zooming out a bit, though, we see William struggling to engage with the task as presented due to one of the addends appearing symbolically rather than quantitatively (Thomas et al., 2010). For this addend, the student does not have perceptual unit items with which to interact, nor is he yet able to construct perceptual replacements for that numeral. Ultimately, he arrives at a (somewhat noncommittal) response of "10 or 11" and remains at a strategic impasse regarding his own thinking on this task. Contrast this activity with that of Sarama. We see her pause (ten seconds) to gather her approach, and then initiate a counting-on strategy (from 17). Although she continues her count past the correct answer (19), she catches herself and attempts the counting sequence again, this time tracking that count using her fingers as motor re-presentations (Steffe et al., 1988). In summary, William struggles with a key aspect of the task, is unable to negotiate a pathway forward, and ultimately disengages, whereas Sarama encounters some initial struggles and strategic challenges, but ultimately completes the task tentatively but successfully. While each child was facing a distinct task, these interactions illustrate the difference between tasks that are positioned optimally for activity (i.e. just beyond the cutting edge) and those that are a bit too distant from a student's conceptions and result in disengagement or frustration. It's also easy to imagine a third scenario where the task is too easy for the student. Likely, with some experience, Sarama's counting-on strategy will solidify and the task she faced in the exchange (and similar tasks) would provoke disengagement or even boredom as the solution requires minimal effort and reasoning. All of this is to say that in our mathematics teaching and learning, productive instruction hinges on finding the right task, for the right student, at the right time.

Difficulty and the Cutting Edge

For many, there is a deep, intuitive congruence with the notion that learning or development is predicated on some manner of challenge or difficulty. Without the experience of struggle, conventional wisdom suggests, there would be no occasion for growth. However, facing too much difficulty is also not productive. We have likely all engaged in and ultimately abandoned tasks that, from the onset, were beyond our capabilities. Many unfinished home-improvement projects stand as testament to this observation. The same is true for mathematics teaching and learning – some difficulty is desirable, but too much is counterproductive. Indeed, there is an optimal cutting edge for the amount of difficulty with respect to the learning of mathematical concepts and processes and this edge is unique to every learner at any given moment. Why this is so is a deeper matter that we will explore in this section.

Beginning with the role of difficulty in mathematical learning, Sfard (2003) provides a compelling argument for its necessity. She writes:

As has been said before in many different ways, true learning implies coping with difficulties. Because people fear difficulty and instinctively try to escape it, I want to stress that when it comes to learning, difficulty is, in fact, a good thing, provided it is basically manageable. One may say that difficulty is for learning what friction is for movement: It is the condition for its existence. On the one hand, without difficulty, no learning occurs, just as no movement occurs without friction. On the other hand, of course, too great a difficulty makes any learning impossible, just as too much friction stops any movement. (p. 366)

Diving deeper into the relationship between struggle and learning, we arrive at the foundational writing of Lev Vygotsky. His work provides something of a source code with respect to the nature of challenge in learning contexts. As a prelude to examining Vygotsky's (1978) crucial identification of a *zone of proximal development*, referred to as one's ZPD, consider the following scenario.

Jaden and Mateo are both six years old and entering first grade. On an initial assessment for arithmetic ability, they achieve remarkably similar scores, with both children relying on perceptual unit items to negotiate addition tasks (Wright and Ellemor-Collins, 2018). At this point, we might say that Jaden and Mateo are mathematically alike because, when problem-solving on their own, their reasoning and strategies are quite similar. To better support their development, Jaden and Mateo both begin working with their teacher in one-to-one sessions. In these sessions, the teacher presents a range of task presentations including partially screened collections, they put forth probing questions, and adjust tasks based on cues (both verbal and non-verbal) from the students. In short, the teacher is in mathematical dialogue with Jaden and Mateo. Very early on, they learn that Jaden is capable of constructing re-presentations to negotiate arithmetic tasks involving concealed collections beyond finger-range (>10) whereas Mateo still relies heavily on perceptual unit items and will occasionally attempt to construct a perceptual replacement for concealed items using his fingers (Wright and Ellemor-Collins, 2018). Now, the students look fairly dissimilar in their mathematical capabilities. Working in concert with another, more knowledgeable individual (the teacher) allows us to see the students' reasoning in a different light. The ZPD refers to this difference: it is the space between what one can do individually and when in mathematical dialogue with a teacher.

Vygotsky (1978), in his descriptions of social constructivism, a key learning theory across all disciplines, elaborates on ZPD. He writes:

> When it was first shown that the capability of children with equal levels of mental development to learn under a teacher's guidance varied to a high degree, it became apparent that those children were not mentally the same age and that the subsequent course of their learning would be obviously different. This difference … is what we call the *zone of proximal development. It is the distance between the actual developmental level as determined by problem solving and the level of potential development as determined through problem solving under adult guidance or with more capable peers* [emphasis in the original] … what is in the zone of proximal development today will be the actual developmental level tomorrow – that is, what a child can do with assistance today, she will be able to do by herself tomorrow. (pp. 86–7)

In this passage, Vygotsky describes the difference we observe quite frequently when we engage in problem-solving dialogue with our students. That engagement sometimes seems to unlock or bring to light strategies or reasoning that has yet to emerge on work or assessments completed on their own. Also important is Vygotsky's notion that the ZPD provides a window into a student's future capabilities without assistance (i.e. ZPD today will be actual development tomorrow). While this assertion is somewhat metaphoric in that capabilities observed while in mathematical dialogue with a teacher do not necessarily solidify in 24-hour periods, Vygotsky's general notion that a student's activities when working in concert with a more knowledgeable counterpart is a preview of what that student will soon be able to do on their own, is quite sound. Key to this aspect of teaching and learning, though, is the skilled work of the teacher to craft and shape that dynamic space which, in turn, pushes the student as far beyond their solo capabilities as productively possible. It is in this dynamic space that we see a waypoint on the student's development and how their learning is actively taking shape. Thus, we arrive at the notion of a cutting edge, that for each student, there is an optimal task space, not too easy, not too difficult, that allows for meaningful conceptual development. On this point, Sfard (2003) asserts that the "zone of proximal development (ZPD) epitomizes the belief that the child's intellectual development can be accelerated by carefully planned learning ... Truly substantial learning can occur only when the child experiences a certain difficulty" (p. 366).

As we conclude this section, we find it worth noting that these ideas regarding difficulty, active problem solving, dynamic mathematical dialogues, and an individualized cutting edge run somewhat counter to the histories and traditions of mathematics teaching and learning. While, over the last few decades, reform-oriented guidance and curricula from professional organizations reflect these ideas (NCTM, 2000, 2014), the longer arc of mathematics education history is more conflicted. Tracing these histories through the lens of cognitive science, Glaser (1984) writes:

> ... still, the utilization of older [behaviorist] theories was widespread, and their impact and limitations are manifest today ... In mathematics, there appears to be an increase in the performances associated with basic skill and computation, but little improvement and even a reported decline in mathematical understanding and problem solving. (p. 94)

While Glaser was reporting from 1984, the manner in which teacher preparation is, at times, "washed out" and practices tend to be more heavily shaped by one's own experiences in school (Zeichner and Tabachnick, 1981) has resulted in only incremental changes toward systems and supports for instruction predicated on ZPD and optimizing for an individual student's cutting edge. All of this is to say that, in this area, we are still swimming upstream, but with thought and energy, teaching congruently with this principle is not only attainable but also richly rewarding for all involved.

Learning Theory and Teaching Practice: Making Connections

In the preceding section, we dove deeply into the manner in which students (and all individuals, for that matter) learn. In other words, we explored learning theory. However, the practice of teaching is something different. Certainly, teaching is intended to be, and often is, deeply connected to learning, but this is not always necessarily the case. Indeed, we can all likely think of moments when a teacher (perhaps ourselves) expended great efforts which resulted in minimal apparent learning. Nevertheless, learning theory is a key consideration which we may use to inform our teaching practice. Thus, while it is technically inaccurate for one to say, "I am a constructivist teacher" or "this lesson is socially constructivist", the deeper notion that we may align our teaching practices to such ideas has considerable merit. Sound practice rests upon sound theory, and this assertion certainly holds true in mathematics education. As such, the theoretical concept of an individual's ZPD (within the larger domain of social constructivism) is a worthy foundation upon which we may shape our instruction. Regarding our teaching practice, there are many different ways we can identify a student's cutting edge and optimize experiences therein. Let's dive back into a few examples (see Figure 9.2).

Returning to the language of noticing, we can think about our teaching moves, our decisions, as falling within three very broad categories. One possible type of decision we could make is to relieve the student from the obligation of the task. In the example involving Shane, we observe Shane's struggle to negotiate a task involving concealed items. Shane appears to be unable, as yet, to construct some representations and relies upon perceptual replacements (fingers) to reason in this

RELIEVE THE TASK OBLIGATION	ADJUST THE TASK/SCAFFOLD	WAIT
TEACHER: So, nine under here, and six under here, how many altogether? **SHANE:** Nine and six? [*voice trails off*] **TEACHER:** Yup, nine on this side, and six on this side. [*motions to screened collections*] **SHANE:** [*raises nine fingers slowly, sequentially and looks at them - whispers*] One, two, three ... eight, nine. Nine. **TEACHER:** What about these over here? [*motions to screened collection of six counters*] **SHANE:** I don't have enough. I don't think ... Nine? **TEACHER:** OK, I like how you were thinking hard on that one. Let's try another one.	**TEACHER:** So, nine under here, and six under here, how many altogether? **JULIE:** [*touches the top of the screened collections*] One, two, three ... thirteen, fourteen, fifteen, sixteen, seventeen, eighteen, nineteen ... **TEACHER:** [*interjects*] So, you are at nineteen, are there a lot more to count? **JULIE:** I don't know. I kinda lost my place. **TEACHER:** What if we start over like this? [*removes the screen from the collection of 9 counters*] **JULIE:** [*touches each of the 9 counters*] One, two ... seven, eight, nine [*touches the screened collection slowly*] ten ... eleven, wait, there's six, right? **TEACHER:** [*nods*] **JULIE:** [*touches the top of the screened collection*] Ten [*whispers "one"*], eleven [*whispers "two"*], twelve [*whispers "three"*] ... fifteen [*whispers "six"*]. It's fifteen, right?	**TEACHER:** So, nine under here, and six under here, how many altogether? **AUBREY:** [*touches the screened collections nine times*] **TEACHER:** So, nine under here, and six under here, right? **AUBREY:** [*looks at teacher*] **TEACHER:** Take your time. How would you get started? **AUBREY:** [*stares intently at the screened collections*] **TEACHER:** I want you to think on this. We have time. Just give it a go.

Figure 9.2   Primary decision categories

problem space. Concluding that Shane is unlikely to engage productively with the task, the teacher simply moves on, presumably to a task better matched with Shane's cutting edge. Another decision category involves making some modification or adjustment to the task. This might be layering in some scaffold (e.g. introducing a tool), removing a constraint (e.g. uncovering a collection), or providing some additional verbal direction. Key to this decision category is that the task itself is changed in some key way that, ostensibly, propels further activity. Note, these adjustments may also aim to make the task more difficult rather than less difficult. We might remove a scaffold or introduce a constraint should we deem a task too easy for a student. Whatever the case, when making these task adjustments, the goal is to optimize the problem-solving space with respect to the student's cutting edge. In the example involving Julie above, we see the teacher remove a task constraint (i.e. uncover a collection) which prompts Julie to revisit her counting strategy and be better able to keep track of the second collection. The last broad deciding category at our disposal is merely to wait. In the typically fast-paced activity in the mathematics classroom, the gift of time is often in short supply. Depending upon cues gained through our attending of a moment and considered through our interpreting, we may simply elect to wait with the student and see if they are able to develop a strategy of their own accord. In the case of Aubrey, we see how such wait-time is deployed. Moreover, these deciding categories may be considered in concert with one another. As mathematics teaching and learning is a very dynamic space, we might begin with one category, move to another, and then another. For example, we might present a task and note some initial struggle, then decide to wait, then (based on observed unproductive struggle) decide to modify the task in some way, then (noting continued unproductive struggle) relieve the student from the obligation of the task. Perhaps we introduce an additional modification and then decide to wait again. The point is that we, as teachers, are not bound to a single decision category within an instructional sequence; rather, these categories provide us with some way to consider and structure the types of decisions we make, and how we might leverage such decisions to match our instruction with a student's mathematical cutting edge.

Mathematical Tools and Models

While waiting and relieving students from the obligation of the task are important decision categories, when working to optimize our instructional space for students, arguably the most frequent type of decision making in which we are engaged involves task modification of some sort. Throughout this book, we have presented different examples from the classroom and many of them involved the use of some manner of tool. Counters and screens, dice, whiteboards, even maps (see the example in Chapter 11) are used to mediate students' mathematical reasoning in these examples; moreover, these are but a fraction of the tools at our disposal as teachers. Likely, we have base-ten blocks, linking cubes, balance scales, calculators, and all manner of apparatus in our classrooms that might be used in our teaching. Given the power and importance of these tools and how tool selection and use can be crucial for task optimization, we find it useful to spend some time examining their nature.

Like a hammer hanging by a workbench, a mathematical tool requires activity in order to promote growth. Mathematical reasoning is not to be found in blocks or technology, but in the students themselves as they act in concert with a tool (Wertsch, 1998). When used in this manner, a mathematical tool serves as a model of the student's thinking. Fosnot and Dolk (2001) wrote:

> To mathematize, one sees, organizes, and interprets the world through and with mathematical models. Like language, these models often begin as simply representations of situations, or problems, by learners. For example, learners may initially represent a situation with Unifix cubes or with a drawing … These models of situations eventually become generalized as learners explore connections between and across them. (p. 12)

In this example, the authors describe how a particular tool (e.g. a unifix cube, a drawing) becomes a model of or for thinking when it is employed for a mathematical purpose by the student. Fosnot and Dolk further explain that "models cannot be transmitted any more than strategies or big ideas can be; learners must construct them. Just because we plan a context with a certain model in mind does not mean that all learners will interpret, or assimilate, the context that way" (2001, p. 79). Quite simply, tools are often necessary but insufficient for the creation of a student's mental model of a concept or an idea.

This perspective has several implications for the mathematics classroom. First, given that the mathematical model is constructed by a student, then anything that a student can use for mathematical reasoning has the potential to become a model for their thinking (Thomas and Harkness, 2013). In other words, "there are virtually no limits on what may be considered a mathematical tool" (Thomas and Harkness, 2013, p. 237). Additionally, and perhaps more importantly, as educators "exercise much control over the learning environment, some informed judgement must be made regarding which tools have the most potential to become models for children" (Thomas & Harkness,

2013, p. 237). Indeed, teachers may employ tools as settings or contexts for a particular task with the aim that the student will, after some consideration, act mathematically with the materials. For example, an emergent counter may be presented with a certain number of chips (creating the potential for the student to construct a model of a collection) and asked to determine the numerosity of the collection. As we have described in this chapter, tool use of this sort should exist at the cutting edge of a student's knowledge; however, it is important that the use of tools not be construed as overly prescriptive by the student. In describing how the Dutch method of Realistic Mathematics Education (RME) employs potential models, Gravemeijer (1999) wrote, "[a]ctually, the students are to *discover* the mathematics that is concretized by the designer" (p. 159, emphasis added). Quite simply, teachers set the stage for growth through the selection and deployment of tools that are well matched with a student's understanding, which may transform into models when used by the student for mathematical purposes.

Lastly, it is often easy to confuse tools and strategies:

> Unifix cubes or fraction bars or paper and pencil are not different strategies. They are different tools. Representing the problem with stacks of Unifix cubes or with fraction bars, or by drawing twenty-four dollars and circling eighteen of them are all the same mathematically. No benefit is derived by changing tools unless the new tool helps the child develop a higher level of schematizing. (Fosnot and Dolk, 2002, p. 27)

What Fosnot and Dolk suggest, first, is that there should be clear lines drawn between a tool and its use. For example, stating that a child used her fingers to solve a particular problem only gives information about a tool. One would have to determine how the child was using her fingers to ascertain the strategy. Secondly, the authors asserted that simply using different tools does not necessarily indicate advances in student strategies. Similarly, continued use of a particular tool does not necessarily indicate stagnation. Consider the dramatic shift between a perceptual counter using their fingers as a replacement and a figurative counter using their fingers as motor representations. In the first instance, the strategy relies on fingers as countable objects whereas the second instance positions fingers as a tracking mechanism for a visual image. Quite simply, a tool does not connote a single strategy. Again, tools are the medium through which students will engage in mathematical activity (thus transforming tools into models) and their strategies provide insights into their current understanding. Or from a different perspective, models (internal activity) are the product of strategic tool use (external activity), and we may gain glimpses of an individual's internal mathematical conceptions through observing their external work with mathematical tools. It is this view into the student's mind that helps us better match our teaching with their instructional cutting edge.

The Role of Assessment

In Chapter 6, we examined the nature and purpose of initial and ongoing assessment which intends to provide an informed understanding of students' knowledge and strategies. While we don't intend to revisit all of those ideas in their entirety, our discussion of optimizing instruction for individual students' development would be remiss without some mention of assessment.

Toward that end, recall our exploration of formative assessments, or assessments for learning. These types of assessments are aimed at determining what students understand so that we are able to shape subsequent instruction productively. While such assessments may influence decisions at more macro levels (e.g. lesson and unit planning), information gleaned through assessments may, and should, also shape our in-the-moment instructional decision making. Our individual task selections, the tools we select to mediate those tasks, whether we wait or relieve the child of the obligation to do the task, and so forth may all be informed by meaningful assessment. Further, assessment typically involves gathering information regarding the students' reasoning and strategies on their own (Wright et al., 2006a). Thus, assessing for conceptual understanding, which we described in Chapter 6, makes visible the entryway to a student's ZPD, the cutting edge where the student's individual capabilities end, but their reasoning may persist in concert with another. As such, assessment-driven teaching is designed so that experiences are "carefully chosen to elicit [mathematical] thinking that is just beyond the limitations of the child's current knowledge" (Wright et al., 2006a, p. 4).

Connecting and Reflecting

While each chapter in this book represents something foundational (a principle, if you will) to rich and productive mathematics teaching and learning, arguably the ideas of challenge, disequilibrium, and positioning mathematical activity precisely and optimally for conceptual development are the cornerstone upon which many other activities rest. For example, noticing as a practice is aimed at identifying (i.e. attending) key moments of activity, making sense of those moments (i.e. interpreting), and shaping subsequent activities (i.e. deciding) so that instruction is optimized in the ways we describe in this chapter. We notice so that we can shape our instruction to match a student's cutting edge. In this section, we will examine how such optimized instruction connects to other ideas and practices presented in this book. Although we could likely draw myriad meaningful connections to every chapter, we find it useful to call out some of what we feel are the more impactful links.

Beginning with the importance of tasks being inquiry or problem based (Chapter 2), we note the centrality of problem solving, rather than procedure following, to any experience aimed at creating mathematical struggle. The type of optimal productive struggle we describe in this chapter, by definition, should be mathematically problematic for the student. Particularly noteworthy is the assertion that our sense of problems, as teachers, and our students' sense of problems may be very different. We return to Thompson's (1982) quote in Chapter 2:

> I recently discussed with a prominent problem solving researcher a taped interview of a missing addend problem, and commented that his behavior led me to believe it was an ill-structured problem. The other party couldn't understand how I could say that, since a missing addend problem is certainly well-structured. I remarked that from his perspective it may be, but the problem that the child was solving seemed to be ill-structured. (p. 155)

In the context of this chapter and considerations of a student's cutting edge, it is important to remember that our perceptions of a task's difficulty (and how we anticipate students will respond) is often distant from how students actually perceive a task and how they actually respond. Indeed, an individual's ZPD isn't always where we think it is or where we think it should be.

Another fundamental connection worth examining and mentioned earlier in this chapter relates to the topics we explore in Chapter 3, specifically the use of learning progressions, frameworks, and trajectories. Research conducted over decades has illuminated many different pathways that students take as they construct and refine their mathematical knowledge, and our understanding of these pathways should directly inform the teaching decisions we make to optimize students' learning. Whether we are thinking in terms of a broad and generalizable progression (i.e. concrete to pictorial to abstract) or something far more detailed and topic- or construct-specific such as the Learning Framework in Number (Wright and Ellemor-Collins, 2018), these progressions and trajectories provide us with a roadmap to consider the position of a student's reasoning in developmental terms, and to better understand where to go next with our instruction to meet the student's cutting edge.

Expanding upon different types of decisions one might make to optimize instruction, a valuable connection may be found in Chapter 4 where we explore different teaching practices aimed at developing students' mathematical strategies. Indeed, extending the range, distancing the setting, and increasing complexity are all valuable ways to adjust tasks so that they are optimized for the individual learner. Related, our examination of the teaching and learning cycle in Chapter 5 provides a model for how to incorporate this manner of teaching into our instructional routines and productively plan meaningful mathematical experiences. Additionally, it's worth noting that the intrinsic mathematical satisfaction described in Chapter 8 is directly related to the sort of mathematical challenge of tasks that match well with a student's ZPD.

Lastly, and perhaps most importantly, equitable teaching of mathematics and dimensions of equity (Chapter 11) should be front of mind with respect to any consideration of optimizing instruction. The dominant dimensions of access and achievement prompt us to question how well our decisions (aimed at optimizing instruction) create or constrain learning pathways for students who have been marginalized in mathematical spaces. Similarly, to what extent are we broadening our conceptions of optimal instruction to include learning experiences that connect to students' identities and empower them toward agency and autonomy in mathematical spaces? In summary, any endeavor to match instruction well with students' mathematical conceptions must realize the inextricable connection between equitable experiences and cognitive development.

Questions for Reflection

As we conclude our exploration of instruction aimed at and just beyond students' cutting edge, we find it productive to reflect upon a few questions that might help further shape our practice. Note, these questions may not have easy or ready answers, but we hope they serve as useful launching pads which might propel our thinking further.

- What assessment processes, systems, or tools do you use to determine your students' ZPD or cutting edge? How often do you do this? How reliable are your processes – that is, do your assessments reliably reflect your students' mathematical capabilities?
- How and to what extent do you make adjustments to your instruction (or to individual tasks) while teaching? What information do you use to guide these adjustments? How well do your adjustments match students' cutting edge? How do you know when an adjustment was productive or not? How do you know if an adjustment enhanced or constrained equitable access to the mathematics at hand?

- How do you manage instructional modifications or differentiation at the individual level within a regular classroom setting involving many students? What strategies can we use to accommodate an individual's developmental needs while still operating as a classroom community?

References

Fosnot, C. and Dolk, M. (2001). *Young Mathematicians at Work: Constructing Number Sense, Addition and Subtraction*. Portsmouth, NH: Heinemann.

Fosnot, C. and Dolk, M. (2002). *Young Mathematicians at Work: Constructing Fractions, Decimals, and Percents*. Portsmouth, NH: Heinemann.

Glaser, R. (1984). Education and thinking: The role of knowledge. *American Psychologist, 39*(2), 93–104.

Gravemeijer, K.P.E. (1999). How emergent models may foster the constitution of formal mathematics. *Mathematical Thinking and Learning, 1*(2), 155–77.

National Council of Teachers of Mathematics (NCTM) (2000). *Principles and Standards for School Mathematics*. Reston, VA: National Council of Teachers of Mathematics.

National Council of Teachers of Mathematics (NCTM) (2014). *Principles to Action: Ensuring Mathematical Success for All*. Reston, VA: NCTM.

Sfard, A. (2003). Balancing the unbalanceable: The NCTM standards in light of theories of learning mathematics. In J. Kilpatrick, W.G. Martin and D. Schifter (Eds), *A Research Companion to the Principles and Standards for School Mathematics* (pp. 353–92). Reston, VA: NCTM.

Steffe, L.P., Cobb, P. and von Glasersfeld, E. (1988). *Construction of Arithmetical Meanings and Strategies*. New York: Springer.

Thomas, J. and Harkness, S.S. (2013). Implications for intervention: Categorising the quantitative mental imagery of children. *Mathematics Education Research Journal, 25*(2), 231–56.

Thomas, J., Tabor, P.D. and Wright, R.J. (2010). Three aspects of first-graders' number knowledge: Observations and instructional implications. *Teaching Children Mathematics, 16*(5), 299–308.

Thompson, P.W. (1982). Were lions to speak, we wouldn't understand. *Journal of Mathematical Behavior, 3*(2), 147–65.

Vygotsky, L.S. (1978). *Mind in Society: The Development of Higher Psychological Processes*. Cambridge, MA: Harvard University Press.

Wertsch, J.V. (1998). *Mind as Action*. New York: Oxford University Press.

Wright, R.J. and Ellemor-Collins, D. (2018) *The Learning Framework in Number: Pedagogical Tools for Assessment and Instruction*. London: Sage.

Wright, R.J., Martland, J. and Stafford, A.K. (2006a). *Early Numeracy: Assessment for Teaching and Intervention*. London: Sage.

Wright, R.J., Martland, J., Stafford, A.K. and Stanger, G. (2006b). *Teaching Number: Advancing Children's Skill and Strategies*, 2nd edition. London: Sage.

Zeichner, K.M. and Tabachnick, B.R. (1981). Are the effects of university teacher education 'washed out' by school experience? *Journal of Teacher Education, 32*(3), 7–11.

10

The Role of Children's Reflection in Mathematics Learning

> ## Guiding Principle: Sustained thinking and reflection
>
> "The teacher provides the child with sufficient time to solve a given problem. Consequently, this child is frequently engaged in episodes, which involve sustained thinking, reflection on [their] thinking and reflecting on the results of [their] thinking." (Wright et al., 2006, p. 27)

Introduction

Educators often have limited time, pressing them to decide between covering content in time and allowing the children in their classroom more time to engage with and reflect on their mathematics, providing depth to each content strand. It seems there is more to teach and less time to allow children the time necessary to sit and productively struggle with a difficult mathematics problem. Given this, educators often feel tension between giving their children the time they need to sit and struggle effectively with a problem and moving their children along to the next mathematics topic. Striking that balance is difficult. Mathematical learning theories suggest that striking that balance is essential when giving children sufficient time to construct meaningful mathematical concepts and make connections between mathematical concepts.

Jean Piaget ([1968] 1970) suggested that when young children struggled with a mismatch between their conceptual understandings of mathematics and their perceived experiences in mathematics, they were experiencing *disequilibrium*. Disequilibrium explains how children respond to this mismatch. As teachers, we often see children struggle to make sense of something new. This struggle can be seen in productive ways (i.e. "Let me think about this more") and unproductive ways (i.e. "Ugh! I am just not good at math!"). Teachers will want their children to struggle productively and reflection on their thinking helps them do this. By reflecting on their thinking, children are more able to handle the unsettling feeling that disequilibrium causes them to feel, compelling them to establish equilibrium. By reflecting on their thinking, children struggle productively and respond appropriately so that their reasoning and the mathematical experience more closely match. Thus, disequilibrium and reflection on their thinking allow young children to struggle productively when they are trying to make sense of a new mathematical idea. This productive struggle is at the root of meaningful mathematics learning. In fact, by giving young children time to reflect on their reasoning while they productively struggle, educators are able to promote clarity in their thinking and the ability to move towards more abstract approaches to mathematics.

To capture the emergent development of children's mental activity, Piaget ([1977] 2001) described different types of abstraction – empirical and reflecting. Essentially, as children experience disequilibrium in a mathematical experience, Piaget explains that they need to accommodate their conceptual understanding (adapting reasoning to new perceived outcomes). When children assimilate their conceptual understandings of a mathematical experience, they integrate their physical actions with their mental actions or develop new mental actions. Gruber and Vonèche (1986) explain that Piaget's assimilation/accommodation learning theories evidence that young children's learning falls along a continuum between their perceived need to accommodate or assimilate their own mathematical understandings, allowing for connections between their actions, ways of reasoning, and mathematical outcomes (see Figure 10.1).

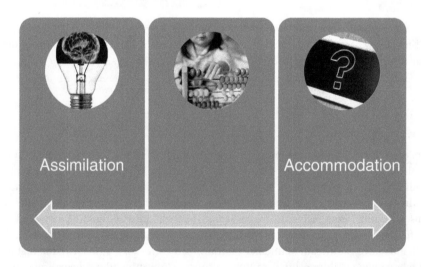

Figure 10.1   Illustration of the continuum of assimilation and accommodation that may exist when children make sense of their environment

Images: left: created by pixel2013 / Pixnio.com; center & right: images by rawpixel.com. All images used under CC0 license

These conceptual understandings (formed through connected actions and reasoning in mathematics) allow for more sophisticated reasoning that allows for long-term learning benefits. For instance, by learning how counting actions both create a sequence of number words and a group of items, children connect their counting to their addition/subtraction activity. These connections can then be leveraged to promote counting by groups to promote early multiplication/division understandings. By constructing these conceptual understandings with physical actions and mental actions, children are also given an opportunity to refine their reasoning and assumptions (i.e. all products are larger than factors).

To leverage the development of children's conceptual understanding, educators must provide children with opportunities to discuss their expectations before solving a problem and reflect on their actions and results throughout and after a mathematics activity. This allows young children to bring to the foreground their strategies and the effectiveness of their strategies.

To frame this work, we first explain abstractions, as described by Piaget (1977/2001). Next, we explain how children's reflections on their activity become evident in mathematics classrooms and can be leveraged in educators' planning and teaching. Finally, the chapter concludes with some questions to reflect on and connections to other books in the Math Recovery series.

Abstractions in Mathematics Learning

Inhelder and Piaget ([1955] 1958) described a learning theory, about *equilibrium*, which explained that children's learning goals were often designed to establish equilibrium between their conceptual understandings and mathematical experiences. This meant that children would often engage with a mathematical experience with anticipated goals, actions, and outcomes. When children perceived an experience with different goals, actions, and outcomes, they experienced disequilibrium. This is often unsettling to young children, provoking an accommodation of their reasoning. For instance, when children count a set of objects with a series of counting words (one, two, three, six), but then subitize the set of items as four, because it looks like a square, they may experience disequilibrium because their ending counting number was not the same as their subitized number.

By experiencing disequilibrium, children engage in what many scholars (NCTM, 2016) describe as a *productive struggle*. A productive struggle often characterizes students' tenacity when solving a problem. Some scholars explain that when students stick with a difficult problem or puzzle, they do so because they are struggling productively (Pasquale, 2016). In fact, the *Common Core* practice standards describe the importance of young children's ability to persevere and make sense of problems when solving them (NGA Center and CCSSO, 2010). To develop children's capacity for productive struggle, Pasquale (2016) explains that young children need to develop an awareness of their strategies as being at the center of their mathematical activity. By reflecting on their engagement with a mathematics problem, young children become more aware of their emergent strategies and develop a disposition that enables them to focus on their reasoning instead of the accuracy of their solution.

For example, a child in third grade might solve a multiplication task, 64 times 5, by first breaking apart a two-digit number, 64, into 60 and 4 to multiply by 5 (an example of partial products). This "breaking apart" of number is an effective strategy when learning how to develop multiplication procedures from conceptual understandings. However, when transitioning towards division, an educator may want this strategy refined further. For example, an educator may provide a true or false question:

$$\text{Is } 120 \div 4 = (120 \div 2) + (120 \div 2)?$$

Here children would need to revisit their conceptual understanding of the reasons for breaking apart numbers and how this strategy relates to their multiplication solutions. By revisiting this activity, children would then need to refine their break-apart actions and make sense of them in relation to division. For instance, some children may first believe this statement to be true because by breaking apart numbers in multiplication, they understand the solution is *true*. By reflecting on their activity, some children may consider this statement to be *false*. In fact, children may revisit their earlier experiences that formed the break-apart strategy and reconsider them in this context. Some children may say something like, "This doesn't make sense. If I had 120 pieces of candy and wanted to divide them into groups of two, I would not have any more pieces of candy to divide again." Another way a child may reason about this is, "If I were to divide 120 into 4 groups, I would get something like 30 but 120 divided into 2 is 60. 60 and 60 is not 30." By productively struggling, children are often accommodating their conceptual understandings and mental activity to better fit these new experiences. These productive struggles evoke a need to develop different types of abstractions associated with their mathematical reasoning.

Empirical Abstraction

Moessinger and Poulin-Dubois (1981) explain that empirical abstraction and reflecting abstraction are often opposed systems but not polar opposites. *Empirical abstraction* describes situations in which a child abstracts qualities of physical objects "contained" in their reality. Examples of these types of physical qualities might include color, shape, or weight. These physical qualities evoke physical activity, allowing the child opportunities to engage in actions that can be later internalized and associated with mental objects, such as the concept of number. In opposition to empirical abstractions, *reflecting abstraction* plays an important role in learning, which empirical abstraction becomes dependent upon for equilibrium to be established. Glasersfeld (1995) explains that the empirical abstractions become connected, forming unstable patterns before being assimilated in the construction of mental actions and operations. By developing mental actions and operations, children are establishing equilibrium and rely on mental actions to form operations. To better define reflecting abstraction, it is important to discuss the components of reflecting abstraction.

Reflecting Abstraction

Reflecting abstraction is composed of *a projection* and *a reflection*. To project an abstraction, a child would need to project or transpose a set of actions onto a superior level. For example, returning to the "true or false" problem, a child who revisits the content related to the break-apart strategy would reorganize their conceptions of why this break-apart strategy works with multiplication and how this strategy is limited with division. By reorganizing and refining their conceptions in this way, children can project their mental actions associated with the break-apart strategy to a higher level by allowing division to be included in the strategy.

A child's reflection is also critical in reflecting abstraction. To reflect on sets of actions, a child would need to be aware of their actions to develop a system to reorganize their actions to better fit different situations. By engaging in reflecting abstraction, a child reflects on their own strategies and actions associated with different contexts to make meaningful connections in mathematics. For example, the children who first believed the "true or false" problem to be *true* would need to revisit their earliest abstractions for the break-apart strategy in the multiplication context to reorganize this for the division context. After hearing other children's reasons for why this statement is *false*, a child might reflect on the strategy in both contexts. By giving children time to discuss and reflect on their strategies, an educator is providing children with opportunities to refine their reasoning, make connections between strategies in different contexts, and develop systems of mathematical understandings.

Children's Reflection in a Mathematics Classroom

To close this chapter, we want to exemplify how reflection and sustained thinking play a role in children's learning in a mathematics classroom. For example, let's visit a first grade classroom. The teacher, Mr. Lunt, is engaging the children in his classroom in a lesson that includes a five-frame and focuses on different additive combinations that sum to five. To meet this goal, he shows the children a five-frame with varying blue and red dots and the children are asked, "How many dots?" and "How many dots are missing?" With each task, Mr. Lunt provides children ample wait time. This gives them an opportunity to develop solutions, reflect on their solutions, and to possibly develop an awareness of patterns between their solutions.

For example, in one task Mr. Lunt engages the children in a classroom discussion after showing them one dot in a five-frame (see Table 10.1). In the excerpt, two children reflect on very different reasoning. Consider carefully how the teacher helps connect the children's reasoning, provides wait time for sustained reasoning over time, and encourages children to reflect on their actions and reasoning.

Table 10.1

Teacher and Child Engagement	Reflection and Sustained Reasoning
Now Mr. Lunt places a blank five frame vertically and places one dot in the frame.	
Mr. Lunt: How many do you see? How many are missing? *Providing students wait time. Students hold up their white board for Mr. Lunt to see.*	Mr. Lunt allows children to think and reflect on their thinking.
Mr. Lunt: Emmanuel, how many do you see?	
Emmanuel: One.	
Mr. Lunt: How many are missing? *Mr. Lunt points to the one dot provided in the frame.*	
Emmanuel: Four.	
Mr. Lunt: How did you figure that out? How did you figure out there were four missing?	Mr. Lunt asks Emmanuel to reflect on his strategy.
Emmanuel: I counted the four empty spaces and then I saw the one dot.	By sharing his strategy, other children are given an opportunity to compare their strategy to Emmanuel's strategy. This gives children opportunities to experience equilibrium or disequilibrium.

(Continued)

Table 10.1   (Continued)

Teacher and Child Engagement	Reflection and Sustained Reasoning
Mr. Lunt *repeats while pointing to the four empty boxes*: So, you counted these first and then one more.	
Mr. Lunt: Did anyone else look at it a different way?	By introducing additional strategies, Mr. Lunt brings children's strategies to the center of their mathematical activity.
Everett: I looked at two boxes and then another two boxes and put them together.	By sharing his strategy, other children are given an opportunity to compare their strategy to Everett's strategy. This gives children opportunities to make connections between strategies and develop patterns in their reasoning.
Mr. Lunt: And what did you get?	
Everett: Four, and then put the one and mixed it altogether and it was 14.	
Mr. Lunt: 14? Oh. How many were missing, did you say?	
Everett: Four.	
Mr. Lunt: And then how many did you see?	
Everett: One.	By asking Everett to revisit his physical activity, Mr. Lunt prompts Everett to reflect on his counting in relation to his construction of 14.
Mr. Lunt *records a four on the board then an addition sign while saying*, So, if you were to count the four empty spaces and the counter, would you reach 14?	
Everett: I would get five.	

This excerpt evidences several different types of effective teacher moves made by Mr. Lunt. For instance, at the onset of Mr. Lunt's launch of the task, he gives the children wait time. This allows the children to reflect on their own thinking and consider both their solutions and their strategies. Next, he asks the children to share their solutions and asks how they developed them. This allows the children to reflect on their reasoning and on other children's reasoning. By making the comparison reasoning, children can assimilate or accommodate their conceptual understandings. For instance, when Everett shared a different strategy and solution, he may have experienced disequilibrium, which encourages him to accommodate his reasoning. However, by revisiting his counting actions, he is also able to make connections between his counting and number construction.

In the excerpt in Table 10.2, Mr. Lunt is teaching the same lesson. He asks the children how many dots they see and how many are missing after showing them four dots in a ten frame. Everett accommodates his reasoning to explain how he knows four and six three different ways. All of this flexible number understanding is constructed through his reflection on his past strategy, Caroline's strategy, and his current counting actions. Look for where Everett is assimilating his reasoning and accommodating his reasoning.

Table 10.2

Teacher and Child Engagement	Reflection, Assimilation, and Accommodations
Mr. Lunt: Caroline, what did you do?	Mr. Lunt presses Caroline to reflect on her actions.
Caroline: Counted by twos.	
Mr. Lunt: OK, come on up here and show us how you counted by twos.	By asking Caroline to evidence her counting, Mr. Lunt presses children to compare their strategies to Caroline's strategy.
Caroline pointed to the four red dots to do 2+2=4, then she counted the bottom squares on her fingers by one.	
Everett: I knew you had two fours and then I knew two and two and two make six. *Everett comes to front to show his strategy.*	Everett takes up Caroline's counting by twos. This evidences an assimilation, as Everett extends Caroline's reasoning to construct six.
Everett: I know the top is five (*points to the top row in the ten frame*), and take one away is four …	Everett takes up his past strategy to construct a 4 and 1 relationship. This evidences an assimilation.
Then he points to two empty squares at a time to show the three twos.	
Everett: … wait, I see three and three empties make six.	By revisiting his counting actions, Everett accommodates his reasoning to include a third strategy when constructing four and six relations.

Everett assimilates and accommodates his "two by two" strategy from the first excerpt to construct six with a "two and two and two" strategy. Everett also uses his new four and one strategy from the first excerpt to construct four. Finally, Everett accommodates his reasoning in the moment when sharing his counting activity by relating "three and three" to his "two and two and two" strategy. By giving Everett time to reflect on his own reasoning, his own actions, and the reasoning and actions of others, Everett is able to develop varying patterns to conceptualize one through six in very flexible ways. These conceptualizations allow him to begin making connections between his counting and early additive reasoning. These connections will also serve as a basis for his systems for number and operations later.

In conclusion, the foci of this chapter related to educators' use of wait time and children's ability to reflect on their thinking connect to Chapters 2 and 8. Chapter 2 focuses on educators' use of inquiry. At the heart of inquiry-based instruction, educators strive to provide opportunities for productive struggle, sustained thinking time, and opportunities for reflection. For example, as we begin to consider how to adapt the curriculum, we need to consider how sustained think time and reflection on activity afford children opportunities to struggle productively with a challenging mathematics task. Chapter 8 focuses on feedback and discourse in mathematics. By designing and posing purposeful questions for feedback and discourse, educators are connecting strategies that children develop and providing opportunities for children to experience disequilibrium, questions like, "How do you know?" and "How is your strategy similar or different compared to _____'s strategy?" These types of questions place children's reasoning at the center of the mathematics lesson and allow children an opportunity to reflect on their reasoning in comparison to others' strategies. Considering how sustained thinking and reflection on reasoning are leveraged throughout a lesson allows educators to better develop inquiry-based lessons and orchestrate meaningful discourse.

Connections to Other Math Recovery Books

Throughout this chapter, we have related many of the discussions to other books in the Math Recovery series. We describe these connections below. This allows educators to draw on more detailed sets of questions, tasks, and instructional moves that this book is not intended to discuss.

The following provides details of students' reflections and instructional tips that educators can use to sustain thinking time:

- The brown book, *Numeracy for All Learners: Teaching Mathematics to Students with Special Needs* (Tabor et al., 2021): Focus on pp. 32–4 and Chapter 11.

These sections of the brown book provide detailed ways that children reason when problem solving and ways in which educators can design meaningful instruction.

Questions for Reflection

In closing, let's consider some questions that may guide us in our use of sustained thinking and reflection during a mathematics lesson. These questions may challenge you and ask you to consider these instructional moves in relation to children's mathematics learning in unique contexts. Our goal is to prompt you to reflect on your own instructional moves and how your own children learn in relation to these instructional moves.

- How do you frame *wait time* for children? Do you consider the wait time too long or too short? Do all your children engage in whole-class and small-group tasks? How could you use wait time to ensure all children are prepared to engage and draw from their reasoning *and* their solutions?
- In what ways can you help your children's actions and reasoning to progress in your classroom discussions? How might children in your classroom assimilate and accommodate their reasoning when reflecting on other children's actions and reasoning?
- How does wait time change for different populations? For instance, when working with children identified with different processing needs or emergent bilingual children, how can wait time be leveraged to allow all children opportunities to fully reflect on their reasoning?
- Children are often taught to memorize procedures in mathematics. How might reflection on their activity allow them more conceptual connections to their procedures?

References

Glasersfeld, E.V. (1995). *Radical Constructivism: A Way of Knowing and Learning*. London: RoutledgeFalmer.

Gruber, H.E. and Vonèche, J.J. (Eds) (1986). *The Essential Piaget*, 2nd edition. New York: Basic Books.

Inhelder, B. and Piaget, J. ([1955] 1958). *The Growth of Logical Thinking from Childhood to Adolescence*, 2nd edition (Translated by A. Parsons and S. Milgram). New York: Basic Books.

Moessinger, P. and Poulin-Dubois, D. (1981). Piaget on abstraction. *Human Development*, *24*(5), 347–53.

National Council of Teachers of Mathematics (NCTM) (2016). *Process*. Standards and Policy. Retrieved November 12, 2021 from www.nctm.org/Standards-and-Positions/Principles-and-Standards/Process

National Governors Association Center for Best Practices and Council of Chief State School Officers (NGA Center and CCSSO) (2010). *Common Core State Standards for Mathematics*. Washington, DC: Authors.

Pasquale, M. (2016). *Productive Struggle in Mathematics: Interactive STEM Research + Practice Brief*. Waltham, MA: Education Development Center.

Piaget, J. ([1968] 1970). *Genetic Epistemology* (Translated by E. Duckworth). New York: Columbia University Press.

Piaget, J. ([1977] 2001). *Studies in Reflecting Abstraction* (Translated by R.L. Campbell). New York: Psychology Press.

Tabor, P.D., Dibley, D., Hackenberg, A.J. and Norton, A. (2021). *Numeracy for All Learners: Teaching Mathematics to Students with Special Needs*. London: Sage.

Wright, R.J., Martland, J., Stafford, A.K. and Stanger, G. (2006). *Teaching Number: Advancing Children's Skill and Strategies*, 2nd edition. London: Sage.

11

Equitable Mathematics Practices

> ## Guiding Principle: Equitable mathematics practices
>
> "Ensuring that all children construct meaningful mathematical knowledge and practices requires a profound commitment to equity in our teaching practices. Accounting for and connecting to children's abilities, cultures, and lived experiences is essential for the creation of broad pathways for learning and fostering positive identities as capable mathematical thinkers. Equity also involves addressing systems and practices that contribute to inequitable outcomes amongst children, particularly those historically marginalized in mathematical spaces."

Introduction

It is a self-evident truth that the enterprise of mathematics education, at its core, aims to develop the mathematical reasoning of all who are engaged. In practice, however, achieving such development amongst *all* students has warranted increasing attention and energy over the past decade. Inequities, both historical and current, are being examined through more critical lenses to examine how certain student groups are often sidelined from meaningful learning. We ask ourselves what we might do differently, as educators, to create more meaningful, accessible, inclusive, and relevant spaces for students who are typically marginalized in the mathematics classroom.

Here, we note that the early texts of the Math Recovery book series (Wright et al., 2006a, 2006b, 2015) did not include a Guiding Principle explicitly focused on equitable mathematics instruction. Arguably, though, the theoretical and philosophical underpinnings of Math Recovery are based upon providing accessible and meaningful mathematical experiences for those who are underserved (or outright neglected) by traditional forms of classroom mathematical instruction. Indeed, the deeply constructivist and student-centered foundation of Math Recovery directly connects to equitable dimensions such as access, achievement, identity, and power (Gutiérrez, 2009).

In the Math Recovery text by Tabor et al. (2021), the authors present each of the nine Guiding Principles in concert with guidance from other professional organizations such as the Council for Exceptional Children (CEC) and the National Council of Teachers of Mathematics (NCTM). Here, the NCTM position statement (2014) is particularly noteworthy in that it not only provides guidance for mathematics teaching and learning such as "being responsive to students' backgrounds, experiences, cultural perspectives, traditions, and knowledge" when implementing instruction and conducting assessments, but also "acknowledging and addressing factors that contribute to differential outcomes among groups of students," which moves educators towards a more critical stance with respect to systems and structures.

Returning to their portrayal of the Guiding Principles at certain points, Tabor et al. (2021) offer a perspective that represents a significant change in direction for math teaching. For example, the emphasis on inquiry-oriented problem solving in the first Guiding Principle is placed in conflict with a gradual release of responsibility models such as "I do, we do, you do" (see p. 20 for an explication). In other places, the authors augment the original principle to create more expansive and equitable practice. When discussing the seventh Guiding Principle, supporting and building upon students' strategies, they describe the varied expressive pathways that students might take. For example, the authors write that "non-verbal students may express their strategies in a variety of means such as sign language … drawing pictures or demonstrating with manipulatives" (p. 22). This elaboration of the Guiding Principles is further operationalized by Math Recovery authors Grindle et al. (2020) in their text on numeracy teaching and learning amongst students with developmental disabilities.

Given this historical foundation coupled with more recent expansions and refinements to Math Recovery traditions, we offer a formalized Guiding Principle for equitable mathematics teaching and learning to complement the other principles we examine in this book. We note, however, that these expansions, thus far, focus primarily on students with special needs (Tabor et al., 2021) and more specific types of disability (Grindle et al., 2020). In this chapter, we will further enlarge our lens of equity to include gender, race, ethnicity, socioeconomic status, and other cultural dimensions through which inequities and marginalization may flow. As such, we open this chapter by proposing a principle that aims to encompass equitable mathematics teaching and learning, broadly construed, and that is consistent with guidance from other professional organizations and the fundamental ethos of Math Recovery.

This chapter will focus on the nature and importance of equitable mathematics instruction and how, as teachers, we may view our learning communities through different equitable lenses. Further, we will examine instructional experiences aimed at capitalizing on the lived experiences of our students, enlarge avenues for access, and generate space for community, critique, and human flourishing (Su, 2020) for all involved. We will situate such equitable practice in history and the research landscape and also explore some practical examples of mathematics teaching and learning that enhance, or perhaps constrain, opportunities for students to equitably engage in rich mathematical learning.

How Might Equity Concerns Manifest in Practice?

Before diving into historical and contemporary examinations of equitable teaching and learning, let's consider a small-group interaction around the task 400 – 198. This is a good opportunity, as you read the exchange (see Figure 11.1), to enact some of the noticing practices (i.e. attending, interpreting, deciding) described in Chapter 7 of this book. Consider students' access to the mathematics at hand, their sense of self as mathematical thinkers, their empowerment to express their thinking and ideas, and how ideas of right and wrong (and who gets to be right and wrong) shape their experience. Perhaps there are other aspects within this transcript where you see opportunities missed or capitalized upon by the teacher which relate to equity in some way. In any event, notice not only the mathematical moves of the teacher and students, but also how the experience may relate to considerations such as access, achievement, identity, and power.

TEACHER: "So before we talk answers, I want to hear about favorite strategies. Who wants to tell me about their favorite?"

JADEN: "I like to use these blocks [*points to base-10 blocks on table*] and I got four of these flat ones, and then I imagined taking off nineteen of these rows and then another eight of the little guys. That gives me two hundred and two left."

ALIYAH: "There's an easier way than with those things." [*motions to the base-10 blocks*]

TEACHER: "Okay, let's listen to Aliyah's strategy and see if you agree that it's easier."

ALIYAH: "I think the easiest way to think about it is to think about a number line. Like, you start at four hundred and then jump back two hundred. But then you've got to put some back. You've got to put two back, so it's two hundred two. Or you could just go up from one hundred ninety-eight to two hundred, two jumps, and then another two hundred. That's two hundred two."

TEACHER: "What do you think about Aliyah's strategy, Ethan?"

ETHAN: "I don't get why you put two back, Aliyah, in that first one. It's subtraction. It's take away. Shouldn't it be two more jumps back?"

ALIYAH: "No. I took too many away at first, now I got to put them back."

ETHAN: "But that's not easier. Going forward and backward is confusing. I think counting the blocks like Jaden makes more sense [*reaches out and touches the base-10 blocks*]. The problem with those blocks is you can't take them apart. You have to do a bunch of swapping and I think that makes it harder. They should be like Legos and you could count each one."

TEACHER: "What about you, Mateo?"

MATEO: "I think the way we are supposed to do it is to stack them up and then cross out the zeros [*moves finger in the air as if writing numbers*]. If you trade, then ten minus eight is two, but then you have to trade again, so ten minus nine. . . wait, no, it's nine minus nine, so it's zero, and then the four turns into a three. So, the answer is two hundred two."

ALIYAH: "You like that way, Mateo?"

MATEO: "Yeah, that's the right way to do it."

TEACHER: "I get your method, Mateo, but let's hold off on it being the only right way. There are other right ways, too. And, they're all interesting strategies. Now, Aliyah, I want you and Ethan to pair up, and I want Jaden and Mateo to pair up. I want you all to spend the next five minutes getting really familiar with each other's strategies. Talk them through. Ask questions of each other. When I come back, I want each person to be able to walk me through the other's strategy and be able to try it out with a new task."

Figure 11.1 Small-group exchange around 400 – 198

As you read this transcript, what sorts of things did you notice related to equity? Perhaps the ready availability (but not the compelled use) of manipulatives stood out. Maybe the teacher's gentle push against a student's tendency to think about strategies in terms of "correct" or "incorrect" struck you as important. Perhaps it was the empowerment of students to engage with and critique one another's thinking around the task that you found noteworthy. Indeed, there are many different angles within this exchange that we might connect to certain dimensions of equity (Gutiérrez, 2009), and in the following sections of this chapter, we will explore these dimensions in more detail. Before diving into that discussion, though, we find it useful to trace the history of equitable mathematics teaching as well as more contemporary conceptualizations.

A Historical Case for Equity

Equitable teaching and learning have been of interest to educational philosophers, theorists, and practitioners for centuries. Historically, many (but sadly not all) of those involved in shaping the educational enterprise come to realize that how students experience instruction in varying ways depends upon a host of factors ranging from the systemic (e.g. school funding processes) to the tactical (e.g. a teacher's propensity to call on certain students in a class). Further, such realizations typically grapple with how culture, ethnicity, race, religion, gender, ability (to name but a few considerations) enhance or constrain students' mathematical participation and conceptual development within a given environment.

On this point, one of the most impactful education reform theorists of the previous century, John Dewey (1938), wrote:

In a word, we live from birth to death in a world of persons and things which, in large measure, is what it is because of what has been done and transmitted from previous human activities. When this fact is ignored, experience is treated as if it were something which goes on exclusively inside an individual's body and mind. It ought not to be necessary to say that experience does not occur in a vacuum. There are sources outside an individual which give rise to experience … A primary responsibility of educators is that they not only be aware of the general principle of the shaping of actual experience by environing conditions, but that they also recognize in the concrete what surroundings are conducive to having experiences that lead to growth. Above all, they should know how to utilize the surrounding, physical *and social* [emphasis added] that exist so as to extract from them all that they have to contribute to building up experiences that are worthwhile. (pp. 34–5)

Here, Dewey, writing on the importance of the instructional experience, describes how such experiences must be viewed through a larger lens which includes consideration of the social context in which such education occurs. Indeed, Dewey describes the active role (i.e. "primary responsibility") of teachers to not only be aware of such surrounding social context but also to leverage these social contexts to create experiences which lead to student growth.

Similarly, William James (1899), an influential pioneer of psychology, described how students experience teaching from a psychological perspective:

We have thus fields of consciousness – that is the first general fact; and the second general fact is that the concrete fields are always complex. They contain sensations of our bodies and of the objects around us, memories of past experiences and thoughts of distant things, feelings of satisfaction and dissatisfaction, desires, and aversions, and other emotional conditions, together with determinations of the will, in every variety of permutation and combination. (p. 8)

In this passage, James is describing, from his late-1800s vantage, the manner in which a student's consciousness of schooling is mediated by all manner of factors beyond the classroom itself. The "permutation and combination" of "experiences," "thoughts of distant things," "desires," and "determinations of will" are fundamentally connected to modern conceptions of identity, culture, and agency. Further, James goes on to explore models of education in different countries (i.e. Germany, England, Sweden) with explicit attention being paid to the cultures which gave rise to such models.

Moving forward in time, Paulo Freire, a Brazilian educator and philosopher, channeling his own experiences of navigating economic and political turmoil, guided these foundational connections between education, the individual, and culture toward more critical spaces. Writing in his seminal work *Pedagogy of the Oppressed* (1970), Freire describes a "banking" concept of education thusly:

> The teacher talks about reality as if it were motionless, static, compartmentalized, and predictable … "four times four is sixteen; the capital of Pará is Belém." The student records, memorizes and repeats these phrases without perceiving what four times four really means, or realizing the true significance of 'capital' … it turns [students] into "containers", into "receptacles" to be "filled" by the teacher. The more completely she fills the receptacles, the better a teacher she is. The more meekly the receptacles permit themselves to be filled, the better students they are … This is the "banking" concept of education, in which the scope of action allowed to the students extends only as far as receiving, filing, and storing deposits. (pp. 71–2)

Freire laments that manner in which systems of education reflect a static and "objective" view of knowledge which is merely transferred to students similar to a bank deposit. He goes on to argue compellingly that such an education is necessarily dismissive of one's agency, identity, experiences, and culture, and is ultimately oppressive. Indeed, Freire asserts, we are much more likely to see banking models of education offered up to those who are typically marginalized in society, students of color, students with more limited resources, students with disabilities, students who do not speak the dominant language, and so on. Other contemporary, prominent scholars such as Ladson-Billings (1995) and Delpit (1995) have operationalized these ideas into educational practices (i.e. culturally relevant pedagogy) befitting modern teaching and learning contexts. As mathematics educators and enthusiasts, we may synthesize these ideas to form a productive vision for equitable mathematics instruction. Such a vision must dispense with the notion of passive and objective knowledge that is merely to be "deposited" into a child's mind. Rather, mathematical knowledge and practice are culturally situated activities in which we as teachers may make profound connections to the lived experiences of students, to their perceptions of the world around them. We may create experiences where mathematics is a vehicle to explore virtues (see Chapter 8 for a deeper exploration) as well as a lens to both critique and potentially solve the human challenges and inequities that they face as individuals and/or groups.

Equity in Mathematics Teaching and Learning

Mathematics teaching and learning has been organized such that all students may develop an enriching understanding of the discipline and this focus has been essential to research and practice for at least a century (Judd, 1928). However, over the past two decades, organizations and scholars have invested in more critical, productive, and actionable visions such as teaching and learning.

Referenced earlier in this chapter, the NCTM (2014) position on access and equity in the mathematics classroom:

> requires that all stakeholders – ensure that all students have access to a challenging mathematics curriculum, taught by skilled and effective teachers who differentiate instruction as needed; monitor student progress and make needed accommodations; and offer remediation or additional challenges when appropriate.

Further, they have developed a suite of resources individualized to particular groups and communities (e.g. students with disabilities, non-native English speakers) who have been historically marginalized in mathematical spaces. Similarly, the Association of Mathematics Teacher Educators (AMTE, 2022) has developed an equity-focused research division and published position statements regarding mathematics teachers':

> freedom to use their expertise and professional judgement to meet the individual needs of all learners in their complex classrooms as they work to teach mathematics in equitable and anti-racist ways. We recognize that [the] mathematics curriculum is multifaceted and needs to represent the diverse experiences, histories, and identities that make up our world.

In summary, there is considerable momentum to investigate and refine mathematics education systems and practices such that they improve outcomes for marginalized individuals.

This energy has resulted in myriad scholarly lenses through which we might consider equity in mathematics education; however, we find the work of Gutiérrez (2009, 2018) to be a fruitful place to connect these ideas to our teaching practice. Gutiérrez (2009) proposed four broad dimensions in which equitable mathematics teaching and learning might be framed: Access, Achievement, Power, and Identity. We might think of these dimensions as *lenses* through which some aspect of our mathematics instruction or a student's experience therein may be viewed and considered.

Access connects to:

> [the] resources that students have available to them to participate in the mathematics, including such things as quality mathematics teachers, adequate technology and supplies in the classroom, a rigorous curriculum, a classroom environment that invites participation. (Gutiérrez, 2009, p. 5)

In this sense, we can think about access as the arena within which mathematical activity occurs. What avenues exist for participation and success? How wide and inclusive are such avenues? How well supported are students in these spaces? These and similar questions might guide us toward considerations of access in our classrooms.

Achievement references:

> [the] tangible results for students at all levels of mathematics, including such things as participation in a given class, course taking patterns, standardized test scores, and participation in the mathematical pipeline (e.g., majoring in mathematics in college; having a math-based career). (Gutiérrez, 2009, p. 5)

We can think of achievement as centered on mathematical "rightness" and "wrongness" and the extent to which particular thinking or activity is elevated and celebrated or demoted and disdained. What type of mathematical activity is "good" or "correct"? What constitutes a mathematical misconception? How do these ideas of correctness sort our students and influence how we think of their abilities and prospects? These and similar questions connect us to the dimension of achievement.

Identity denotes not only the "personal, cultural, or linguistic capacities of students … [and] focusing on students' pasts (e.g., including the contributions of their ancestors). But, the identity dimension also concerns itself with the balance between self and others in a global society" (Gutiérrez, 2009, p. 5). Further, identity:

> acknowledges the way students are racialized … gendered, and classed … It includes whether students have opportunities to draw upon their cultural or linguistic resources (e.g., other languages and dialects, algorithms from other countries, different frames of reference) when doing mathematics. (p. 5)

Fundamentally, the dimension of identity is grounded in the lived experiences of our students and guides us to consider the extent to which those lived experiences (with attention to culture, race, gender, language, ability, etc.) connect to and are reflected within mathematical spaces. How relevant is a mathematical experience to one's students? What types of individuals are elevated as mathematical thinkers? How might students see mathematical activity as human activity grounded in many different cultures? How welcoming is a mathematical experience and one's classroom to diverse ideas and ways of thinking? These and similar questions lead us to consider mathematics instruction through an identity lens.

Power refers to the "voice in this classroom (e.g., who gets to talk, who decides the curriculum) … opportunities for students to use math as an analytic tool to critique society … and rethinking the field as a more humanistic enterprise" (Gutiérrez, 2009, p. 6). In a very real sense, this dimension is focused on who wields power in a mathematical space and how power might be distributed not only amongst teachers and students, but within student constituencies. Who gets to talk and why? Who makes decisions and upon what criteria? Who leads a student small group and whose voice is lost in the shuffle? When are students' explanations and ideas welcome, and when are they not? These and similar questions ground us in the dimension of power.

Gutiérrez (2009) continues this explication of equity dimensions by pairing and positioning certain dimensions as *dominant* and *critical*. Access and Achievement are described as dominant in that they prepare "students to participate economically in society … privileging a status quo … where access is a precursor to achievement" (p. 6). Gutiérrez refers to this dominant dimensional pairing as *playing the game* of mathematics. By this, she means attending to existing features of mathematics teaching and learning and considering the extent to which these features are consistent not only with conceptual development but also students' flourishing as human beings (Su, 2020). Power and identity are described as existing on a critical axis "where identity can be seen as a precursor to power [and] ensures that students' frames of reference and resources are acknowledged in ways that help build critical citizens so that they may *change the game* [emphasis added]" (Gutiérrez, p. 6). Indeed, all four dimensions are important lenses through which we might consider a mathematical moment or our instructional contexts more broadly:

Learning dominant mathematics may be necessary for students to be able to critically analyze the world while being able to critically analyze the world may provide entrance into dominant mathematics. It is not enough to learn how to play the game, students must be able to change the game. (p. 6)

In the next section, we will put our knowledge of these dimensions into practice and use them as lenses through which we might consider a mathematical moment.

Dimensions of Equity in Practice

To consider how one might use these dimensions of equity to consider a mathematical moment (while also synthesizing the practice of noticing – see Chapter 7), let's return to the exchange from earlier in this chapter (see Figure 11.1). Jaden, Aliyah, Mateo, and Ethan are again working together as a table group. Their teacher has tasked them with trying to find as many strategies as they can to solve the task 400 – 198. Further, each student is to identify their favorite strategy. Using our practice of noticing (i.e. attending, interpreting, deciding), we can consider different aspects of this moment through each dimension of equity.

Access

Beginning with access, we can attend to the availability of physical resources (i.e. base-10 blocks) and the extent to which these resources supported some students' mathematical thinking. Further, the well positioned task along with the small-group setting allowed for each student to participate in the activity and engage in mathematical reasoning. Similarly, we might interpret Ethan's remarks about not being able to take the base-10 blocks apart as signaling a desire for more adaptable models (e.g. unifix cubes). Thus, one possible decision might be to introduce a new model for Ethan to enact his strategy or perhaps invite Ethan to further describe his ideal model or tool and how he might use it.

Achievement

Returning to the idea that achievement is fundamentally grounded in the presence or absence of value judgements when considered in the context of a specific mathematical moment, attending to this exchange reveals very little (if any) signaling from the teacher regarding correct answers or preferred strategies. Indeed, at one point the teacher presumably attends to Mateo's description and gesture and then interprets this activity as a description of the standard algorithm. The teacher then decides to explicitly push back on Mateo's assertion that the standard algorithm is the correct strategy for solving the task. This decision creates space for the strategies of other students to also be considered correct, and in turn, for those students to achieve mathematically.

Identity

Looking at this moment through the lens of identity, we see some positioning of individual students as capable mathematical thinkers. Attending to the teacher's posing of the task, students are able to explore varying pathways and explorations of their own reasoning and the reasoning of others. We might interpret Aliyah's statements as a willingness to critique her peers' strategies and claim capability. We might also interpret Ethan's responses to Aliyah similarly – as a willingness to critique Aliyah's strategy and claim capability regarding his own thinking. While this particular moment did not explicitly draw in students' cultural backgrounds or connect to broader societal impacts, subsequent decisions might layer in these considerations via the introduction of more contextualized tasks that draw on the backgrounds and lived experiences of the students.

Power

At its core, power is about the apportionment of control and authority within a mathematical moment. In this instance, the teacher appears to deliberately position herself as a facilitator of the mathematical conversation and speaks infrequently. Thus, we see students in the group claiming power to voice their ideas and critiques. Attending to Aliyah's response to Jaden's use of the base-10 blocks ("There's an easier way than with those things"), we might interpret that as Aliyah having an alternate strategy that she might describe to the group. The teacher made a responsive decision to invite Aliyah to share more about her strategy, which also elevated her voice at this moment as a valuable contributor to the mathematics discussion. Indeed, skillful facilitation of student discourse is a key practice to develop mathematical reasoning (Smith and Stein, 2011). We argue that being mindful of power dynamics in the moment allows for the more deliberate apportionment of agency and authority between students and teacher – that teachers may be more aware of how much power they wield in a mathematical moment, and identify opportune times to cede such power to students by extending them space to share their own ideas.

Making Connections

Going one step further, we might connect multiple dimensions when examining a moment which allows us to perceive and respond with greater nuance and care. Returning to our example, we might attend to the way achievement interacts with access – how pushing back on assertions of correctness may open space for others to participate in a mathematical moment. The teacher's decision to push back on Mateo's notion of correctness signals validity to the other students around the table and their reasoning making them more likely to share and participate. Another example of such a connection might be to attend to the interaction between Aliyah and Ethan via identity and power. Recall that Aliyah described strategies of jumping both forwards and backwards on a number line while Ethan expressed a preference for counting individual blocks. Attending to these remarks, the teacher interprets a contested space regarding the two students' mathematical ideas. Leaning into this contested space, the teacher decides to pair Aliyah and Ethan and task them with becoming familiar with each other's strategy. Looking at this moment through the lens of identity, we see how the teacher's decision positions students as mathematical thinkers capable of teaching one another (vs. passively receiving information from a teacher). Similarly, putting on the lens of power, this decision also reflects the distribution of power from teacher to students as the instructional activity and talk (i.e. peer teaching) are now positioned between Aliyah and Ethan. These are but two examples of how multiple dimensions of equity may be connected and considered when engaging in professional noticing, and such considerations increase the potential for increasingly sophisticated and equitable mathematical activity in the classroom.

In summary, each of these dimensions provides us with a powerful lens to consider our teaching and how it shapes students' mathematical experiences in different ways. In this example, we were examining an individual moment with respect to equity or looking for meaning within the micro. However, these dimensions also serve as powerful lenses that allow us to zoom out and examine structures and systems (e.g. curricula, scheduling, assessments) not only to help students play the game, but also to facilitate the changing of the game.

Going Deeper and Rehumanizing Mathematics

Building upon these foundational dimensions of equity, Gutiérrez (2018) provides a series of more detailed ways in which we might practically think about our mathematics teaching such that we move beyond "merely tinkering or basically repeating the same approaches" (p. 2). She goes on to write:

> [We] begin with the assumption that people throughout the world already do mathematics in everyday ways that are human ... Yet schooling often creates structures, policies, and rituals that can convince people they are no longer mathematical. In this way, those structures, policies, and practices can be experienced as dehumanizing. Take the notion of students' misconceptions. Many teachers have been trained to anticipate the misconceptions that students have so that they can address them in their lessons. Yet, students don't have misconceptions. They have conceptions. And those conceptions make sense for them, until they encounter something that no longer works. They are only "misconceptions" when we begin with the expectation that others need to come to *our* way of thinking or viewing the world. (p. 2)

Here, Gutiérrez provides a strident critique of current ways that mathematics teaching and learning are often enacted in schools and, building upon the previously discussed dimension of equity (i.e. access, achievement, identity, power), puts forth a series of practices that rehumanize mathematics for students (see Table 11.1).

Table 11.1   Aspects rehumanizing mathematics

Rehumanizing Practice	Description	Equity Dimensions
Participation and positioning	Examining roles, power, and authority in the mathematics classroom	Achievement; Identity; Power
Windows and mirrors	Examining the power of seeing oneself in a mathematical experience	Access; Power; Identity
Cultures and histories	Tracing the cultural and historical roots of students' strategies and situating mathematical thinking within different contexts and cultures, particularly those that have been historically marginalized or erased	Access; Identity; Power
Broadening mathematics	Developing a vision of mathematical practice beyond the school curriculum and identifying how mathematics may be used to make the world more just and equitable	Access; Achievement; Identity; Power

Rehumanizing Practice	Description	Equity Dimensions
Living practice	Identifying moments to enliven the mathematical experience through divergent thinking, "rule breaking," and seeing mathematics as a verb (rather than a noun)	Access; Achievement; Identity; Power
Creation	Finding opportunities to invent, build, and share mathematical creations	Access; Identity; Power
Body/Emotions	Connecting mathematics to other aspects of self and society including emotion, intuition, voice, and vision	Access; Achievement; Identity; Power
Ownership	Exploring mathematical play and discovery to create intrinsic ownership of the discipline	Access; Identity; Power

Source: Adapted from Gutiérrez, 2009, 2018

Some of these ideas have emerged in previous chapters. For example, the rehumanizing practice of ownership is deeply related to the principle explored in Chapter 8 – "Children gain intrinsic satisfaction from their problem-solving, from their realization that they are making progress, and from the verification methods they develop" (Wright et al., 2006b, p. 27). In that chapter, we operationalized that principle and provided some examples of putting those ideas into practice. Similarly, Su's (2020) portrayal of mathematics for human flourishing, mentioned in a number of chapters, connects to many of these rehumanizing practices such as body/emotions, windows and mirrors, and living practice, just to name a few. There are other rehumanizing practices, though, that have not yet been explored thus far, and we find it advantageous to examine two in particular to provide an example of how these ideas may layer into the mathematics classroom.

Cultures and Histories

Connecting our mathematical experiences to the cultures and histories of our students or beyond our own individual/school contexts can be an incredibly enriching experience for students. At times, our curriculum may provide embedded opportunities for this work, but more often, it requires us to be good students of the mathematical world and braid our own learning and knowledge into our instruction.

For example, you may or may not know that doubles are culturally important and significant in many African cultures: twins are especially esteemed, blacksmiths use twin bellows, a double iron hoe is presented during a bridal ceremony, and the world is understood as a dual world of spirit and matter. The divination system or fortune telling in African religion such as the *Ifa* system uses a base of two. West African tailors traditionally used the technique of doubling to do large mental multiplications. It is a complex procedure. The tailors double a factor multiple number of times and match them up with corresponding powers of two (Eglash, 1958; Zaslavsky, 1973).

This knowledge could provide a context for engaging students in measuring practices while also shining a light on culturally situated mathematical thinking that may otherwise remain veiled. We might test a few rules of thumb employed by such tailors, such as *once around the waist, twice around the neck* or *once around the neck, twice around the wrist*. These sayings, developed through a cultural lens that focused on the power of doubling, allow tailors to take a few key measurements and extrapolate other measurements when constructing a garment. In our mathematics classroom, we might put these to the test.

Similarly, you may or may not be aware that:

> unlike Western cultures, in Africa finger counting usually starts with the left-hand palm facing up. Counting starts with all fingers bent and counting to five involves extending the little finger followed by the ring finger in that sequence until all fingers are extended. Numbers six through ten are counted on the right hand in a similar sequence. (Zaslavsky, 1973, p. 47)

In our early counting work with students (Wright and Ellemor-Collins, 2018), we might experiment with such finger patterns in lieu of our own native patterns. Creating space for these sorts of activities not only connects to the mathematics of other cultures (and potentially our students from such cultures), but also illuminates rich and historic mathematical traditions and thinking that would otherwise remain hidden.

Broadening Mathematics

This practice of rehumanizing mathematics allows us to think of how we might create experiences for students to look critically at the world around them and imagine ways to make that world a better place. Toward this end, we might use those virtues described in an earlier chapter as a guide (Su, 2020). Justice, for example, might be the foundation for our work in this practice. While justice and mathematics intersect in countless ways, one context relates to historic forms of the financial oppression of African Americans whose effects linger to this day – *redlining*.

Likely, you may be familiar with the term redlining or perhaps you have heard it in passing somewhere:

> The term 'redlining' … comes from the development by the New Deal, by the federal government of maps of every metropolitan area in the country. And those maps were color-coded by first the Home Owners Loan Corp. and then the Federal Housing Administration and then adopted by the Veterans Administration, and these color codes were designed to indicate where it was safe to insure mortgages. And anywhere where African-Americans lived, anywhere where African-Americans lived nearby were colored red to indicate to appraisers that these neighborhoods were too risky to insure mortgages. (Gross, 2017)

These color-coded maps were ubiquitous in towns and cities throughout the U.S. and inequalities in wealth distribution in such areas is, in large part, a result of these discriminatory policies.

This tragic history provides educators with a mathematical opportunity, though. We can couple historical and mathematical knowledge to examine our world to shine a light on lingering injustice. We can go further as a mathematical community and imagine ways to address these injustices. For example, we might examine the historical zoning maps of our own communities and examine how these zones reverberate today. Note, these maps are often available on the internet for larger communities. For smaller communities, this might require an email to a county clerk. Nevertheless, these resources are readily available to those who seek them. The map in Figure 11.2 represents one author's community with respect to historical zoning. This map, coupled with other technological tools, allows us to explore a key question related to food availability and *food deserts* (Shaw, 2006). For those not familiar with the term food desert, this refers to the often-observed unavailability of healthier food within economically oppressed areas, with residents relying more on small retail stores (e.g. convenience stores) and fast-food restaurants for nutrition. Armed with this knowledge, we might ask ourselves, as a mathematical community, to what extent do residents in a historic zone (green, red) have access to a grocery store? In this example, we might use distance as a proxy for access (see Figure 11.2).

How many grocery stores are within one mile of a given address in a particular historic zone?

How many grocery stores are within two miles of a given address within a particular zone?

How would you determine an average distance to the nearest grocery in a particular zone?

On a scale of 1–10 (1 least important; 10 most important) how would you rate the importance of the distance from a person's house to a grocery store and why?

Figure 11.2   Historic zoning in author's community, as captured by Google Maps

Likely, this activity would involve the use of other tools – technological tools in particular. Students may deploy internet searches and mapping tools to determine distances, but key to this experience is that the context allows for an examination of injustice and how injustice shapes their own world today.

Another feature of this example is that students are not given a signal with respect to process or procedure. There is no "right way" or "wrong way" to dive into these prompts, which relates to the equity dimension of achievement. Consider two different students' responses (see Figure 11.3).

While both Kayden and Brianna arrived at the same determinations of grocery store presence with respect to zoning, their reasoning around how to find the average distance to a store within a particular zone varied considerably. Kayden adopted something of a random-sample type of approach while Brianna partitioned each zone into quadrants and selected a residence from each of the quadrants. These two approaches (coupled with the other varied approaches of their peers) provide us with ample terrain to discuss the affordances and constraints of a given method. More importantly, we are doing so within the context of historical and contemporary economic oppression. Particularly noteworthy is that concluding prompt (On a scale of 1–10, how would you rate the importance of

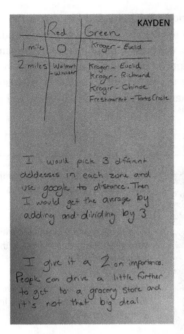
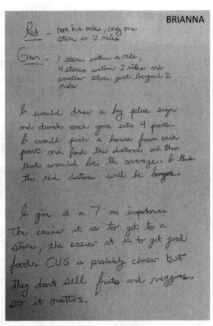

Figure 11.3 Students' responses to zoning tasks

Note: These are author-created examples inspired by student work

the distance from a person's house to a grocery store?). Again, note the differing responses of Kayden and Brianna. From Kayden's perspective, driving a bit further is "not that big deal" while Brianna argues that it is important because more accessible stores (i.e. "CVS" [a pharmacy]) don't sell produce and obtaining healthy food is more challenging in historic red zones. This broadening of the activity creates space not only for students to engage in mathematical reasoning, but also to situate that reasoning in relevant societal spaces that invite critique.

Connecting, Reflecting, and Getting a Bit Uncomfortable

Creating, supporting, and sustaining cultures of equity are the foundations upon which the other Guiding Principles of this book are based. Being responsive to children's backgrounds, abilities, experiences, cultural perspectives, traditions, and knowledge when designing and implementing instruction, propels our teaching and learning toward a place where all children may find a mathematical home and realize their own success. Additionally, our acknowledgement of and work towards refining structures and systems that contribute to inequities, ensures a brighter future for the next generation of children and their teachers. Undoubtedly, having read thus far in the book, you have recognized many connections to these ideas throughout. Indeed, we tried to make a few of these connections explicit within those chapters. More importantly, you have likely made several connections of your own which relate to your own students and setting, and all of our ideas, together, will help us realize a more just and equitable mathematics classroom.

Important to this work, though, is the understanding that engaging in the deep and critical reflection required for equitable mathematics teaching may place us in some uncomfortable places from time to time. Perhaps, as we scrutinize our teaching, we become more aware of our own questioning patterns and how we might favor certain groups of students. Or maybe we begin to notice how we signal, in subtle or unsubtle ways, the correctness of a certain strategy or way of thinking. At times, we might be reluctant to relinquish control of a particular aspect of a lesson and create space for student voices. We might reflect on our own instructional designs and realize that they lack a real connection to the lived experiences of our students. Finally, pressing for equitable change in our school structure may create new tensions amongst colleagues and leaders. These are but a few examples that might push us into uncomfortable realizations with respect to our teaching. Certainly we, as mathematics teachers ourselves, have experienced the discomfort and tension that come with these realizations and efforts. However, they are actually opportunities for growth – both personal and systemic. We encourage you to press forward toward equity and justice and know that we and many others will be walking alongside you on this journey.

Questions for Reflection

To conclude this examination of equitable mathematics teaching, we find it useful to consider a few key questions that might guide us in this area. Note, these questions are designed to carry your thinking further and help you envision how you might act upon these ideas in your own practice.

- How would you describe your mathematics classroom, curricula, and teaching methods with respect to *access*? How accessible are the mathematical experiences to different groups of learners? Do students have the support they need to be successful?
- How would you describe your mathematics classroom, curricula, and teaching methods with respect to *achievement*? What signals do students receive about "right ways" and "wrong ways" of mathematical thinking and problem solving? How often do you create alternative pathways aside from traditional "correct" procedures or ways of thinking? How do your assessments signal "right" and "wrong" ways of thinking?
- How would you describe your mathematics classroom, curricula, and teaching methods with respect to *identity*? How does your instruction relate to the lived experiences of your students? To what extent is the mathematical thinking of non-dominant and historically marginalized groups examined by you and your students?
- How would you describe your mathematics classroom, curricula, and teaching methods with respect to *power*? When are you willing to cede control of discussions and other activities to students? When are you less willing to cede such control and why? How empowered do your students feel to engage in their own mathematical exploration and thinking? When and how often do you ask students to await step-by-step guidance as they engage in problem solving?
- How would you describe the systems and structures at your school with respect to equitable outcomes? Which student groups tend to be more successful and which tend to be less successful and why? If you were to make change in this area, what is the very first thing you would do? What is the challenge of doing that "first thing" and how can you overcome it?
- Who, in your school or broader professional community, could you talk to about these ideas? What are some wonderings you have, and who, amongst your group, would be a good thought partner for these wonderings?

References

Association of Mathematics Teacher Educators (AMTE) (2022). *Statement on Equitable and Inclusive Mathematics Teaching and Learning*. Position Statement. https://amte.net/news/2022/04/press-release-amte-statement-equitable-and-inclusive-mathematics-teaching-and-learning

Delpit, L. (1995). *Other People's Children: Cultural Conflict in the Classroom*. New York: New Press.

Dewey, J. (1938). *Experience and Education*. New York: Collier.

Eglash, R. (1958). *African Fractals: Modern Computerized and Indigenous Design*. New Brunswick, NJ: Rutgers University Press.

Freire, P. (1970). *Pedagogy of the Oppressed*. New York: Herder and Herder.

Grindle, C.F., Hastings, R.P. and Wright, R.J. (2020). *Teaching Early Numeracy to Children with Developmental Disabilities*. London: Sage.

Gross, T. (2017). A "forgotten history" of how the US government segregated America. *Fresh Air – National Public Radio*. www.npr.org/2017/05/03/526655831/a-forgotten-history-of-how-the-u-s-government-segregated-america

Gutiérrez, R. (2009). Framing equity: Helping students "play the game" and "change the game." *Teaching for Excellence and Equity in Mathematics*, 1(1), 4–8.

Gutiérrez, R. (2018). Introduction: The need to rehumanize mathematics. In I. Goffney, R. Gutiérrez and M. Boston (Eds), *Rehumanizing Mathematics for Black, Indigenous, and Latinx Students* (Annual Perspectives in Mathematics Education; Vol. *2018*). Reston, VA: National Council of Teachers of Mathematics.

James, W. (1899). *Talks to Teachers on Psychology and to Students on Some of Life's Ideas*. Mineola, NY: Dover.

Judd, C. (1928) The fallacy of treating school subjects as "tool subjects." In J.R. Clark and W.D. Reeve (Eds), *Selected Topics in the Teaching of Mathematics* (pp. 61–79). New York: Teachers College.

Ladson-Billings, G. (1995). But that's just good teaching! The case for culturally relevant pedagogy. *Theory into Practice*, 34(3), 159–65.

National Council of Teachers of Mathematics (NCTM) (2014). *Access and Equity in Mathematics Education*. Position Statement. www.nctm.org/uploadedFiles/Standards_and_Positions/Position_Statements/Access_and_Equity.pdf

Shaw, H.J. (2006). Food deserts: Toward the development of a classification. *Geografiska Annaler Series B Human Geography*, 8(2), 231–47.

Smith, M.S. and Stein, M.K. (2011). *5 Practices for Orchestrating Productive Mathematical Discussions*. Reston, VA: National Council of Teachers of Mathematics.

Su, F. (2020). *Mathematics for Human Flourishing*. New Haven, CT: Yale University Press.

Tabor, P.D., Dibley, D., Hackenberg, A.J. and Norton, A. (2021). *Numeracy for All Learners: Teaching Mathematics to Students with Special Needs*. London: Sage.

Wright, R.J. and Ellemor-Collins, D. (2018). *The Learning Framework in Number: Pedagogical Tools for Assessment and Instruction*. London: Sage.

Wright, R.J., Martland, J. and Stafford, A.K. (2006a). *Early Numeracy: Assessment for Teaching and Intervention*, 2nd edition. London: Sage.

Wright, R.J., Martland, J., Stafford, A.K. and Stanger, G. (2006b). *Teaching Number: Advancing Children's Skill and Strategies*, 2nd edition. London: Sage.

Wright, R.J., Stanger, G., Stafford, A.K. and Martland, J. (2015). *Teaching Number in the Classroom with 4–8-Year-Olds*, 2nd edition. London: Sage.

Zaslavsky, C. (1973). *Africa Counts*. Boston, MA: Prindle, Weber & Schmidt.

12

Connecting back to NCTM Mathematics Teaching Practices and Common Core State Standards of Mathematics Practices

Introduction

This book has focused on the connections between mathematics education learning theories and mathematics education practices. By bringing these connections to the foreground of the mathematics education community, we aimed to show why the Guiding Principles in the Math Recovery community are so important to mathematics educators and mathematics teacher educators. Largely, these connections are absent in the wider mathematics education community, preventing real depth to develop around educators' instructional practices in relation to effective student learning of mathematics. This lack of depth can often lead to inequitable and uneven mathematics learning opportunities for students around the world. In fact, the resources needed to help mathematics educators to support all students are often lacking in those schools with fewer financial resources and schools with relatively larger proportions of students from lower socio-economic status households. Given these issues, many standards in the United States have established effective teaching practices for mathematics teachers (NCTM, 2014) and effective learning practices for mathematics students (NGA Center and CCSSO, 2010). Therefore, in this final chapter we first describe the connections between effective teaching and effective student practices in mathematics education before exploring connections between these practices and the Guiding Principles. Second, we broadly explain how particular practices, which evidence these Guiding Principles, can be used to explain the three main themes in this book: effective mathematics teaching, assessments in responsive mathematics teaching, and inclusive and equitable mathematics teaching. We conclude this chapter with a series of reflective questions that mathematics educators can consider when incorporating these standards, practices, and principles into their own mathematics teaching.

Effective Teaching and Student Practices

In the United States, the National Council of Teachers of Mathematics (NCTM) developed a series of eight effective mathematics teaching practices. These practices are often coupled with a series of effective mathematics student practices, as delineated by the *Common Core State Standards for Mathematics* (NGA Center and CCSSO, 2010). By considering the relationships between effective teaching practices and effective student practices, educators can reflect on how their instructional moves may evoke particular effective student practices.

Effective Student Practices

Effective Student Practices in the United States are outlined fully in the *Common Core State Standards* (NGA Center and CCSSO, 2010). These eight effective student practices are meant to reflect mathematics education research findings that focus on student learning in mathematics. These findings evidence effective student learning practices in mathematics, connect to learning theories, and echo effective mathematics learning found around the world (see Table 12.1). Often in the United States, educators will use these effective teaching practices in mathematics to determine if their students are engaging with mathematics tasks in meaningful ways. In a sense, these effective student practices guide many of the mathematics educators' instructional choices. Therefore, from this work, eight effective student practices were created to explicate important classroom activity that mathematics educators should look for in their classroom.

Table 12.1 Effective mathematics student practices

(1) Make sense of problems and persevere in solving them
(2) Reason abstractly and quantitatively
(3) Construct viable arguments and critique the reasoning of others
(4) Model with mathematics
(5) Use appropriate tools strategically
(6) Attend to precision
(7) Look for and make use of structure
(8) Look for and express regularity in repeated reasoning

Source: Common Core Standards for Mathematical Practice. © Copyright 2010. National Governors Association Center for Best Practices and Council of Chief State School Officers. All rights reserved.

Similar to the Guiding Principles, each of the effective student practices shows the importance of active student learning in a mathematics classroom. For instance, when teaching mathematics, educators should design lessons that promote students' ability to use tools appropriately to better model with mathematics, make sense of problems, reason abstractly, construct viable arguments, and look for and express regularity in repeated reasoning. By engaging with mathematics actively, students are assured of opportunities to develop conceptual mathematical ideas that allow for more sophisticated reasoning in future school experiences.

Effective Teaching Practices

To best support their students' development and use of these effective student mathematical practices, mathematics educators and mathematics teacher educators often reflect on what instructional moves they can intentionally design and use to support their students' conceptual mathematics learning. This type of reflective activity is the basis for the *Principles to Action* discussion and the creation of the effective mathematics teaching practices (NCTM, 2014). Broadly, the effective teaching practices are based on the five interrelated strands that the National Research Council describes as evident of students' mathematical proficiency (Kilpatrick et al., 2001). The following strands are what the *Principles to Action* explain are used to form a basis for the effective student practices (see Table 12.1):

- Conceptual understanding
- Procedural fluency
- Strategic competence
- Adaptive reasoning
- Productive disposition

By drawing on these, we can begin to think broadly and around the details that describe effective student practices. For instance, by considering conceptual understanding, we can look at particular activities that support students' development of conceptual understanding, such as: "(3) Construct viable arguments and critique the reasoning of others" and "(4) Model with mathematics." By making these connections between mathematical proficiency and students' practices, mathematics educators can see a clear purpose for why they might use these student practices. The next step that the *Principles to Action* authors sought to explicate were the effective mathematics instructional practices.

The eight effective teaching practices (see Table 12.2) were designed to best support mathematics educators and mathematics teacher educators as they designed mathematics instruction that would broadly promote their students' mathematics proficiency. These practices were also created as a result of findings in the mathematics education research field. Often, mathematics educators have a lot of information to support what their students' learning should look like but it is rarely detailed guidance on how to support effective student learning. For instance, we know we want our students to "(4) Model with mathematics" but might wonder how to support this practice. By examining the effective mathematics teaching practices, one might consider using the following instructional moves: "(2) Implement tasks that promote reasoning and problem solving," "(7) Support productive struggle in learning mathematics," and "(8) Elicit and use evidence of student thinking." However, by implementing tasks that promote reasoning, an educator might wonder, how should I implement a mathematics task to promote reasoning and what characteristics should this task encapsulate? Given this, we will also discuss these effective mathematics teaching practices in relation to the Guiding Principles.

Table 12.2   Effective mathematics teaching practices

(1) Establish mathematics goals to focus learning
(2) Implement tasks that promote reasoning and problem solving
(3) Use and connect mathematical representations
(4) Facilitate meaningful mathematical discourse
(5) Pose purposeful questions
(6) Build procedural fluency from conceptual understanding
(7) Support productive struggle in learning mathematics
(8) Elicit and use evidence of student thinking

Note: Adapted from information located at the Common Core State Standards for Mathematical Practice (2010), www. corestandards.org/Math/Practice

Broad Connections between Effective Student Practices and Teaching Practices with the Guiding Principles

The eight effective teaching practices more closely relate to the Guiding Principles. In many ways, the Guiding Principles can be regarded as a conduit mediating effective student practices and effective teaching practices in mathematics, making so many hidden acts in elementary mathematics classrooms visible. For instance, as shown in Figure 12.1, inquiry-based teaching (Guiding Principle 1) can explain connections between teachers' ability to support students' productive struggle as well as students' ability to make sense of problems and persevere in solving them. Taking time to consider the details of each Guiding Principle can better support teachers' development of effective teaching practices in the pursuit of leveraging effective student practices.

The example provides a possible connection between one effective student practice, one Guiding Principle, and one effective teaching practice. However, when considering how particular practices relate to the Guiding Principles, we can consider multiple connections between multiple practices. In this section, we explore these possible connections in more detail.

Effective Mathematics Teaching, Assessments in Responsive Mathematics Teaching, and Inclusive and Equitable Mathematics Teaching

The Guiding Principles were organized in this book around three main themes: (1) Effective Mathematics Teaching, (2) Assessments in Responsive Mathematics Teaching, and (3) Inclusive and Equitable Mathematics Teaching. To better understand the detailed relationship these Guiding Principles have with effective teaching and effective learning standards, and in relation to the three

Effective Mathematics Student Practices

(1) Make sense of problems and persevere in solving them
(2) Reason abstractly and quantitatively
(3) Construct viable arguments and critique the reasoning of others
(4) Model with mathematics
(5) Use appropriate tools strategically
(6) Attend to precision
(7) Look for and make use of structure
(8) Look for and express regularity in repeated reasoning

Guiding Principles

(1) The teaching approach is inquiry based
(2) Teaching is informed by an initial, comprehensive assessment and ongoing assessment
(3) Teaching is focused just beyond the "cutting-edge" of the child's current knowledge
(4) Teachers exercise their professional judgment
(5) The teacher deliberately engenders the development of more sophisticated strategies
(6) Teaching involves intense, ongoing observation by the teacher and continual micro-adjusting
(7) Teaching supports and builds on the child's intuitive strategies
(8) The teacher provides the child with sufficient time to solve a given problem ... reflecting on [their] thinking
(9) Children gain intrinsic satisfaction from their problem solving, their realization they are making progress, and from the verification methods they develop
(10) Equitable mathematics practices

Effective Mathematics Teaching Practices

(1) Establish mathematics goals to focus learning
(2) Implement tasks that promote reasoning and problem solving
(3) Use and connect mathematical representations
(4) Facilitate meaningful mathematical discourse
(5) Pose purposeful questions
(6) Build procedural fluency from conceptual understanding
(7) Support productive struggle in learning mathematics
(8) Elicit and use evidence of student thinking

Figure 12.1 Relationships between effective teaching and learning practices with the Guiding Principles

Note: The Guiding Principles have been synthesized by the authors for easier discussion. Adapted from Wright et al., 2006, NCTM, 2014, and NGA Center and CCSSO, 2010

main themes of this book, we will close this chapter with a discussion around the potential effects of these principles in mathematics teaching, assessments, and equitable practices.

Effective Mathematics Teaching

Effective mathematics teaching was captured in this book by focusing on Guiding Principles (synthesized by the authors for easier discussion): (1) The teaching approach is inquiry based, that is, problem based, (4) Teachers exercise their professional judgement in selecting from a bank of teaching procedures …, (5) The teacher understands children's numerical strategies and deliberately engenders the development of more sophisticated strategies, and (7) Teaching supports and builds on the child's intuitive, verbally based strategies … (Wright et al., 2006, pp. 26–7). By focusing on these four Guiding Principles, we were able to have the potential to enact six of the eight effective teaching standards: (1) Establish mathematics goals to focus learning, (2) Implement tasks that promote reasoning and problem solving, (4) Facilitate meaningful mathematical discourse, (6) Build procedural fluency from conceptual understanding, (7) Support productive struggle in learning mathematics, and (8) Elicit and use evidence of student thinking (see Figure 12.2). By enacting these six effective teaching practices, mathematics educators have the potential to support five of the eight effective student practices: (1) Make sense of problems and persevere in solving them, (4) Model with mathematics, (5) Use appropriate tools strategically, (7) Look for and make use of structure, and (8) Look for and express regularity in repeated reasoning.

These sets of Guiding Principles elicit the most teaching and student practices, suggesting that some of the biggest impacts may stem from effective teaching practices in mathematics. Interestingly, the most common effective student practice leveraged by these Guiding Principles was "look for and make use of structure." This suggests that by enacting many of these effective teaching practices, educators are providing students with more opportunities to construct and use mathematical structures more often when solving problems. This may be because educators are being asked to attend to structures in their students' mathematics learning, which echo the mathematical structures and relationships the students are developing. Thus, by designing and enacting effective teaching practices – which include inquiry-based mathematics instruction, promote educators' ability to plan effective mathematics teaching, help educators understand relationships between teaching and learning, and utilize learning progressions and trajectories – mathematics educators can put in place many of these effective teaching and student practices that draw from connections and structures in mathematics and mathematics learning.

Assessments in Responsive Mathematics Teaching

Assessments designed and used in responsive mathematics teaching were captured in this book by focusing on the following Guiding Principles (synthesized by the authors for easier discussion): (2) Teaching is informed by an initial, comprehensive assessment and ongoing assessment …, (6) Teaching involves intense, ongoing observation by the teacher and continual micro-adjusting …, and (3) Teaching is focused just beyond the cutting-edge of the child's current knowledge (Wright et al., 2006, pp. 26–7). By focusing on these three Guiding Principles, we were able to have the potential to enact four of the eight effective teaching standards: (3) Use and connect mathematical representations, (4) Facilitate meaningful mathematical discourse, (5) Pose purposeful questions, and (8) Elicit and use evidence of student thinking. By enacting these four effective teaching practices,

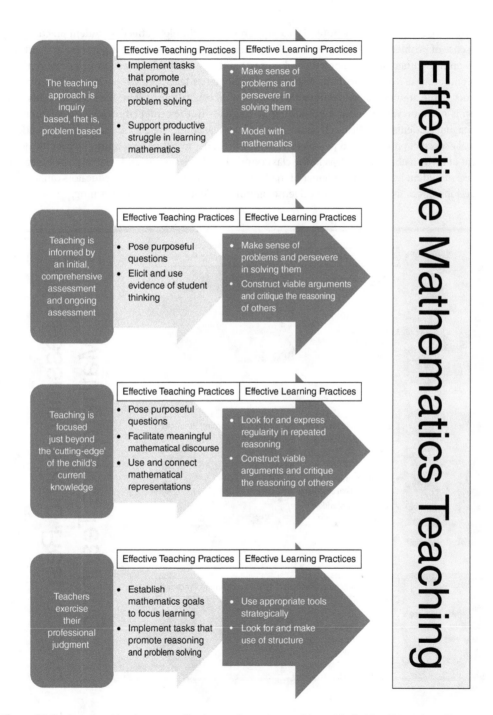

Figure 12.2 Relationships between effective mathematics teaching with Guiding Principles, effective teaching practices, and effective student practices

mathematics educators have the potential to support three of the eight effective student practices: (1) Make sense of problems and persevere in solving them, (3) Construct viable arguments and critique the reasoning of others, and (8) Look for and express regularity in repeated reasoning (see Figure 12.3). When educators use assessments in responsive mathematics teaching, we posit that students will construct viable arguments and critique the reasoning of others most often. We posit that this connection is more prevalent because by placing assessments in the center of responsive teaching, we are engaging students in critical reflection of their own reasoning. We also argue that many students may make sense of problems and persevere in solving them because they have authority over the development of their mathematical ideas in the classroom. Thus, by designing and enacting assessments in response to student learning at the center of mathematics teaching, mathematics educators can leverage the development of many of these critical lenses around students' mathematics learning.

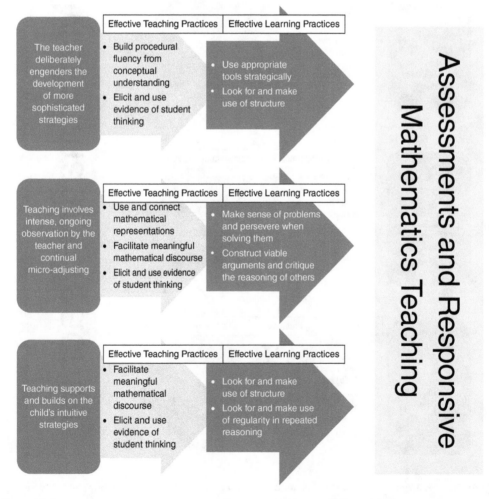

Figure 12.3 Relationships between assessments and responsive teaching with Guiding Principles, effective teaching practices, and effective student practices

Inclusive and Equitable Mathematics Teaching

Finally, by focusing on inclusive and equitable mathematics teaching practices, we focused on Guiding Principles (synthesized by the authors for easier discussion): (9) Children gain intrinsic satisfaction from their problem-solving, their realization they are making progress, and from the verification methods they develop, (8) The teacher provides the child with sufficient time to solve a given problem … reflecting on [their] thinking (Wright et al., 2006, p. 27), and (10) Equitable mathematics practices (introduced Guiding Principle in this book). By focusing on these three Guiding Principles, we were able to have the potential to enact five of the eight effective teaching standards: (2) Implement tasks that promote reasoning and problem solving, (3) Use and connect mathematical representations, (4) Facilitate meaningful mathematical discourse, (7) Support productive struggle in learning mathematics, and (8) Elicit and use evidence of student thinking

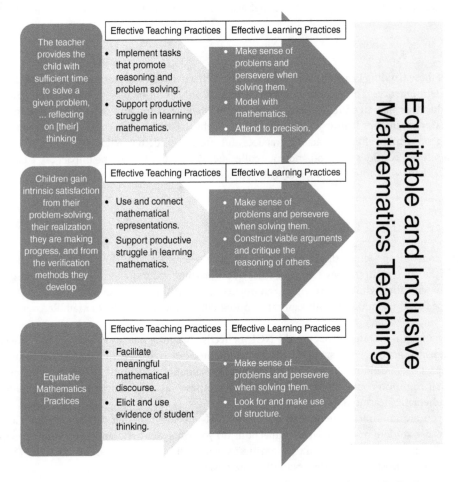

Figure 12.4 Relationships between equitable and inclusive mathematics teaching with Guiding Principles, effective teaching practices, and effective student practices

(see Figure 12.4). By enacting these five effective teaching practices, mathematics educators have the potential to support five of the eight effective student practices: (1) Make sense of problems and persevere in solving them, (3) Construct viable arguments and critique the reasoning of others, (4) Model with mathematics, (6) Attend to precision, and (8) Look for and express regularity in repeated reasoning. Interestingly, each of these Guiding Principles not only allow for more access points in mathematics tasks for students, but also directly leverage opportunities to promote students' productive struggle when learning mathematics. What this means is that when educators provide students more inclusive and equitable mathematics instruction, more students gain access to the mathematics in the classroom without sacrificing the rigor involved in the mathematics learning. Thus, by designing mathematics instruction that considers inclusive and equitable approaches, educators are more able to utilize grouping strategies for productive struggles in mathematics learning, encourage students to take more time to reflect on their mathematics activity, and explicitly draw on equitable mathematics instructional approaches. By drawing on these Guiding Principles, mathematics educators can leverage the development of many of these effective teaching and student practices, providing more equitable and rigorous mathematics learning opportunities.

Summary

Many of these Guiding Principles may evoke different effective teaching practices and different effective student practices. These connections are suggested only as an exercise in how we can consider what educators may need to consider is effective in their teaching and what is effective in their students' mathematics learning. In reality, many of these Guiding Principles may be capable of utilizing many more effective teaching practices and effective student practices. Therefore, in the following section, consider how you and your colleagues can best reflect on the impact these Guiding Principles have with your teaching and with your students' learning.

Reflecting on Practices

In this concluding section of the book, we will pose several key questions for you to reflect on around the three main themes. Consider these questions and add more to this discussion, allowing for more ways these Guiding Principles can impact your teaching and your students' learning. It is our hope that these questions will explicate school mathematics in relation to Math Recovery.

- If you as an educator *do not* use the NCTM effective teaching practices or the CCSSM effective student practices, what standards and/or guidelines can you draw on when determining the impact these Guiding Principles have in your mathematics classroom? Draw your own visuals. What common connections do you see between these Guiding Principles and your students' mathematics learning?
- If you are an educator who *does* use the NCTM effective teaching practices or the CCSSM effective student practices, what connections do you often see between the Guiding Principles and your students' learning of mathematics? What would you include and/or exclude? Discuss particular classroom experiences to illustrate these connections.

- For each of the three scenarios below, consider the questions that follow:
  - When designing effective teaching practices (theme 1) for the mathematics in your classroom
  - When designing assessments in responsive mathematics teaching (theme 2)
  - When designing inclusive and equitable mathematics teaching (theme 3)

How often do you draw on these Guiding Principles? Why are some Guiding Principles used more often than others? Why are some Guiding Principles used less often than others? By knowing the frequency and method for using these Guiding Principles, do you contemplate changing your mathematics teaching? Why or why not?

- How do these Guiding Principles change from school to school or from group to group?
- In using these Guiding Principles for whole-class instruction rather than small group and one-on-one instruction, how might these Guiding Principles change? In this new context, what might the impact of these Guiding Principles be on students?

References

Kilpatrick, J., Swafford, J., Findell, B. and National Research Council (US) (2001). *Adding It Up: Helping Children Learn Mathematics*. Washington, DC: National Academy Press.

National Council of Teachers of Mathematics (NCTM) (2014). *Principles to Action: Ensuring Mathematical Success for All*. Reston, VA: NCTM.

National Governors Association Center for Best Practices and Council of Chief State School Officers (NGA Center and CCSSO) (2010). *Common Core State Standards for Mathematics*. Washington, DC: Authors.

Wright, R.J., Martland, J., Stafford, A.K. and Stanger, G. (2006). *Teaching Number: Advancing Children's Skill and Strategies*, 2nd edition. London: Sage.

Index

Printed in the USA
CPSIA information can be obtained
at www.ICGtesting.com
LVHW052334290923
759592LV00009B/150